Food Cultures of the United States

FOOD CULTURES OF THE UNITED STATES

Recipes, Customs, and Issues

Bruce Kraig

The Global Kitchen

 GREENWOOD

An Imprint of ABC-CLIO, LLC

Santa Barbara, California • Denver, Colorado

Library of Congress Cataloging-in-Publication Data

Names: Kraig, Bruce, author.
Title: Food cultures of the United States : recipes, customs, and issues / Bruce Kraig.
Description: Santa Barbara, California : Greenwood, an Imprint of ABC-CLIO,
    LLC, [2020] | Includes bibliographical references and index.
Identifiers: LCCN 2019041067 (print) | LCCN 2019041068 (ebook) |
    ISBN 9781440866586 (hardback) | ISBN 9781440866593 (ebook)
Subjects: LCSH: Food habits—United States. | Food preferences—United States.
Classification: LCC GT2853.U6 K73 2020 (print) | LCC GT2853.U6 (ebook) |
    DDC 394.1/20973—dc23
LC record available at https://lccn.loc.gov/2019041067
LC ebook record available at https://lccn.loc.gov/2019041068

ISBN: 978-1-4408-6658-6 (print)
        978-1-4408-6659-3 (ebook)

24 23 22 21 20   1 2 3 4 5

This book is also available as an eBook.

Greenwood
An Imprint of ABC-CLIO, LLC

ABC-CLIO, LLC
147 Castilian Drive
Santa Barbara, California 93117
www.abc-clio.com

This book is printed on acid-free paper (∞)

Manufactured in the United States of America

Contents

Series Foreword

Imagine a typical American breakfast: bacon, eggs, toast, and home fries from the local diner. Or maybe a protein-packed smoothie, sipped on the go to class or work. In some countries in Europe, breakfast might just be a small cookie and a strong coffee, if anything at all. A South African breakfast might consist of a bowl of corn porridge with milk. In Japan, breakfast might look more like dinner, complete with rice, vegetables, and fish. What we eat varies from country to country, and even region to region. The Global Kitchen series explores the cuisines of different cultures around the world, from the history of food and food staples to main dishes and contemporary issues. Teeming with recipes to try at home, these volumes will delight readers by discovering other cultures through the lens of a treasured topic: food.

Each volume focuses on the culinary heritage of one country or one small group of countries, covering history and contemporary culture. Volumes begin with a chronology of major food-related milestones and events in the area, from prehistory to present. Chapters explore the key foods and meals in the country, covering the following topics:

- Food History;
- Influential Ingredients;
- Appetizers and Side Dishes;
- Main Dishes;
- Desserts;
- Beverages;
- Holidays and Special Occasions;
- Street Food and Snacks;
- Dining Out; and
- Food Issues and Dietary Concerns.

Chapters are textual, and each chapter is accompanied by numerous recipes, adding a hands-on component to the series. Sidebars, a glossary of important terms, and a selected bibliography round out each volume, providing readers with additional information and resources for their personal and scholarly research needs.

Whether readers are looking for recipes to use for classes or at home, or to explore the histories and traditions of world cuisines, the Global Kitchen series will allow readers to fully immerse themselves in other cultures, giving a taste of typical daily life and tradition.

Introduction

Every day, multiple times, almost all Americans think about food. What to eat, when to eat, and where to get food is so deeply embedded in American people's existence that they scarcely realize that they are thinking about it. A lot of ordinary conversation is about food in all of its aspects, from eating out to discussions about recipes. Meal planning—including reading cookbooks and watching television cooking shows—shopping, food preparation, and actual eating take up hours of almost everyone's day. Of all biological functions, eating and what follows from it, are the ones with the most "culture" around them. From personal and group identification to taboos and taste and distaste, jokes, stories, movies, television programs, and much more, food is central to people's lives. And yet Americans usually take all these for granted as normal behaviors in everyday life.

Different peoples around the world have not eaten in the same ways as everyone else, though today, international contacts have made those differences smaller. Nonetheless, America is unique in many ways. Those who study foodways (meaning the economic, social, and cultural habits of a people) ask why do Americans eat what they eat? Where does the food come from and why do they like it, or not like it? Why do they dine at certain times of the day and what rituals do Americans use for eating, such as using forks or eating out of hand?

American food, what is eaten and what is not, comes mostly from immigrant origins. Cattle (beef and dairy products made from cows' milk), pork from pigs, chickens, sheep (lamb), and goats (mostly dairy), wheat, barley, rye, oats, rice, apples, peaches, watermelons, pears, broccoli, spinach, chard, kale, and many others, are imports from the Old World (Europe, Africa, and Asia). Of the relatively few plants native to North America that we eat, corn is the most important. Animal feeds, corn oil, corn meal, corn starch, corn syrup, high fructose corn syrup, and sweetened and plain popcorn, this seed is in about 60 percent of American food. Beans are next, followed to much lesser extents by squash and pumpkins as native foods seen regularly on American tables. What is eaten at meals to this day is really based on European, specifically British and German, tastes: meat, potatoes, bread, some vegetables, and sweets at the end.

How American food is produced, processed, and sold has changed over time. Most of the changes have come from the demand for quantity, convenience, and cheaper foods. From the Colonial period well into the nineteenth century, most food came from small family farms. Farmers fed themselves and the rural communities in which they lived, while city people got food mostly from local farms in the vicinity. With the rise of large-scale farming and meat production, food could be produced in one part of the nation and shipped everywhere. At first, this was by canal boats and railroads and, from the mid-twentieth century onward, by trucks using the interstate highway system. With large-scale farming came new food processing and preservation technologies. Meat could be packed in central locations and shipped in refrigerated railway cars and trucks everywhere: the packaged meats in grocer's cases today are ready for cooking or, if preserved, eaten immediately. Almost any food was canned from the Civil War period onward. Canned vegetables, meats, soups, milk, and sweets filled grocery store shelves giving families convenient ways to prepare meals at low prices. After World War II, there was a frozen food boom as home freezers became widespread. Today, almost every food imaginable can be found in frozen food cases, from fish to meats, vegetables, prepared meals, pizzas, many snacks, and plenty of cakes and ice creams. To cook them, new devices such as the microwave oven were devised and are now standard in almost every home kitchen. Toasters and toaster ovens, slow cookers, pressure cookers, air fryers, and many more cooking tools came on the market to make breakfast, lunches, dinners, and snacks quickly and easily. Just as machines were invented to prepare new foods, companies that process foods adapted their products to new apparatuses. For example, fruit-filled tarts and pies could be cooked in toasters and breakfast cereals cooked in their packages in microwave ovens. Cookery publications, in print and online, boast of how swiftly meals can be prepared, completely unlike cookery in centuries past when nothing was convenient and women spent long hours raising food in gardens and preparing meals.

Americans typically take three meals a day for granted: breakfast, lunch, and then a large dinner, often followed by dessert. Health and nutrition authorities have been recommending this regimen since the nineteenth century and it makes sense to break up a workday into four or five-hour intervals with a protein-rich breakfast at the start. But eating times, numbers of meals, and quantities at each meal have changed over time. In the eras before industrialization, when most Americans lived on farms, breakfast might have been a minor meal, perhaps leftovers from the day before or just bread or biscuits and coffee or milk. Because farm chores began very early, preparing a large breakfast may have been desired but not always possible. Sometimes, snacks or sandwiches were taken into the fields, especially during planting and harvest season. The largest meal of the day was around noon when all the farm workers sat down to a hearty meal of meat and potatoes or some other starches with bread and some vegetables on the side. At the end of the day, the final supper was often leftovers from the large midday dinner or other lighter foods. For poor people, such as slaves in the Antebellum era, meals were often less elaborate and not so rich on proteins. For them, the stewpot cooking slowly the whole day through with whatever could be grown, hunted, or found sufficed for all the day's meals.

The Industrial Revolution of the nineteenth century created the modern eating order. Upper-class dining habits and rules of etiquette moved down the social scale into the newly emerging middle classes. If a family could afford good china, silver, or silver-plated serving and eating utensils, fancy tablecloths, sideboards, and dining room sets they purchased them in the new department stores that were established after the Civil War. Or they could be bought from mail order catalogues such as Sears, Roebuck and Company, or Montgomery Ward. Rules of decorum prohibited people from using just knives to cut and put food in their mouths as had been done in rural and frontier America. Instead, forks were to be held in the left hand, food cut with a knife in the right, and then the knife set down, the fork with food impaled on it transferred to the right hand and then brought to mouth. The reason for this cumbersome way to eat was to slow down Americans' propensity to eat very fast. Like upper-class Europeans, Americans were supposed to engage in polite table talk while dining in leisurely fashion. This was meant as a sign of civility and, of course, of differentiation of social classes.

Cities and large towns with their factories and businesses rapidly grew as people left farms and joined large numbers of immigrants in urban areas. Factory and business office work required long hours away from home, so lunch was eaten nearer the workplace and evening dinner was the day's main meal. Breakfast came to be more quickly eaten giving rise to a new category of American food: breakfast cereals. Invented in the later nineteenth century, these featured whole grains processed into flakes or small nuggets and served cold with milk or hot cooked versions. They arose from health food advocates such as the Kellogg family and were promoted as a good nutritious breakfast. All of today's breakfast cereals and the habit of eating them in the morning are descendants of the innovations, though their creators would be horrified at the amounts of sugar in most cereals today.

In the late nineteenth century, whole new classes of lunch restaurants appeared, from dairy restaurants meant for working women to self-serve smorgasbords (the ancestor of the modern salad bar), diners, lunch-counters, and cafeterias. Soups and sandwiches became mainstays of these quick service outlets. Soups, tuna fish, ham and cheese, melted cheese, macaroni and cheese, iceberg lettuce salads and pies of every kind were to be found on these menus along with soda fountain drinks such as colas and root beer. In many a movie from the 1930s, scenes of someone sitting at a diner or lunch counter ordering a piece of pie and coffee are common. Today, most of these older lunch venues have been replaced by fast food chains serving a wide variety of dishes ranging from hamburgers to fried chicken parts to Asian and Mexican food.

The evening meal came to not only be the most substantial but the most meaningful for family life. In the ideal, born in the 1950s, and seen universally in print media, radio, movies, and television, the father of the family comes home from work to find dinner being prepared by his wife, a stay-at-home mother. The children would be home from school, probably having snacked right afterward on cookies and milk, ready to sit and eat dinner at the dining table. The meal itself would be the standard, a main protein dish such as roasted meat, with potatoes on one side and a cooked vegetable on the other. There would be a savory thickened liquid, gravy, to pour over the meat and potatoes, and rolls with butter to accompany the food. A sweet always followed, perhaps a pie or cake made from a cake mix or with preprepared fillings, along with a dollop of ice cream or artificial whipped cream.

The evening dinner is the place for the family gathering and a way to solidify family values. If the evening meal sounds like a holiday feast, such as at Thanksgiving, it is not an accident. Thanksgiving is usually seen as a larger family gathering, the sharing of food and stories, creating a bond among the extended family members. The dinner plate has the same pattern as the regular dinner, only with more food additions such as cranberry sauce, poultry dressings, and certain kinds of rich dessert. Many Americans still have holiday meals in this way, though not observing the model daily family meal.

Modern families rarely follow the model family dinner. Surveys show that 40 percent of families eat dinner together three times a week but 88 percent do eat with at least one member of their family most of the time. With parents working full time and children engaged in activities all day and into evenings, getting all family members together can be difficult. Cooking an old-fashioned meal is also hard; some 80 percent of Americans using conveniently prepared foods for dinners. These may be take out from restaurants or grocery stores or dishes ready to be microwaved or heated in conventional ovens or pans. The old standard meat and accompaniment plate may also differ, especially with today's interest in vegetarian, gluten-free, dairy free, and other non-traditional diets. A dinner of pizza is a common quick meal that might be consumed while sitting in front of a television set. The famous TV dinners invented in the 1950s were a precursor of a common American dining practice. Nor are the old rules of etiquette followed. Most pizza need not be eaten with a fork—Chicago's deep-dish pizza is an exception. Neither do sandwiches of all kinds from hot dogs to hamburgers and even delicate hors d'oeuvres at receptions and fancy dinners. American meals and the ways to eat them are ever evolving to meet social and cultural changes. It has always been so.

Chronology

American cookery begins not in kitchens as we know them today, but around open campfires, in the mouths of caves, and in huts. Hunting implements such as spears and knives made from stone are the technologies that the first migrants into the Americas used to capture, gather, and prepare foods. Over the course of centuries, Native Americans exploited local food sources, developed agriculture, invented pottery for food storage and cooking, and created local cuisines. European and African immigrants after 1500 CE brought new plants and animals to the Americas along with new food production and preparation technologies. These were developed over the next 500 years to become the modern industrialized food systems and dishes that Americans know and use each day.

20,000–18,000 BCE
The first Americans, small groups of hunter-food collectors, begin to migrate from a homeland in Beringia, a landmass linking Asia to Alaska, sometime after 22,000 years ago. They travel down the continent by boat and on foot reaching Chile by at least 16,000 BCE.

10,000 BCE
Later migrations of hunter-gatherers bring Na-Dené-speaking peoples and Aleut-Eskimo speakers as late as 4000–2000 BCE. The southern group of Na-Dené speakers include Navajos of the American Southwest.

10,000–8000 BCE
Paleo-Indians, as they are commonly known, find late Ice Age animals such as woolly mammoths, mastodons, giant sloths, and giant beavers. These are widely hunted and at the end of the Ice Age all but bison have disappeared.

9000–8000 BCE
As ice sheets disappear, the North American landforms and biomes that exist more or less today are formed. Native American peoples fill every ecological zone, hunting large and small game and gathering numerous wild plants for food.

6000–2000 BCE
Native peoples intensively gather wild foods such as nuts and process them using grinding stones to produce bits and flour for boiling into stews and porridges. Hunting and fishing are major food sources.

4000 BCE onward
At least six distinctive regional culinary traditions emerge based on local ecologies, such as northwest coast peoples remaining hunter-food collectors and southwestern peoples taking up small-scale agriculture.

4000 BCE
First domesticated squashes appear in villages near the Mississippi River. They spread across the continent to become a major food source.

3000 BCE
Corn (maize) appears in the American southwest as a supplement to people's food supplies. Corn spreads across most of North America to become a dietary staple.

c.2500 BCE
The earliest pottery used for food storage and cooking is made by peoples in the American southeast and spreads slowly to other peoples in the Midwest and Northeast. The great southwestern pottery traditions among the Pueblo peoples began in the first millennium CE.

500 BCE
Domesticated beans come to North America and are combined with corn and squash to become the famous "three sisters," the basic diet for many Native American peoples.

125–600 CE
Polynesian peoples from the Marquesas Islands settle in Hawaii bringing pigs, chickens, dogs, taro, coconuts, sugarcane, and many other edible plants. After 1200, a later wave of Polynesian people arrive with bananas, likely varieties of sweet potatoes, and other foods typical of native Hawaiian cuisine.

1492
Spanish arrive in the Caribbean and begin their subjugation of the Americas including today's American southwest and Florida. Their political conquest is also biological because they bring new animals and plants including cows, pigs, chickens, horses, wheat, barley, oats, apples, peaches, pears, and numerous others.

1608
The French begin permanent settlement of North America with the founding of Quebec in Canada. Claiming the whole Mississippi River valley, they create towns

such as St. Louis (Missouri) and create a wine industry, some of which is exported to France.

1603

English colonists found a settlement at Jamestown, though it takes more than a decade for Virginia to become permanently settled by Europeans. They bring European animals and food plants.

1615

Dutch colonists begin settlements on the Hudson River, founding New Amsterdam (later New York) in 1624. Dutch dishes such as doughnuts and cookies become iconic American foods.

1619

The first Africans are brought to Virginia by Dutch merchants. They are indentured servants but later in the century become slaves. Hundreds of thousands followed over the next two centuries.

1620

English pilgrims found the Plimoth Plantation in Massachusetts, followed a decade later by Boston. The Pilgrims and their Native American friends hold the first Thanksgiving feast.

1670s

English plantation owners from the Caribbean found rice (and indigo) farms in South Carolina that are worked by African slaves. African foods such as rice, okra, black-eyed peas, sesame seeds, and watermelons come to America.

1680

Native peoples of the Plains acquire horses from Spanish America and transform their lives to become the classic migratory Plains Indians bison hunters.

1681–1682

William Penn is given a charter, forms Pennsylvania, and founds Philadelphia. The colony becomes a major wheat grower making it one of the "Bread Colonies."

1718

French settlers found a city famous for its complex culinary culture in Mississippi River delta: New Orleans.

1769

Spanish missionaries and ranchers establish settlements in California, raising large numbers of cattle, and planting citrus crops and grapevines that will become major food exports to the rest of the nation in the next century.

1776–1783

The American Revolution leads to independence and opens the way for Americans to cross the Allegheny Mountains and settle what are now the Midwest and interior regions of the South.

1783

The mechanical genius, Oliver Evans, builds the first automated flour mill on the Brandywine River in Pennsylvania. By 1790, it is perfected and becomes a foundation for the industrial production of food in America.

1803

Known as the Louisiana Purchase, France sells the middle of the North American continent to the United States, opening it for settlement and development of America's agricultural heartland.

1825

The Erie Canal opens linking the rich agricultural lands of the Midwest via the Great Lakes to New York City. The city of Chicago becomes the entrepôt, making it the food shipping and processing center of America by the late nineteenth century.

1826

The Atwood & Bacon Oyster House (Union Oyster House) opens in Boston serving local seafood, baked beans, and other regional fare. It remains one of the oldest public dining establishments in America and widely copied.

1837

Blacksmith John Deere invents a polished-steel plow pioneer that lets farmers cut through tough prairie soils of the Midwest. The plow and other farming technologies create enormous agricultural abundance.

1847

Cyrus McCormick of Virginia perfects his grain reaping machine and moves his company to Chicago. McCormick and other companies revolutionize planting and harvesting grain, making America the world production leader.

1849

Immigrants from the Canton (Guangzhou) region of China arrive, mainly to work on the new railroad systems being built. They create Chinatowns and classic Chinese American dishes such as chop suey and chow mein.

1850

Increasingly large numbers of Germans immigrate bringing with them a number of items that become signature American foods and beverages, such as sausages and beer.

1858

Connecticut native, Gail Borden, perfects canned condensed milk and in the same year John Mason patents his glass canning jar. Both are landmarks in food preservation.

1861

Needing to feed the Union army during the Civil War, canning manufacturers ramp up production, devising new ways to safely can and process foods. By the late

1870–1880s, canned foods become cheap enough for ordinary people to make them staples on pantry shelves.

1865
Chicago's Union Stock Yards are established, becoming the main industrialized meat processing and shipping center in the nation. Other regional stockyards, such as Kansas City, are modelled on it.

1869
The first transcontinental railroad is completed, linking California's growing agricultural abundance to the East Coast.

1877
Henry Seymour and William Heston create the first quick cooking oat cereal and register its symbol, a Quaker man, making it the first branded breakfast cereal.

1877
Cadwallader C. Washburn and John Crosby form a flour milling company in Minneapolis, later to be America's milling center. Their company becomes General Mills in the next century and, along with the Pillsbury Company, dominate the packaged flour and cake mix industry.

1898
A consortium of major baking companies combine to form the National Baking Company (Nabisco), putting their crackers in packaging to keep them fresh. All American cookie and cracker manufacturers follow suit.

1906
Reacting to an expose of appalling conditions in the meat packing industry, Congress passes the Meat Inspection Act and Food and Drug Act. Package labelling is also regulated, upheld in a 1924 Supreme Court decision. Food labelling will become more detailed over the next century.

1913–1918
Home refrigerators are invented and perfected with automatic controls by several manufacturers. Refrigeration changes the way that Americans shop for food.

1916
Piggly Wiggly, the first self-service grocery store, opens in Memphis Tennessee. The word "supermarket" appears in large California warehouse-type stores in the 1920s.

1917–1918
America enters World War I and begins publicity campaigns encouraging food economy with simplified recipes, thus changing the way that Americans prepared food.

1919–1920
The Eighteenth Amendment to the Constitution followed by the Volstead Act prohibit the manufacture and sale of alcoholic beverages with some exceptions. Many

restaurants go out of business, soft drinks become popular, and gangsters make fortunes on illegal liquor sales.

1929
A stock market crash exposes deep structural weaknesses in the American economy resulting in a decade-long "Great Depression" that impoverishes the nation.

1930
Clarence Birdseye invents "flash freezing" technology for food. When home freezers become widespread in 1950s, frozen food becomes a major part of the American diet.

1930
Drought hits the Great Plains, drying out over-plowed lands and creating the infamous "Dust Bowl." Millions of tons of topsoil are blown away, millions of acres of land become useless, and 2.5 million people migrate out of the affected areas.

1933
The nation's first farm bill, the Agricultural Adjustment Act, supports farm prices and helps farmers retain their farms. The federal government creates large infrastructure projects such as tree planting, dam building, and soil conservation to rebuild the rural economy.

1941
Entering World War II, America mobilizes vast manufacturing and food production resources in a victorious effort. Food rationing is in effect for four years.

1945–1950s
Acute housing shortages and consequent federal loan programs lead to a boom in suburbanization. Within 50 years, one-half of the American population will live in suburbs and with them go food stores and restaurants.

1954
Ray Kroc signs an agreement with Richard and Maurice McDonald of San Bernardino, California, to franchise their fast food operation. In 1961, Kroc buys the brothers out and massively expands the chain into the world's largest. Other chains follow.

1956
President Dwight D. Eisenhower signs the Federal-Aid Highway Act creating the Interstate System, the largest infrastructure project in American history. Everything changes as food processing becomes decentralized and fast food restaurants line the new highways.

1958
Frank and Dan Carney of Wichita, Kansas, found a restaurant featuring a dish once known only in Italian communities, pizza. The next year, they franchise Pizza Hut, which becomes a worldwide chain.

1965

Congress passes The Immigration and Naturalization Act that lifts most restrictions on immigration from Asia, Latin America, and Africa. At least 18 million people come to the United States during the next 30 years bringing their food customs with them. American food is transformed with Mexican and Asian cuisines becoming highly popular.

1972

American farmers sell a huge surplus of wheat to the Soviet Union. This leads to overproduction, consolidation of farming by agribusiness, and the increased use of corn for biofuels and animal feed, many of them raised in confined feeding operations.

1975

Microwave ovens, first introduced to the commercial market in 1954, reach 1 million home sales. The way that Americans cook is once again transformed.

1993

The Food Network broadcasts live cooking shows, initiating an age of celebrity cooks and a boom in food and food preparation products for the home market.

2002

Organic foods are recognized as a growing part of the food system with the passage of the National Organic Program.

2007

With acquisitions of other companies, Chicago's Kraft Foods becomes the largest food company in America; in 2015, it merges with Pittsburgh's Heinz to become a major force in food processing and sales.

2008

The beer company Anheuser Busch is bought by Belgian-Brazilian company InBev to become the world's largest brewer; seven years, later it buys SABMiller, becoming even larger.

2017

Food conglomerates dominate the American market, Tyson Foods, PepsiCo, Nestle, Coca-Cola Company, and JBS (meat processing) join Kraft-Heinz Company as the market leaders.

2019

In a time of cultural ferment, worries about food lead to new ideas and changes in diets, from environmental concerns, to agriculture, food processing, and ethical treatment of animals, and diet crazes such as keto and paleo.

CHAPTER ONE

Food History

The human food history of the United States actually begins with migrations of peoples to the North and South American continents. The first immigrants may have arrived as early as 20,000 BCE during the last Ice Age. They were hunters-gatherers who originated in northeast Asia but had lived for thousands of years in Beringia, the cold lands that once lay between Asia and modern Alaska. Living in small bands, they preyed on megafauna such as mammoths, mastodons, and horses that lived on the dry tundra along the edges of the great ice sheets, as well as on fish and seals along the unglaciated coasts. Over time, as the ice sheets began to melt away, groups moved slowly southward into the continent, reaching Chile in South America by 14,500 BCE.

Because historically, America's food comes from the land and water, much depends on geography and climate. This was especially the case before food was industrialized—mass produced—and before transportation systems were invented that could carry products over long distances. The foods of the classic Native American tribal groups often reflect the lands on which they lived. Great Plains Indians differed in their way of life and language from those from the Southeast or Pacific Coast. In similar ways, the earliest European and African settlers also originally adapted to the lands that they settled. None of these differences could have taken place without massive climatic events from the end of the last great Ice Age, beginning about 12,000–13,000 years ago onward.

The modern American aquatic systems, such as freshwater seas called the Great Lakes and the many river systems of the continent's northern half, are the results of these events. Immense prairies and plains cover the central part of North America—gifts left by the retreating ice. As the first Americans advanced across the continent, century by century, they found lands that were increasingly rich with millions of plant and animal species that had evolved in isolation from the other continents. Upon finding abundant food sources, peoples eventually settled in every part of both American continents, forming tribal nations large and small.

The United States is a country with examples of almost every climate and landscape on Earth. The northeastern states making up New England have seven ecological zones alone. The East Coast runs from the rocky shores of Maine; down through the seafood-rich Chesapeake estuary; through the marshes and tidal swamps of South Carolina, where rice was once a major product; and finally to the swampy, subtropical Florida flatlands and the 1,000-mile-long sandy coastlines along the Atlantic Ocean and Gulf of Mexico. To the west rise the Appalachian Mountains, which stretch from New York State into Georgia. Within them are fertile river valleys, such as the Hudson, Allegheny, Connecticut, and upper Ohio, and the wheat-growing regions of Pennsylvania and Ohio. In the South, a wide coastal plain covers Florida on the east and stretches into western Texas and northeastern Mexico. The upper part of the South is hillier, dry land. Both areas eventually turned to cotton production, and with it, the slave plantation system surrounded by poor farmers in the uplands.

West of the Appalachians are flat prairies that cover most of the continent. The long grasslands of the Midwest are cut by the Mississippi River and its many tributaries, whose deep soils are among the most fertile in the world. To the west is the short grass country of the Dakotas and Montana, its immense herds of bison later replaced by cattle and wheat. The Rocky Mountains form the continent's western wall, cut by passes and rivers such as the Colorado and the mighty Columbia. West of those mountains is a series of smaller ranges with fertile valleys between them, and

The Previous Ice Age

When the first Americans arrived in North America during the last Ice Age, more than 20,000 years ago, they found giant animals such as wooly rhinoceroses, wooly mammoths, mastodons, giant ground sloths, and horses. As the Ice Age ended around 13,000 years ago, most of the big animals disappeared, including horses. Horses were reintroduced in the sixteenth century by Spanish colonists. Researchers conclude that climate change and human hunting were the main causes. Because the animals' main food supply declined, their breeding populations became too small to reproduce. As animal populations dwindled, human hunters killed enough of many species to ensure extinction. Remains on kill sites of the period include mammoths, giant sloths, and horses.

then, pressed against the Pacific Ocean, are the agriculturally rich lands of California, Oregon, and Washington State. All these larger areas contain different ecological zones that Native American peoples exploited. The European and African settlers who followed did the same, creating cuisines that differed from one another. New England lobster boils were nothing like the fried prairie chicken of the Midwest. What eventually linked all the regions together were the plants and animals that the newer immigrants brought with them. And by establishing these new life forms, the new Americans changed America's biomes.

Native Americans' Food History

The Native American peoples knew their environments intimately, and from the Archaic Period (after 9000 BCE) onward, they gathered and processed a broad range of plants and animals. In the Southwest, Plains, and Great Basin tubers such as biscuit roots and yampa (a member of the parsley family) were gathered, dried, and ground. In desert areas, agave plants served as both food and fiber to be woven into clothing. Even more important were highly nutritious nuts such as the piñon, or pine nut in the West. In the regions that became the American East and Midwest, there was a rich supply of wild foods. Widely eaten were oily seeds such as squash, sumpweed, and sunflower, starchy seeds the likes of maygrass, amaranths, and chenopodia, and plenty of nuts. Pecans and hickory were major food sources, as were acorns from the millions of oak trees that covered North America. Tubers such as Jerusalem artichokes (also called *sunchokes*), groundnuts, King Solomon's seals, onions, asparagus, sorrel, wild turnips, and types of lilies were all eaten fresh or dried and pounded into flour to be made into flatbread.

Many greens were also on the menu, of which mustards, purslane, watercress, ramps (wild leeks), and edible nightshades are best known. Wild strawberries, chokeberries, huckleberries, and (in the northern areas) cranberries were widely used, often as flavorings for dishes. Other fruits such as paw paws, American persimmons, black cherries, American grapes, and American plums were also consumed in season. One estimate of what plants of the chenopodium family such as goosefoot and marsh elder were capable of is that a 70-by-70-meter field (a little less than the size of a football field) planted with them could feed a household of ten people for six months. Wild game and fish were always on the menu as well. Relatively large populations lived on wild resources, especially in California and the Northwest Coast, where fish remain a major part of native diets, but almost none of the plants are used today. Neither do modern Americans live on wild game, by and large. Some plants have been commercialized, meaning that they are grown on farms for sale in markets; examples include Jerusalem artichokes, mustard greens, watercress, and purslane (the latter used mainly in Latin American communities). The many varieties of wild plants have been supplanted by narrower varieties of European imports, and most of them were raised to be sold as well.

Domesticated plants created even more food that was valuable in pre-Columbian America, especially corn (maize), beans, and squash. Corn was a staple of Central American civilizations such as the Mayans and Aztecs. Early forms of the plant, looking more like popcorn than the modern varieties, was likely brought to the American Southwest by at least 2500 BCE. Over the subsequent centuries, farmers developed new breeds of corn that yielded many more edible seeds (corn kernels) than earlier ones. By about 200 CE, corn became a major part of people's diets. Corn mixed with beans and squashes, including pumpkins (also introduced from Mexico around the same time as corn), became the backbone of the Native American diet. Called the "three sisters" by peoples of the northeast, they were planted together and grew symbiotically. Eventually, the "sisters" moved into the rest of the continent, reaching the East Coast after about 1300 CE. By the time of Old World contact, about 1,000 varieties of corn, 100 types of beans, and several dozen kinds of squash were being raised by native peoples throughout the continent.

Yet broad-range food collecting remained important in the Americas. Northeastern peoples such as the Narragansetts of coastal Massachusetts lived in woodland environments, mainly in small social groupings that were often organized into loose-knit tribes. Many of their villages were moved seasonally depending on wild food supplies, though small-scale horticulture was common. The Narragansetts fished in the season when their prey were running, hunted for game, gathered birds during migration season and eggs at nesting time, and collected many greens, fruits, nuts, and berries. The crops raised were the "three sisters," along with tobacco. The early New England settlers who encountered these foods remarked on how abundant the crops were when planted in the native way: corn and bean in a small mound of earth, with the beans putting nitrates back into the soil, the corn stalks proving uprights for climbing bean vines, and wide squash leaves shading away weeds. The Native influence on early northeastern colonists can be seen in names and some preparations. The name *squash* comes from the Narragansett *askutasquash,* meaning something raw or uncooked; and succotash, a stew of corn and beans, descends from msíckquatash, or boiled corn. Succotash looked like European vegetable stew and was immediately adopted by European settlers.

Succotash

Yield: Serves 2–4

Ingredients
12 ounces young lima or kidney beans, shelled
Water to cover
1 tsp salt
12 ounces corn kernels, cut from the cob
½ pint milk or cream
1 Tbsp butter
Salt and pepper to taste

1. Place beans in a deep, lidded pan.
2. Cover them with water and stir in 1 tsp salt.
3. Bring water to boil, reduce heat to simmer, and boil 25 minutes, or until the beans are tender and water has almost evaporated.
4. Add corn kernels.
5. Add milk or cream and butter.
6. Stir mixture continually for 5 minutes.
7. Add salt and pepper to taste.

Serve as side dish.

Adapted from S. T. Rorer, 1886. *Philadelphia Cook Book: A Manual of Home Economies.* Philadelphia: George H. Buchanan and Company.

The native peoples of the southeast (known later as the Five Civilized Tribes, among them Cherokee, Choctaw, Creeks Chickasaw, and Seminole) farmed on a larger scale among highly organized communities. Early visitors commented on large field systems, some a mile square, that produced maize, beans, and squash. No ploughs existed, only hoes and planted hillocks, as in the rest of the Americas.

In the southern uplands, horticulture and hunting resembled the Northeast and Midwest. Corn was boiled whole to become hominy, with the name *hominy* coming from the Powhatan (peoples who lived on the Virginia coast) word for corn. The word also means corn soaked in wood ash, a process that allows the absorption of vitamin B_3. Without adding wood ash or lime, using corn as a main food leads to pellagra and actual malnutrition. Corn was ground into cakes, the ancestor of hominy grits and hoe cakes, while thickened stews looked like European and African preparations and were readily adapted by Old World immigrants.

The indigenous peoples of the Americas gave the world roughly 60 percent of its modern food crops, especially maize, potatoes, corn, manioc, chilies, tomatoes, most varieties of beans, and many kinds of squash. Most of these originated in Central and South America, but early European and African colonists of North America picked up some of them from native North Americans. Corn, beans, squashes, and several types of berries became staples of colonial and later foodways. Pumpkin pie, for instance, is a blending of European and Native American cooking. But hundreds of native food plants disappeared from the colonial American table. Instead, Old World animals and plants such as cows, pigs, chickens, wheat, barley, rye, apples, peaches, broccoli, spinach, lettuces, and many others came to dominate the American food landscape.

The European and African colonization of North America dramatically changed the continent's ecological systems, mostly because of the foods that the new peoples wanted. For instance, the American prairies that stretched from the rolling foothills west of the Alleghenies to the Rocky Mountains were once a sea of wild grasses. Now they are wide areas of corn, soybeans, and wheat. Old World immigrants brought three new elements of food production: new plants and animals, new means of raising and processing foods, and new ways of cooking them.

The process by which Old World plants and animals conquered the Americas has been called *ecological imperialism*. Where the climate and land were conducive to growing what the new settlers wanted, new plants were established. Sometimes the invasive species just spread naturally, replacing native species. Wheat, barley, rye, oats, peas, chickpeas, lentils, sesame, rice, turnips, carrots, radish, brassicas such as broccoli and cauliflower, cabbage, onions, cucumbers, many mustards, rapeseed, olives, raspberries, various wine grapes, apples, peaches, cherries, apricots, pears, melons, citrus fruits, figs, sugarcane, almonds, cumin, basil, coriander, and fermenting yeasts came from various parts of the Old World. Wheat was the most prized of all grains—the main cash crop. It grew well in New World climates that the Middle Atlantic colonies—especially Pennsylvania and New York—came to be called the *Bread Colonies*. Later, wheat was planted on the American prairies and plains, where it replaced wild grasses and the old wild food crops of the Native peoples. Similarly, rice was brought from Madagascar to the so-called low country of the Carolinas, where waterlogged land and a warm climate created perfect rice paddies. Carolina rice became a household staple until the late twentieth century.

Where native plants produced more food than European ones, they were adapted by the new settlers in a process called *creolization*. There are two ways that creolization took place (and still does). One is where immigrants adapt the native foods that they found because they had to. In New England, where good farmland was not abundant and wheat was harder to grow than elsewhere, corn was adapted into dishes such as Indian pudding and hasty pudding. Boston to this day is famous for its baked beans, made sweet with molasses made from sugarcane. Corn was the staple of many Southern diets, especially in mountain regions and among poorer farmers (including African American slaves), where it was eaten with pork, also called *hog and hominy*.

A second means of creolization is where old and new foods came together to be cooked in Old World ways. The most famous American creole cuisine is along the Gulf of Mexico coast, centered on New Orleans, a city founded in 1718. Here, people from Europe, Africa, the Caribbean, Central and South America, as well as Native Americans mixed their foods and cooking preparations into a true American melting pot. Gumbo and jambalaya, which are basically African dishes made with some French cooking techniques, are great examples. On the other hand, today's popular barbecues descend from Native American cooking traditions.

There is a third means of creolization. Plants and at least one animal were taken from the Americas to the Old World, modified there, and then introduced to North America. Potatoes, sweet peppers, turkeys, and perhaps tomatoes are examples. Potatoes were taken by the Spanish conquerors of Peru and other Andean kingdom to Europe in the sixteenth century. They were not eaten in most of Europe until the eighteenth century, but in Ireland, they had become the single most important food for ordinary people a century earlier. Potatoes from Northern Ireland were brought to Canada and Americas by Scotch-Irish immigrants in the early eighteenth century, but it took another century for them to become the staple food that they are today.

The turkey found on holiday tables today is not usually the North American wild turkey, but a domesticated breed from Mexico. It was brought to Spain, and from there it spread to other parts of Europe. English settlers eventually imported the fowl, and over time, new breeds were developed for the U.S. market. The sweet peppers we eat today were once hot chilies from Mexico that were tamed in Spanish gardens and then spread across Europe (Hungarian paprika comes from them via Turkey) and back to the Americas. And tomatoes, also from Central America, were brought to Spain and other Mediterranean countries and may have been introduced to

Rye and Injun Bread

Yield: Makes two loaves

Ingredients
3 cups water
2 cups cornmeal
¼ cup lukewarm water
0.75 ounce dry yeast
1 tsp sugar
4 cups rye flour, divided in half
⅓ cup cornmeal
2 Tbsp cooking oil
2 Tbsp sugar
1 tsp salt
1 cup cornmeal

1. Place water in a deep pan and bring to boil.
2. Stir in the cornmeal and boil for 1 minute.
3. Turn off heat and let cornmeal stand for 30 minutes until lukewarm and water is absorbed.
4. Place lukewarm water in a bowl and stir in sugar and yeast. Let stand until yeast foams up.
5. When yeast is ready, stir it into the cornmeal.
6. Add 2 cups rye flour, cornmeal, cooking oil, sugar, and salt.
7. Stir together and knead gently until a soft dough is formed. Add more warm water if necessary.
8. Place mixture in a large warm bowl, cover with cloth or towel, set in a warm place (75–80°F is best), and allow to rise until doubled in size.
9. When doubled, knead in 1 cup cornmeal and remaining rye flour.
10. Divide the dough in half and place each in a 9 × 5 × 3-inch bread loaf pan.
11. Cover. Let rise until dough reaches twice its bulk.
12. Set in preheated 350°F oven. Bake 45 minutes or until a skewer inserted into the loaves comes out nonsticky.

Adapted from Belle Wood-Comstock, M.D. 1916. *The Home Dietitian.* Pasadena, CA: Scientific Dietetics Practically Applied.

North America from there or from Spanish colonies in the Americas. American food is creole food, and all the plants we eat today have been genetically modified by different groups of people over time. That includes food animals.

Early Settlers and Farm Life

North America had no domesticated animals except for dogs before Old World immigration. Europeans brought cows, pigs, chickens, domesticated ducks and geese, goats, sheep, and horses to the Americas, along with some inadvertent guests—black and brown rats and house mice. Imagine what American food might be without these animals (rodents excepted). Pigs were the first invasive animals set loose in the Americas. Starting with Christopher Columbus in the 1490s, pigs were released into wooded regions of the Caribbean and North America, where they were harvested seasonally. Pigs are highly intelligent (much smarter than dogs and cats), breed prolifically, and can adapt to almost any wooded environment. They spread across North America rapidly, rooted up forests, and gobbled up Native Americans' corn and bean crops. In the nineteenth century, pigs lived openly on American city streets, eating refuse and anything else they could find. Semiwild or feral pigs were staples of colonial tables, especially in the South, where warmer climates allowed more nutritious biomass. In modern times, pigs have been bred into distinct types and are widely factory farmed, unlike their wild siblings, who remain free in their natural state.

Cattle were also early immigrants to the Americas. The nearest equivalents to cattle were bison, but they do not give milk for dairy products, nor are they usually docile. Spaniards introduced cattle into their colonies in the American Southeast and Southwest. In the East, cattle went feral and adapted to American climates, becoming resistant to diseases and heat. In the Southwest, Spanish cattle adapted to the dry, hot conditions and became the famous Longhorns of Texas. Both kinds of cattle were herded in large numbers and supplied meat to beef-loving Americans. At the same time, dairy cattle came to the Northwest, and later the Midwest, where they became the bases for major milk and cheese industries. New York State, Wisconsin, and California became prolific producers of what might be Americans' favorite food—cheese.

Goats, sheep, and especially chickens were all new to the Americas. From the earliest colonial period, no farm lacked chickens. Chickens breed rapidly, can feed themselves when left in pastures, and can be fed cheap grains and seeds when necessary. Throughout American history, chicken eggs have been a main protein source and the basis of many baked sweets. Like almost all other American foods, chickens and their eggs have become industrialized commodities.

For almost 300 years of their history, most Americans lived and worked on farms. Farms, ranches, and plantations advanced across the continent from their seventeenth-century beginnings on the East, South, and West coasts until every fertile region was occupied and exploited. From the start, food production came from two necessities: subsistence farming to feed the people who raised food, and foodstuffs grown or raised for external markets. The latter means such grains as wheat and corn, as well as cattle and pigs that were raised to sell in numerous market towns and then on to cities, where the produce was traded to national and international markets.

A good example is Chicago, which as early as the 1850s collected grain from the Midwest, sending it to Europe and on to British troops fighting Russia in the Crimean War. Later in the century, Chicago became the nation's meat-processing center, while Minneapolis grew into a great wheat-milling city.

Wheat was the prime moneymaker for farmers throughout most of American history because it was and is used for bread and both sweet and savory products. Other grains were also important depending on region. In New England, rye and oats were better suited to the less fertile soil, so dishes such as "rye and Injun" bread (corn and rye) were often on people's tables. Oats were always important crops because they were excellent horse fodder; in the days when horses were the main means of transportation and farm work, one-quarter of all American farm production went to horse feed. Later in the nineteenth century, oats were transformed into human food by the invention of breakfast cereals. Corn was widely used for both human consumption, especially among poorer people, and animal feed. Today, most corn production goes to animal feed.

Processes and Cooking Techniques

Because much of food was meant for sale in markets, new technologies developed over time. The earliest Old World settlers brought metal tools for farming, food processing, and cooking. Inventories of colonial households show iron plows, hoes, shovels, rakes, sickles and scythes, horse gear, hammers, chisels, iron straps for wheels, and especially axes. Plows harnessed to horses and oxen broke the land, allowing wide areas to be planted and agriculture to be scaled up to supply market demands. Scythes were used for harvesting even though it took a great deal of time and human effort to cut fields of ripened grain. The axe might have been the most important tool in the colonial toolbox: settlers would use it to cut down American forests to create open fields of grain and animal pasture. They were also prized trade items for Native Americans, who replaced their flint axes and hatchets with iron ones. To make and service tools, almost every American town and village had a blacksmith whose forge was worked daily. All of these implements were to be improved by farmers and inventors over time as farming became mechanized and industrialized during the nineteenth and twentieth centuries.

Farm economies (meaning what people raised, ate, and sold) differed from region to region, but cooking utensils and techniques were common in all American households. Iron pots and pans, kettles, gridirons, Dutch ovens for baking and stewing, and hooks for hanging pots over cooking fires were important items used by colonial households. Europeans cooked at home using built-in fireplaces by placing iron pots directly on the fire or hanging pots and kettles over it. Cooking ranges came into use beginning in the 1790s with Benjamin Thompson's (Count Rumford) invention of a built-in cooktop. Through the early part of the nineteenth century, the combination cooktop/oven came to be made of cast iron; by the 1850s, almost all households had one. Early colonial households also milled their own grain using hand-turned stone mills. As farming ramped up for the market, grist and flour mills sprang up across the country. Some were horse powered, but many were set in streams using flowing water for more efficient volume production. Efficiency, meaning using less personnel, was the driving force behind the food revolution to come.

In 1790, the brilliant inventor Oliver Evans patented the first automatic flour mill, and soon they were set up along Pennsylvania's Brandywine River. His mill was able to filter, or "bolt," coarsely ground, larger amounts of flour into the finer grades that bakers wanted, and at lower cost. Before long, flour mills spread across the country so that home bakers could afford to buy flour for bread and pastry baking. Evans later built a high-pressure steam engine to run his mills, the forerunner of steam-powered engines used in transportation and agriculture.

Steam power was applied to boats and a new invention, railroad locomotives, in the early nineteenth century, leading to a revolution in the ways that foodstuffs could be shipped. Prior to these, canals such the Erie Canal running from Buffalo to Albany, New York, opened in 1825, allowing Midwestern produce to be brought cheaply to Eastern cities, especially New York. The small village of Chicago became the focus of this trade, eventually becoming the nation's food-handling and -processing center. The new railway networks spread across the nation, with cities such as Chicago being hubs.

Brunswick Stew

This dish is traditionally made in a large, cast-iron pot set over an outdoor fire. It is cooked for a whole day. It can be made on an indoor stove, but a large pot is needed.

Yield: Serves 6–8

Ingredients
Have ready a large, deep 2–3-gallon pot (it does not have to be cast iron)
2 chickens, about 3–3½ pounds each
3 pounds of stewing beef or pork, cut into bite-sized chunks
24 cups water, or enough to cover the meat in the pan
6 large tomatoes, chopped into large pieces
2 cups butter beans or lima beans
6 medium-sized onions, chopped
2 red peppers, seeded and chopped
6 medium-sized potatoes, peeled or unpeeled if they have thin skins, cut in slices
1 Tbsp salt or more to taste
1 Tbsp black pepper or more to taste
6 ears fresh corn, each one cut into 2 pieces. Slit the kernels lengthwise so the juices run out
½ pound of butter

1. Place chickens and beef or pork in the pot, cover with water, bring to boil, reduce heat to simmer, and cook until the chicken falls off the bone, about 1½ hours. The water will have reduced during cooking.
2. Remove chicken and meat from pot, remove chicken meat from bones, and discard bones.
3. Return chicken and meat to the pot and add tomatoes, butter or lima beans, onions, red peppers, potatoes, salt and black pepper. Return to boil, reduce heat, and simmer for 1 hour or until potatoes are fork-tender.
4. Add corn to pot and cook for about 30 minutes. Stir butter into the stew.
5. The liquid will thicken, so stir it from time to time to make certain that the stew does not stick to the bottom of the pot.

Adapted from a recipe in Jacqueline Harrison Smith (Compiler), 1908. *Famous Old Receipts Used a Hundred Years and More in the Kitchens of the North and the South Contributed by Descendants.* Second authorized ed. Philadelphia: John C. Winston Co.

As soon as the transcontinental railroad linking San Francisco and the East Coast was completed in 1869, and another from Los Angeles not long afterward, California began its development into a major food-production center. At the same time, steamboats ran up and down the nation's navigable rivers, linking cities such as New Orleans, St. Louis, and Minneapolis—St. Paul along the Mississippi River, and Cincinnati and Pittsburgh up the Ohio. Food products flowed in ever-increasing amounts from and to every region of the country.

As transportation became available, agriculture expanded with the help of new technologies. The Midwestern prairie lands were composed of deep thick soil and lots of marshes. Plowing them was hard using cast-iron plows, but in 1831, John Deere of Illinois invented a steel plow that cut the prairies cleanly. His plow and others, among them the Oliver Chilled Plow, along with inventions such as riding plows, turned the Midwest into "America's breadbasket." To better harvest the grains, Obed Hussey invented a practical, horse-drawn reaper in 1833. Cyrus McCormick patented a better reaper in 1837, which, with many improvements over time, became the farm standard. Horse-drawn plows, reapers, binders, and mowers, along with many other new machines, increased grain production dramatically.

In 1830, it took almost 300 hours of labor to grow and harvest 100 bushels (6,000 pounds) of wheat grown on five acres. By 1890, the number of hours to produce the same amount of wheat was 40–50, and today, with full mechanization, only 3 hours are needed. With efficiency, prices for food fell dramatically over the course of the nineteenth and twentieth centuries. Cheap bread, vegetables, and meat have been major elements of American diets.

Changes in home cooking came more slowly: homemakers (who were almost universally women) spent long hours growing, processing, and preparing food, along with many other chores such as laundering. Farm women got up early in the morning so they could stoke cooking fires, pump and carry water, make breakfast, clean and wash, tend to domestic fowl, milk cows, care for their gardens that provided the family's fresh vegetables (including potatoes, green beans, corn, turnips, carrots, and greens), and prepare lunch, the largest meal of the day. That meant roasting, boiling, and baking meats, potatoes, breads, and whatever vegetables were available, and serving them in as large quantities as the family could afford.

Afternoons were spent in similar ways, including making butter and making or mending clothes and the endless numbers of other things that needed tending to during the day. Supper usually consisted of leftovers from the main midday meal, but it also took considerable preparation time. In season, women canned fruits and vegetables, salted and cured newly slaughtered meat, and made jams and jellies. In most places, they also added to the family income by selling eggs, cured and salted beef or pork, chickens and turkeys, tallow, beeswax, butter, and cheese. Such cash as a family had was spent on coffee, tea, sugar, molasses, spices, decent cloth (much preferred to homespun), cookware, and china, all of which were sold in town and village stores.

New cast-iron stoves were a great convenience, as were an increasing number of kitchen tools. Iron pans, tongs, spatulas, canning jars and pans, baking pans, toasting griddles, strainers, sieves, corers and peelers, ladles and cooking spoons, kitchen knives, and many more items filled the kitchens of even the very poorest households. Late in the nineteenth century, farm women could get these implements by mail order, sold by the new catalog stores, Sears, Roebuck, and Company and Montgomery Ward. Still, life amounted to grueling work for women farmers in general. It is no wonder that new convenience foods became popular after the Civil War.

African American Food History

One segment of the population may have worked even harder than anyone else—and their diets fell well short of most farm families. Before 1860, roughly four million people were held in bondage in the United States. Of African origin, but American in heritage long before most others, they lived mainly in the South, where they toiled as agricultural workers on plantations. A lot has been written about the lives of black people before the Civil War, and there are some generalities concerning African American food and cookery. First, along with African people, foods from the continent were introduced, including black-eyed peas, okra (called *kingumbo*, and later called *gumbo*), rice, bananas, yams, melegueta peppers, sorghum, and watermelon. When they could not find African ingredients, cooks adapted American ones: peanuts and corn were two of these.

Both on plantations and in cities such as New Orleans, African women became cooks, bringing their spicy, strongly flavored dishes into wide use. One example is gumbo, a famous Creole stew made with meats, seafood, or just vegetables (including okra), and lots of herbs and spices. African American slaves who worked on plantations were rarely given the best parts of food animals and were chronically underfed, so they adapted leftovers, along with whatever wild game and fish they were permitted to catch, vegetables from their gardens, and cornmeal, to create their own dishes. Cooks who worked in "the big house" on plantations brought these cooking techniques and tastes with them and greatly influenced Southern cuisine in particular and American tastes in general. Black cooks became famous

---

Gumbo with Beef and Shrimp

Yield: Serves 4–6

Ingredients
Oil for frying
1 pound stew beef, cut into 1-inch cubes
½ pound andouille sausage, cut into ½-inch slices
1 pound peeled raw shrimp
24 small okra pods
1 large onion, coarsely chopped
1 small serrano pepper, crushed
Water to cover
1 tsp salt, or to taste

1. Heat oil in a deep skillet until hot.
2. Place beef and sausage in hot oil and fry until lightly browned.
3. Lower heat and add shrimp.
4. Add okra, onion, and pepper to the pan.
5. Cook gently over low heat until okra and onions are slightly browned; do not overcook okra or else it will become slimy.
6. Cover the contents of the pan with water, to about 2 inches.
7. Bring to boil, reduce heat, and cook for about 1 hour, or until liquid becomes thick.
8. Add salt and adjust to taste.

Serve with or over rice.

Adapted from Lafcadio Hearn, 1885. *La Cuisine Creole.* 2nd ed. New Orleans: F.F. Hansell and Bro.

---

for their skills working in restaurants and on railways, and appearing as the faces of branded national foods. Aunt Jemima and Uncle Ben are among the best-known examples.

Industrialization

Three elements pushed the United States into its modern industrialized food system: the Civil War (and other wars), urbanization, and immigration. The Civil War (1861–1865) saw the mobilization of about 2 million Union and 1½ Confederate troops that fought in campaigns across the continent. Raising food and supplying it were critical to keeping armies in the field, and in this, the North succeeded while the South faltered. The numbers of agricultural machines used exploded as Northern farmers raised enough grain to feed the armies, the populations of Northern cities, and to export it to Europe. Machines also freed up farm workers to join the army.

Because Union troops campaigning in the South found that their food spoiled quickly, new or improved methods of preservation were employed. Canned goods that were once expensive underwent a revolution in technology that allowed quick production in massive quantities. Gail Borden's small New York condensed milk company, which boomed once given large government contracts, is one example of a food business of that period that became an iconic American brand. Canned food prices plummeted, and these foods became American staples forever afterward. Meat processing also underwent technological changes in preservation. New salting techniques for pork made it possible to keep troops supplied year round, making salt pork and hardtack (a very hard biscuit that lasted indefinitely) a standing soldiers' joke. Meat production became centralized in cities such as Cincinnati and Chicago.

German immigrant Nelson Morris formed a cattle business in 1859, and during the war, he collected and sold large numbers of animals to the army. His success and knowledge of production and distribution led him and others to create the Union Stockyards in Chicago in 1865. There, Phillip Armour, Gustavus Swift, Morris, and others centralized slaughtering, processing, and refrigerated shipping across the nation. By 1900, 80 percent of U.S. meat came from these stockyards.

Led by General Montgomery C. Meigs, the Union set up sixteen supply depots, where massive amounts of food and war materials were collected and distributed. This was the model for future food warehousing systems. Railroads were the means for supplying the depots and for getting food to troops in the field, no matter how far away they were. After the war, railroads systems expanded to accommodate farm products and processed foods. Chicago, with its centralizing meat companies, became the nation's densest railway hub, connecting it to almost every part of the nation. Within a generation of the war's end, national brands of processed foods emerged; some of them still exist, though now they are connected by both rail and the national highway system.

Manufacturing and trade were the engines of U.S. cities, and immigration the motor of population growth. Cities grew rapidly, while the number of people on farms declined. New York City, always the nation's largest, went from around 800,000 in 1860 to 4.5 million in 1910, while Chicago expanded from 112,000 to 2.1 million during the same period. Philadelphia, Baltimore, St. Louis, Boston, Detroit, and Cleveland, among others, also grew enormously. Los Angeles, now the second-most-populous U.S. city, only began its rapid growth in the 1920s–1930s. Today, more than 80 percent of Americans live in and around cities. Urban growth led to major changes in America's food.

Class differences appeared in city populations from at least the 1830s onward. Poor urban working families did not have access to fresh fruits and vegetables earlier in the nineteenth century, nor could they afford much meat or milk. Food became cheaper later in the century, so consumption of meat (always the most prized food), white bread, and sweet baked goods went up depending on a family's income, but many people remained poor and not well nourished. At the same time, growing wealth led to the rise of a small middle class and a really wealthy upper class. At the top, the rich lived in mansions or fancy apartment buildings, had servants who cooked for them, and ate in fine restaurants. Restaurants modeled on French originals, such as New York's famous Delmonico's and Rector's, served multicourse meals featuring staggering amounts of food prepared by European-trained chefs and accompanied by the best French and German wines. Any good hotel in any city served similar meals. Similar kinds of meals, though with fewer dishes, were served in upper-class homes.

Middle-class restaurants appeared in U.S. cities. These ranged from expensive to economical. For instance, in the 1890s a steak dinner at the upper end of the scale might cost $1.25, while other restaurants served "hamburger steaks" (ground beef, the ancestor of the hamburger) for 25 cents. Many of these restaurants also served multicourse meals, starting with appetizers and soups and continuing to main dishes and then desserts. Later in the century, new kinds of food service emerged in cities: cafeterias, food trucks, and street food. Cities became densely packed with workers who did both manual and clerical jobs. Most traveled by new public transit systems into the city centers, where there was a need for food served quickly because lunch breaks were short.

Cafeterias that served preprepared food sprang up in the 1880s. They came in several varieties; some had waiters, but increasingly they had counters with food that diners picked up as they moved along a line. New drugstores and cheap general stores such as Walgreen's and Woolworth's 5 and 10, respectively, added food counters and soda fountains with chairs to their stores, serving cheap dishes well into the twentieth century. Food trucks, originally horse-drawn and then motorized in the 1920s, served crowds just as they do today in many American cities. Further, many cities permitted street food vendors from whose carts everything from hot dogs to peanuts and fresh fruits were sold at very low cost.

Similar dining patterns applied to home cooking, and so did dishes in the late nineteenth century. Women's magazines such as *Godey's Lady's Book* and *Good Housekeeping,* along with newspaper articles and classes given by experts, taught middle-class women about multicourse meals and the proper ways to eat them. Cookery books now contained recipes for each course, and etiquette became an important sign of class. Middle-class families served multicourse meals that lower-class families often could not afford. Like farm meals, there might have been one main dish, such as a soup or stew, and perhaps a main meat dish on a weekend, followed by a sweet. Coffee usually accompanied meals at all levels of society.

Middle-class dishes usually included an appetizer of soup or raw vegetables such as carrots, radishes, or the very popular celery. The main dish was composed of a plate with meat in the center, a starch (especially potatoes) on one side, and perhaps a vegetable such as peas or green beans on the other. The last dish was a dessert, perhaps pastry such as pie, ice cream, or a combination of them called *pie à la mode.* This kind of meal is still the pattern today, even in prepared frozen meals.

America's agricultural production accommodated these preferences. Wheat for breads and pastry filled the prairies and Great Plains, while dairy cattle occupied grazing lands, producing cheese and dairy for everything from macaroni and cheese, Welsh rarebit (a melted cheese sandwich), and any sandwich made for lunch counters and at home. Corn came to be grown mainly for animal feed because the United States has always been among the most carnivorous nations on Earth. Recipes for fried, stewed, and roasted meats made at home are reflected in restaurant dishes, the hamburger, roast beef, and the turkey sandwich among them.

The Melting Pot

Between 1880 and 1920, about 20 million people emigrated from Europe to the United States. Most of them were from eastern and southern Europe, including Poles, Russians, Jews, Czechs, Italians, and Greeks. Most of these new Americans settled in cities or mining and factory towns where they could find work. At the same time, the United States restricted immigration from China and other Asian countries, a policy that changed only in 1965. Mexicans, whose food has always been part of Southwestern cuisine, came in larger numbers after 1910, and then again after World War II, mostly doing manual labor in agriculture and manufacturing. The foods that they brought with them changed American diets. At first, dishes such as pasta and pizza were confined to Italian neighborhoods, bagels to Jewish quarters, sausages to Polish people, and tacos, tamales, and spicy sauces to Mexican neighborhoods. Gradually, however, these foods crossed their boundaries into general usage as the immigrants integrated into American society. Italian restaurants became popular in the 1910s, and pizza became an American national dish after the 1950s. Mexican cuisine is the most popular one in the United States today, with tacos and burritos (a North American invention) on the menus of many quick dining places, as well as eaten at home. Bagels in many varieties are to be found everywhere in supermarkets and in restaurant chains. Most of these foods were Americanized—that is, made in such ways that the general U.S. public would want. The best examples are two Chinese foods: chop suey and chow mein. Although Chinatowns in cities were small, these two Cantonese dishes became immensely popular around 1900. They are nothing like the original versions, but they remain as standard dishes both in the 40,000 or so Chinese restaurants across the United States and in American cookbooks.

At the same time that immigration swelled and enriched the food cultures of U.S. cities, food production technologies advanced rapidly. After about 1910–1920, new machines such as gasoline powered tractors and harvesters replaced the horse-drawn originals. Especially after World War II, chemistry and genetics transformed American food. Animals have always been manipulated by breeding for characteristics that producers wanted, such as plumpness or more milk production. New fertilizers, herbicides, and pesticides greatly increased agricultural production, though sometimes with serious environmental costs. Food processing became ever more mechanized and efficient, ranging from canning to frozen foods (invented by Clarence Birdseye in 1924) to bottling.

Packaging also underwent a revolution from the 1930s onward: chemicals and heavily processed ingredients such as high fructose corn syrup are added to food to enhance flavor and give it a longer shelf life. Food labels often feature a long list of additives that consumers find bewildering. Naturally, there is some concern about the safety of additives, but federal and state food safety authorities have approved almost all of them as safe to eat.

To sell these newer, cheaper goods at greater volume, supermarkets appeared and spread. Americans had always shopped at specialized stores in a neighborhood, such as butchers, bakers, and greengrocers; they were handed their goods by a clerk over a counter. But the new stores changed all that. The first full self-serve store, Piggly Wiggly, opened in Memphis, Tennessee, in 1916 and not long afterward, drive-up supermarkets were born in California.

Cornbread

Yield: Serves 6

Ingredients
4 cups cornmeal
2 tsp baking soda
2 tsp salt
4 eggs, beaten
4 cups buttermilk
½ cup bacon drippings

1. Preheat oven to 450°F. Combine dry ingredients, add eggs and buttermilk, and mix well. Stir in the bacon drippings.
2. Heat a greased 10½-inch cast iron skillet in a preheated oven for about 5 minutes until very hot.
3. Pour in the batter. Bake in preheated oven for 30 minutes or until lightly browned.

American cities always had suburbs, but they exploded in number and size after World War II. Supermarkets soon appeared in increasing numbers to serve these new housing developments. And to get to the new suburbs, a new network of roads and freeways, parts of the new national interstate system, were built beginning in the 1950s. Highway systems had always played an important part of American economic and social life after the invention and widespread adoption of the automobile. Food purveyors from diners to drive-ins and roadside food stands were features of American life. With the interstate system, franchised quick-service restaurants grew rapidly; the best known of these, McDonald's, started in the 1950s. Today, these and other chains have replaced the cafeterias, serving fast food versions of the standard American dish featuring meat, potatoes, and bread to millions: the hamburger and fries.

Chain restaurants of every variety (many ethnically themed) dominate the American dining scene. After Congress passed laws allowing immigration from Asia in 1965, new foods made their way onto the American menu. Over the next half-century, Thai, Japanese, and Korean sushi and Vietnamese, Indian, and Middle Eastern dishes became popular in restaurants and at home. In cities, many other ethnic restaurants have popped up, including West and East African, Caribbean, Ethiopian, South and Central American, Chinese (from five or six regions), Filipino, and many more. Supermarket shelves now routinely stock a long list of varieties of Mexican-inspired hot sauces, sriracha (a Thai-based hot sauce), soy sauces, sesame seed oil, tofu and other soybean-based products, and varieties of Asian and Indian rices. Any American living and shopping in in 1950 would be amazed at how cosmopolitan American cuisine has become, even going as far as knowing how to eat with chopsticks.

Modern industrial-scale farming, food preservation, and transportation systems have overcome most regionalities in food production and taste. At one time, oysters from Puget Sound in Washington State or crabs from the Chesapeake Bay could be eaten only in those places and were considered local specialties. Now they are farmed and transported to every part of the United States. Commodities such as wheat and meats, apples, citrus, grapes, and many others are no longer local, unless grown by specialty farmers. There are many more such foods. America's land has been transformed by technology to produce uniform food for a mass market. Hamburgers are a good example. Still, people like to identify themselves by eating foods that are unique to their communities and families. There are lots of regional dishes and many interpretations of standard foods, such as hot dogs, that make American food more interesting than one might think.

As in the past, American food is undergoing transformations. A rising public interest in healthy eating, concerns about the environmental impact of large-scale farming, and the ethics of animal rearing have led to a rise in vegetarianism, vegan diets, and flexitarian eating (meaning a diet of mostly vegetables, but including some animal proteins). Among health concerns are obesity, a shocking upsurge in diabetes among adults and children, and diseases or allergies possibly caused by foods. Ethics and environmentalism, plus a desire for good-tasting natural foods made locally, have given rise to organic products now widely sold in markets and restaurants. Locally crafted beers, wines, liquors, and many food products go along with a proliferation of farmers' markets. All these items are changing the American food landscape to the extent that even chain restaurants are promoting healthy eating, and even organic foods.

CHAPTER TWO

Influential Ingredients

Because the meals of the United States are mainly based on European culinary traditions, most of the ingredients originated in the Old World; the important exceptions being corn and beans. The subject of a meal's ingredients is not as simple as various individual foods on a plate. Almost all foods are produced by using various modified food ingredients, or artificially made chemicals. Even most organically grown foods use fertilizers and natural pesticides to help plants produce abundantly. Antibiotics, and sometimes hormones, are widely used in the industrial-scale production of animal proteins. The chicken nugget is a good example. Industrial chickens, raised by the hundreds and thousands in large buildings and given antibiotics, are fed corn that is itself grown using chemicals. After slaughter, meat is removed from the bone and some of the meat is sent to packers where it is cut into bite-sized pieces. The best chicken nugget or chicken strip is coated in a mixture of corn meal with corn syrup added and then cooked for packaging and sale. The cheaper nugget varieties contain very finely chopped layers of skin, fat, veins, and gizzard traces and other "leftover" ingredients. In either case, a chicken nugget is really a product of other ingredients, especially corn.

Meats

Proteins supplied by animals have always been at the center of meal plates in the United States and in the middle of most handheld foods. Americans are among the world's leading carnivores, averaging 222 pounds of meat consumption per person in 2018. Though meat preferences have changed over time and differ from place to place, beef, pork, chicken, lamb, and turkey are the leading meats eaten by Americans today with beef historically the most prized of all.

Beef cattle were introduced to the Americas by Spanish settlers and explorers in the sixteenth century. Some of these cattle became feral and became naturalized to the Americas' land and climates; the most famous of these being Texas Longhorns and southern Cracker and Pineywoods breeds. Although these kinds of lean cattle supplied meat locally, the animals used today were imported mainly from England from the seventeenth to the twentieth century. Genetic manipulation by selective breeding for specific qualities that farmers wanted in the animals led to the development of modern types; the process is ongoing as "improved" animals are introduced fairly often.

Shorthorn Durham cattle from Northern England came over to the United States in the early nineteenth century. They became popular because they fattened so well, thus producing more meat, suet for cooking, and tallow for candle making. Even better were the now common white-faced Hereford. These are well muscled, efficient at grazing, and adaptable to varied climates. Purebred Herefords were brought in great numbers after the Civil War, especially to the Midwestern and Western Plains ranches. Herefords did well in the Upper Great Plains because they could withstand winter cold and could feed on varieties of forages. They were also highly successful as cross-breeders with the once feral, now tamed cattle loosed into the wild—the American Texas Longhorn.

Black Angus has become the best-known type of beef today because of advertising. Black-coated Aberdeen and Angus cattle were bred in Scotland in the late eighteenth and early nineteenth centuries and were brought to the United States because they resist harsh climates and mature early. They are thought to yield more high-quality boneless meat than other cattle and when bred with Hereford bulls, Angus cow hybrids live longer and are more efficient at calf production. What makes Angus cattle so good to carnivorous humans is that they yield fine marbled meat. Marbling means the amount of fat globules in steaks cut from the animal's ribs, making for tender meat. So successful has the Certified Black Angus campaign been that cattle with black hides, Angus, or some mixtures of them with other breeds, make up about 60 percent of American beef herds. Meat marketers have made Black Angus synonymous with high-quality and have heavily advertised it to the public.

Steaks have always been at the top of the beef eater's menu as they come in many forms and grades, from expensive to cheap depending on the animal and what part of it is used. Steaks can be broiled or fried, but grilling is the most common in modern America. Whole chunks of beef have always been used for roast and pot roasts (made with liquid and root vegetables) and are still popular. Ground beef is the most popular form with around 8 billion tons sold per year. Hamburgers sold at retail are not the only way of eating beef; since the 1960s, when a ground beef boom began in American home cooking, hamburgers have remained a major food item in food stores. From meatballs to meat loaf, and as additions to sauces, ground beef is more popular than any other beef product.

Pigs came to the Americas in 1493 when Christopher Columbus brought eight of them to the Caribbean on his second voyage. Within ten years, they were in every Spanish-held island and soon in colonies on the North American continent. The first English settlers carried pigs with them as well, so that by the middle of the seventeenth century, there were pigs everywhere in the Americas. Pigs are long lived and breed rapidly and prolifically; females give birth to eight or more piglets several times a year. None of the early pigs were the huge, fat animals seen on today's farms. Instead, they were lean, long-legged animals who were well adapted to the American forests that covered much of the land. Pigs were allowed to forage in woods and even lived freely in towns and cities and then harvested in wintertime. Being highly intelligent, a number of pigs escaped to become the famous wild razorbacks. Today, there are some 5 million wild pigs distributed in North American forests.

Pigs have always been prized for their meat and for the fat that they produce. Before shortening was invented in the early twentieth century, lard was the standard ingredient for pie crusts and for frying. Bacon, the meat cut from the pig's fatty belly and then smoked, has always been popular; Americans eat about eighteen pounds per capita annually. Pork chops can also be fatty, but lean ham prepared in several ways such as smoking is also heavily consumed.

Selective pig breeding for desirable attributes such as greater reproduction and specific qualities of meat began in the late eighteenth century. Most modern breeds are nineteenth-century creations. Thomas Jefferson imported Calcutta pigs for cross-breeding purposes. In England, the same pigs had been used to create the classic Yorkshire breed. This breed produces leaner meat and is thought of as the base for a number of others such as the Hampshire. Yorkshires were brought to Pennsylvania in the 1810s and then spread to farms in the Midwest by the 1830s. Later breeding programs led to the two most popular pig varieties: the Poland China and the Duroc. Neither Polish or Chinese, hardy Poland Chinas was developed in Ohio by a farmer reportedly of Polish descent. Duroc pigs are descendants of African pigs that came to North America as part of the slave trade and interbred with English Berkshires. Durocs were created in New York and New Jersey in the 1830s and became popular with farmers because they rapidly gain weight. Six-hundred-pound pigs are not uncommon. Commercial modern hogs, as mature pigs are called, are often raised in large numbers in confined feeding operations (CAFOs), which is nothing like pig-rearing on traditional farms of the past.

Sheep, mainly in the form of lamb, and goats are only a small part of the American diet today. Brought to North America in the Colonial period for wool production, sheep moved westward into the hilly country south of the Ohio River, such as Kentucky, and then further west onto the Great Plains and adjacent mountain areas. Mutton, a strong-flavored meat from mature sheep, was a common English dish also favored by Basque sheep herders who immigrated to states such as Utah. Burgoo or Brunswick stew made with mutton is still made for festivals in Kentucky, but otherwise has fallen out of favor. Lamb is more common among immigrant communities, such as Greeks and Middle Easterners, because it is a staple of cuisines in their original homelands. Rack of lamb, which is roasted lamb ribs, is often found in restaurants such as steak houses and those serving European cuisine. Goats are mainly consumed by more recent immigrants, such as those from Mexico, the Caribbean, and Africa. Barbacoa, roasted goat, is a common dish in many Mexican restaurants that serve regional cuisine.

Poultry

In 1992, there was a remarkable change in Americans' meat consumption: chicken surpassed beef and pork as the most popular animal protein. In 2018, Americans ate 93 pounds per person annually. For most of North American history, chicken was considered to be a special meat, usually consumed on a weekend or if on a farm eaten during the labor-intense harvesting season. However, changes in poultry breeding, rearing, and processing made chicken into a commodity sold at less than half the price of beef by the 1990s, resulting in a rise in popularity.

Descended from wild fowl native to Southern and Southeast Asia, chickens had been spread across the Old World for several thousand years by the time they arrived in the Americas. As foraging omnivores eating plants, grain, and insects, they are adaptable to many environments, are generally docile (hens can make good pets), and lay every day when in season. Spanish and English immigrants brought chickens with them to the Americas and as they colonized the continent, so did chickens; most farms had them because eggs fed the family and could be sold for cash in local markets. Early American recipes for baked goods usually call for a large number of eggs, showing that home cooks in cities, towns, and villages could buy them fairly cheaply. Chicken farming became industrialized in the 1920s. Genetic manipulation created birds that matured faster with larger breasts that laid more eggs in shorter periods of time. In CAFOs, as many as a quarter of a million chickens can be housed in large buildings, often confined to cages six-inches square, and fed vitamins and antibiotics to keep them healthy enough to slaughter and process within six weeks.

Chicken is eaten in many forms. Whole chickens are widely available, often to be roasted at home, and also popular when precooked in supermarkets. Chicken parts are commonly fried in many styles, both at home and in fast food chains that specialize in the dish. Chicken meat is also cut into strips or formed into shapes, breaded, then fried, then sold frozen or fresh in markets and in food service outlets. Fried chicken wings accompanied by sauces have become a staple snack in many restaurants and sporting venues. Chicken meat, including remnants sucked by vacuum machines from bones, is used in many inexpensive sausages. Virtually no part of a chicken remains unused.

Turkey is a popular meat in the United States but comprises only about 15 percent of the poultry market. Wild turkeys were plentiful in North America but these are not the same fowl as the kind seen on tables at Thanksgiving and Christmas because they do not breed well in captivity. Hunting and loss of wooded habitats brought wild turkeys to the brink of extinction (conservation efforts have brought them back to about 5 million). If Americans wanted turkeys, especially for holiday dinners, then they would have to have been another kind. Domesticated turkeys are birds native to Central America where they were domesticated in pre-Hispanic times. Spanish conquerors of Mexico sent some to Europe where they were bred, later spreading across Europe. English colonists then brought these Mexican types to their North American colonies in the eighteenth century where they became the base for modern turkeys. Unless an heirloom or heritage breed, the turkey served on most tables today is the Broad Breasted White, a genetically manipulated animal created to have large breasts and swift growth. Americans prefer white meat, hence a bird that has little resemblance to its wild cousins. Raised on CAFOS, turkeys are treated the same ways as chickens. Turkey is mostly served in roasted form but ground turkey and sliced cold lunchmeat varieties have become more common.

Ducks are also consumed by Americans, though at about one-third pound per person annually. They are common wild fowl in North America; roughly 45 million strong and divided into ten different species, the mallard being the most common. While wild ducks are hunted in season for food, most ducks found on American tables are farm raised and descended from the long-domesticated white Pekin duck brought over from China in the 1870s. Duck meat is dark and rich in fat and, for Americans, roasting until crispy-skinned is the usual preparation. Duck confit, meaning long

---

Tarragon and Garlic Roasted Chicken

Yield: Serves 4–6

Ingredients
1 roasting chicken, 5–6 pounds
1 Tbsp salt
¼ cup bourbon
¼ cup light soy sauce
1 cup coarsely chopped tarragon
1 cup chopped fresh garlic plants—leaves, bulb, and all
1 small piece fresh ginger, crushed or smashed

1. Clean chicken. Rub salt all over the chicken inside and out. Mix bourbon and soy sauce together. Rub the mixture all over chicken, inside and out. Place chicken in refrigerator for several hours overnight before cooking.
2. Preheat oven to 450°F. Stuff chicken with the tarragon, garlic, and ginger. Place on a roasting rack in preheated oven. Roast for 30 minutes. Reduce heat to 350° and roast for 1 hour. Check from time to time to see that color of the skin does not become too brown—it should be golden.

Remove from pan and serve chicken sliced. Serves 4–6.

Note: When chicken is cooked, use drippings for a sauce:

Ingredients
Chicken drippings
1 tsp tapioca starch
1 cup chicken broth

1. Skim off excess fat, place drippings in a pan, stir in tapioca starch to thicken, and add chicken stock. Bring just to boil and serve with roasted chicken slices.

---

and slow cooking, is a well-known French preparation commonly found in fine dining establishments in the United States and worldwide.

Seafood

Although North America is surrounded by oceans, has the world's largest freshwater seas (the Great Lakes), and contains countless freshwater rivers and lakes, Americans only eat about three ounces of fish each week. When Old World colonists arrived, they found such great numbers of fish on coasts and rivers that seafood was often seen as a cheap food to be eaten when meat was scarce and when religious requirements meant fasting. Still, Americans ate enough seafood to support salt and freshwater fishing industries. New England became famous for cod and lobsters, the Chesapeake was a major producer of oysters, shrimp remains a large industry on the Gulf of Mexico coasts, the Pacific Northwest is a main area for salmon and oysters, and Great Lakes fisheries have always been based on whitefish and other freshwater species. America's many rivers, when not polluted, have been used for both commercial and sport fishing. Catfish, an important part of Southern cuisine, is an example of both kinds of fishing.

Cooking fish depends on flavor, texture, and size. Saltwater flatfish, such as sole, flounder, and fluke, are usually poached and sometimes breaded and fried. Thicker-bodied fish with firm white flesh such as cod, haddock, tuna fish, and red snapper are commonly baked, broiled, and sometimes grilled or fried as in the famous Mexican dish *huachinango mojo de ajo* (fried snapper in garlic sauce). Oily species, salmon the most widely consumed, tend to be grilled or broiled, while smaller oily fish are often pan fried. Freshwater types of fish, such as perch, bass, trout, pickerel, and pike, are also mostly pan fried. Freshwater catfish is most often cut into strips, breaded, then fried; though catfish is also cooked in stews with vegetables. Some common fish are used by certain American communities. Carp, most of which were introduced to American waters beginning in the 1870s (goldfish are carp species), are popular among Chinese and Southeast Asians and also the main ingredient for a well-known Jewish dish called gefilte fish (ground fish balls). Of all preparations, breaded and fried saltwater fish is the most widely consumed in fast food chains and as frozen products called fish fingers.

Shellfish and crustaceans are also important but smaller segments of the seafood market. Oysters were once among the most commonplace American foods, so cheap that they were eaten by poor people but also found as appetizers on the menus of every fine dining restaurant and on the tables of the rich. From the early nineteenth century, Oysters, clams, and mussels were harvested along the East Coast from Long Island to Maryland and on the Gulf Coast and shipped across the country by boat and by train. Fresh oysters were featured in Chicago restaurants as early as the 1830s. Shellfish consumption declined dramatically, beginning in the 1910s, when oyster beds were depleted by overharvesting and severe pollution. Though oysters have made a comeback, especially as Northwest Pacific varieties have become popular, they are minor elements of the American table.

Lobsters and shrimp, on the other hand, have never lost their appeal. Though expensive, lobsters are in demand in restaurants ranging from seafood chains to fine dining venues and as regional specialties such as New Orleans lobster rolls and Po'boy sandwiches. Shrimp consumption is one of America's most popular foods with roughly four and a half pounds per person annually being consumed. Crab is less popular but almost always to be found canned on grocers' shelves across the nation, rather than fresh. Crab cakes made from shredded meat and giant snow crab legs are common restaurant items, but steamed whole crab is a regional specialty on the East Coast around Baltimore and in the Pacific Northwest. Shrimp is used as a component of dishes centered on rice and pasta, but mainly gobbled down as appetizers and as fast food. At 22 million pounds a year, Las Vegas with its many casinos and dining buffets is the highest consumer of shrimp in America. A good deal of modern shrimp production has moved to Asia, but about 100 million pounds still comes from the Gulf of Mexico.

Oven Poached Haddock

Yield: Serves 4–6

Ingredients
2 pounds haddock fillets
1 lemon, sliced
1 small onion, sliced
3 cloves garlic, chopped
3 medium tomatoes, chopped
1 tsp salt
¼ tsp pepper
½ cup white wine mixed with ½ cup water

1. Preheat oven to 350°F. Butter inside of a baking dish large enough to accommodate the fish fillets.
2. Lay fillets in dish. Place 1 or 2 slices of lemon on each fillet. Sprinkle with onion, garlic, and tomatoes. Add salt and pepper and cover fish with wine and water.
3. Cover dish with aluminum foil and bake for 20–30 minutes or until flesh flakes easily. Add water if necessary. If any liquid remains at the bottom of the dish, pour it over the fish before serving.

Other Animal Proteins

Dairy products are another main source of protein in the American diet. European immigrants from every nation brought their love of cheeses with them, while milk has always been considered a healthy food for children. Before the rise of efficient transportation systems such as canals and railroads, the large amounts of milk that cows, and to a lesser extent goats and sheep, produced could not be sent to larger markets before spoiling. Cheese, especially cheddar, can last for much longer periods, so farmers turned it out for markets in cities and towns and for use at home. All cookbooks contained recipes for making cheese-based or cheese-laced dishes and cheese dishes were always served in restaurants. Welsh rarebit, an open-faced melted cheese sandwich, was immensely popular around 1900, becoming today's melted cheese sandwich served in quick service restaurants and also made at home. Cheese was also an early portable food, used for snacking by working people, travelers, and as a staple of picnics. Cheese became more convenient with the rise of processed cheese, most famously by James L. Kraft with his American cheese packed in slices, soft Velveeta, and Cheese Whiz. Fluid milk availability has been in decline for the past 30 years, going from a high of 284 gallon per person in 1964 to 153 in 2017. Cheese consumption, on the other hand, has increased from 34 pounds per capita to more than 42 pounds in 2017. Most of this rise is due to interest in Italian-inspired foods, pizza especially, and Mexican-based dishes that both use melted cheese. Mozzarella consumption alone amounts to about 11 pounds per person. These cheeses are another example of how immigrants made American meals what they are.

Grains

Native Americans gathered, processed, and ate varieties of seeds such as corn, wild rice, amaranths, buckwheat, and sunflowers. Except for corn, most of these became minor crops when Europeans and Africans arrived in North America bringing with them wheat, barley, rye, oats, and rice. Wheat has always been the most valued of all grains because it makes the most preferred baked products. Wheat grew so well in New World climates that the Middle Atlantic colonies—especially Pennsylvania and New York—came to be called the "Bread Colonies." Wheat moved west with American settlements where it was planted extensively on the American prairies and plains, and also in California. There are numerous varieties of wheat for specific climates and landforms but the two main types are hard and soft.

Grown mainly in northern latitudes, hard wheats are used in breads and pasta because of their high gluten content. Soft wheats with lower gluten levels are used traditionally in pastries and biscuits. The wheat flours that most home cooks use are called "all purpose" flours because they are mixtures of soft and hard wheats created by milling companies for use in varieties of baked goods. There is some regionalism in flours, for example Southern cooks using soft wheat flour for their biscuits.

Corn is classified variously as a grain and vegetable. It is actually the fruit of a grass that when dried is treated as a grain, but when fresh on the cob is thought of as a vegetable. It is the most widely used grain in the world because of its versatility and fecundity: an acre produces 15 million calories of food value. Corn is used in almost every conceivable way as a food in itself and as an ingredient in food processing. Corn on the cob is a classic vegetable eaten fresh during the corn harvesting season and in public places such as picnics. Corn kernels—fresh, canned, or frozen—are also common as a standalone item or mixed with other vegetables such as green beans, peas, and carrots. A strain of corn provides one of America's leading snacks: popcorn, served either plain or with sweetening. Dried and ground corn is the main ingredient of a number of baked foods such as cornbread and in fried foods such as hush puppies. It is the basis for one of America's most famous breakfast foods: corn flakes. Because corn is used as a main animal feed, it passes to humans who eat meat. Corn is processed into syrups, flour, and starch, which are used heavily in processed foods. Almost any baked cake, ice cream, candy, and other sweets use high fructose corn syrup, while even hot dogs often contain nonsweet corn syrups. Corn starch

Native Plants

Native Americans flourished for thousands of years on plants that most Americans have forgotten as food. Researchers studying native plants have discovered that many of these plants are more nutritious than the ones now commonly eaten. Among fruits, persimmons, pawpaws, chokecherries, long-leaf ground cherries, ram's horn young green pods, skunkbush sumac, and golden currants all have much higher protein and fiber than any commonly eaten fruits. Some wild plants that people consider mere weeds are highly nutritious. Lambsquarters is rich in calcium, folates, beta carotene, and lutein, while purslane has the highest levels of omega-3 fatty acids of any plant, plus the antioxidants beta carotene, alpha-tocopherol, and glutathione. Raw purslane has a lemony flavor and is also good cooked.

is a leading thickener for manufactured foods and flour is widely used in batters for frying. Americans eat a lot more corn than most of them realize.

Barley and rye have smaller places on the American table. Grown mainly in northern tier states, from Minnesota to the Dakotas, barley can be found in "pearled" form, meaning the husk removed, on most grocers' shelves. It is used in soups and sometimes as a side dish. It is in the brewing industry that barley is most widely used because when allowed to sprout and then dried, a process called malting, it makes excellent beer. Rye, on the other hand, has been the grain used since the eighteenth century for an American alcoholic beverage called rye whiskey. Rye grows on poor soils and endures cold winters so it has been used as a substitute for wheat since agriculture began in Southwest Asia and Europe. Rye bread is commonly made by bakeries, especially those making German (pumpernickel is a whole grain rye bread) and East European breads: rye is a staple of Jewish delicatessens. Oats have been used for food as long as wheat and barley but in modern times mainly as animal feed. Oats were used by people in cooked cereals and in baking such goodies as oatmeal cookies and muffins, but they were not widely used. They first became popular as breakfast food in the 1870s, when rolled oats were invented by the Quaker Mill Company and then again in the 1990s, when the company's successor Quaker Oats publicized their product as a heart-healthy food.

Rice is the world's most heavily used grain because it is the center of most meals in all of Asia and much of Africa. Americans eat far less rice than other nations but it remains an important crop and component of the American diet. There are numerous forms of rice, the main distinctions being short grain, medium grain, and long grain. Long grain rice from Madagascar was brought to North America in the seventeenth century where it became a major crop in the "low country" of the Carolinas. Carolina rice was widely eaten until the mid to late twentieth century when production of rice on the Texas coastlands, Arkansas, and California replaced it. Immigration from Asia and the popularity of Asian cuisine has led to the rise in annual rice consumption to about 26 pounds per person. Most rice sold today is either white rice whose nutritious outer layers have been removed, or brown rice that has more nutritional value. Commercially made parboiled rice is also popular, the best-known brand being Minute Rice and a mix called Rice-a-Roni. Traditionally, Americans eat long and medium grain rice as side dishes or more typically mixed with other ingredients such as vegetables. Since many Asian restaurants serve short grain sticky rice, it has become somewhat more popular in home cooking. At the same time, imported aromatic varieties such as jasmine and basmati have become increasingly popular and are often on grocery store shelves.

Beans and Pulses

Legumes belong to a large plant family that composes important elements of the American food regime eaten directly or as ingredients in processed foods. Pulses are legumes, dried edible seeds that grow in pods. They include dry beans, dry broad beans, dry peas, chickpeas, cow peas, pigeon peas, and lentils. Leguminous plants called beans are the fresh varieties including snap or green beans, fresh peas, and lima beans, among others. However, green beans, peas, and lima beans are also thought of as vegetables. Soybeans and peanuts are legumes but not pulses since they have oily, not dry, interiors. Because beans are high in protein, fibers, vitamins, and minerals they are recommended by nutritionists and, because they are cheap, they have always been substitutes for the more expensive meats. Some of the increasingly popular meat analogue products are made from pea powder and soybeans.

Most of the dried and fresh beans that are consumed in America have native origins. Pre-Columbian peoples of Mexico and the southwest developed scores of different colored and textured beans; today, kidney beans, pinto beans, black beans, white beans, navy beans, and Great Northern beans are the most popular dried beans. Mexican-based cuisine in America uses pinto and black beans as side dishes, refried beans perhaps the best-known version. White beans, including navy and Great Northern, are the base for baked beans. One of America's best-known dishes, baked beans are made in many ways, from vegetarian to barbecue-flavored and a signature Boston dish that is loaded with molasses. Most of the pulses came to America from the Old World. Chickpeas and lentils are major elements of Mediterranean and Middle Eastern cuisines, while black-eyed peas, or cowpeas, are likely African in origin.

Snap or green beans belong to a class of fresh legumes called haricots. They come in numerous varieties, bush or pole beans the most popular of them. Most haricots are processed into frozen or canned products, though fresh beans are found in the produce sections of any market in the United States. They are usually cooked by boiling and then adding butter, mixed with other vegetables such as carrots and corn, and also in casseroles. Peas were an important high-protein plant food in Europe, commonly eaten by peasants who called it "the poor man's meat." Like green beans, peas are widely distributed as frozen or canned vegetables and one of the components of a well-known dish: carrots and peas.

Both soybeans and peanuts are significant contributors to the American table, mostly because of the products made from them. Peanuts are New World natives that were grown and eaten in the American South: Georgia is the nation's leading grower. After the Civil War, their popularity grew throughout the United States because they are a high-protein, nutritious, and cheap snack food. Ground peanut, or peanut butter, was turned into a commercial product in the 1890s and half the peanut crop of today is turned into it. Among the many other products made from peanuts, cooking oil is widely used because it does not burn as quickly as other oils. Soybeans are Asian plants that were a minor crop on American farms until the 1960s. World demand for high-protein soy products and American interest in Asian cuisines and soybean oils has led the United States to become the world's leading soybean producer. Americans eat soybeans in many forms, from tofu products, to soy sauce, soymilk, and as textured soy protein, a meat extender that is used in many processed foods. Oil pressed from soybean makes up about one-half of all cooking oils used in the United States and worldwide.

Vegetables

Vegetables are a large class of edible foods that are usually thought to mean the leaves, roots, and sometimes seeds of plants. Botanically speaking, any plant that contains seeds is a fruit, but fruits such as tomatoes and eggplants are considered to be vegetables as are legumes, peas, and haricot beans. Almost all of the vegetables that Americans commonly eat were imported from Europe. These include carrots, radishes, brassicas such as broccoli and cauliflower, cabbage, onions and garlic, eggplants, cucumbers, spinach, lettuce, celery, chard, kale, turnips and kohlrabi, many mustards, button mushrooms (a fungus that is thought of as a vegetable), and even potatoes. Potatoes originally came from the Andes Mountain region of South America, were taken to Europe, and then came to North America with immigrants. Sweet potatoes, which are not related to South American potatoes, were imported from the Caribbean. The tomato, also a South American native, corn, and beans were already cultivated in North America. Squashes, pumpkins, and other members of the *Cucurbita pepo* family are American in origin but the popular zucchini was developed in Italy in the nineteenth century and returned to North America by Italian immigrants. The same process led to the development of bell and other sweet peppers when they were taken to Spain in the sixteenth century and later returned to the New World.

The United States Department of Agriculture began publishing guidelines for healthy eating in 1916. Since 1980, guidelines have been updated every five years. These recommend that half of Americans' caloric intake be composed of vegetables and fruits. Yet in 2018, only 9 percent ate the

---

Broccoli Casserole

Yield: Serves 4

Ingredients
6–8 ounces broccoli florets
5.2-ounce can cream of mushroom soup
1 cup cooked white rice
1 small onion, diced
½ cup shredded sharp cheddar cheese
½ cup mayonnaise
1 egg, beaten
½–¾ cup bread or cracker crumbs

1. Preheat oven to 350°F. Wash and drain broccoli florets.
2. In a large bowl mix together cream of mushroom soup, cooked rice, diced onion, shredded cheese, mayonnaise, and egg.
3. Add broccoli and mix together.
4. Have ready an 8×8-inch casserole dish. Place the broccoli mixture in the dish.
5. Sprinkle bread or cracker crumbs evenly over the top of the casserole.
6. Place casserole dish in oven and bake for 30 minutes.

Serve as a side dish.

Adapted from *Recipes and Recollections*, Carmi, IL: White Country Historical Society, 2005.

---

recommended amount of vegetables and 12 percent consumed the recommended daily servings of fruit. Americans just do not eat large amounts of green and yellow vegetables; only 2 percent of American farmland is used to grow fruits and vegetables. Of the many vegetables that are available to Americans, potatoes and tomatoes are the most commonly eaten. Three quarters of American food shoppers buy potatoes and almost the same number for tomatoes, compared to 50 percent for salad mixes and broccoli and 40 percent for spinach. Americans devour 117 pounds of frozen (mostly as French fries) and fresh potatoes each year, 12 pounds of which are potato chips. About 22–24 pounds of tomatoes per person are consumed mainly in the form of sauces for Italian and Mexican dishes. In comparison, people eat about 6 pounds of broccoli, about 900 percent more than in 1990. Green leafy vegetables such as lettuces, chard, kale, and spinach are widely used in salads but at about 5 pounds a year with similar amounts for carrots.

There are several ways that vegetables are used: raw, cooked, and cooked in composed dishes. Raw vegetables are used as snacks and in salads. Carrots processed into smaller, bite-sized units and baby carrots are the most familiar snacking vegetable sold. Salads with mixed lettuces and other greens such as Swiss chard and arugula, and perhaps mixed with raw slivered carrots, green onions, and nuts, are regular features of lunch tables and served before or after main courses at dinners. All of the main kinds of vegetables are served cooked as accompaniments to main proteins on dinner plates. Vegetables are also components of cooked dishes such as stews, soups, and roasted meats and poultry. There is hardly a recipe for such dishes that does not include onions and garlic, while soups often call for carrots and onions. Many ethnic dishes liberally use vegetables, from Asian stir-fry to Mexican creations, German and Eastern European pot roasts, French and Mediterranean meat stews, and many more. Of all composed dishes, none are more American than green bean casserole—invented for the Campbell Soup Company in the 1950s.

Fruit and Berries

Americans eat more fruit than vegetables and of these the most popular are transplants from Europe, Africa, and Asia. Americans consume about 116 pounds of fruit and berries annually in the forms of fresh fruit and processed in baked goods and sauces (such as applesauce) and beverages. Traditionally, apples have been the most American of all fruits, although they were brought by European colonists in the seventeenth century. Americans love apples but what of what kind? Apples are extreme heterozygotes meaning that each new apple does not carry the same genes as its parents. Instead each apple can be a new breed. As apples spread across the country by seeding in the early nineteenth century, new kinds appeared, as many as 15,000 varieties by the century's end. Each of them had different flavors and textures. Most were sour because they were made into the most popular beverage of the eighteenth and nineteenth centuries, cider, especially the hard or alcoholic variety. During the nineteenth century, nurserymen bred numerous types, but when the apple industry became industrialized, the Red Delicious became the preferred kind. Largely grown in the Pacific Northwest, this apple is shipped across the nation. New varieties of apples from Asia and New Zealand, along with old American heirlooms, are now popular because of their eating and baking characteristics. New Zealand

Granny Smiths are good cooking apples, while Fujis and their crossbreeds such as Honeycrisps are good for eating fresh. Today, using grafting techniques, only about 10 varieties are grown on an industrial scale for the commercial market. But groups of apple detectives scour the countryside to find old apple varieties and have discovered as many as 4,500. Some already turn up in farmers markets and specialty stores.

Americans consume about 19 pounds of apples each year, but not as much as bananas at about 28 pounds a year. Bananas, native to South and Southeast Asia, were transplanted to Central and South America and the Caribbean in the nineteenth century. They were heavily marketed as healthy food that was portable and cheap. Although there are many banana varieties with different flavors, most of America's bananas are one variety, the large yellow Cavendish.

Citrus fruits such as oranges, grapefruits, tangerines, lemons, and limes account for about 24 pounds per person. All citrus fruits came from Europe, brought by Spanish colonists to California and Florida with their welcoming warm climates. Being bitter, lemons and limes are not eaten whole but are common ingredients in many prepared dishes and beverages. Much of the orange and grapefruit crops go to juice, one of the preferred breakfast beverages, though halved grapefruit was once a mainstay of the breakfast table.

Peaches, pears, cherries, apricots, table grapes, pineapples, and melons are also widely used fruits eaten at rates ranging from 3–8 pounds per person, mostly fresh and some in drinks and in jams and fillings for baked goods. Table grapes were once seasonal fruits but are now heavily imported from South America and are eaten year-round. Grapes are America's highest value fruit because they are used in making wine: 7 million tons are used each year to make 350 million gallons. Melons, like other fruits originally from the Old World, are usually seasonal treats. Watermelon, an African plant, is the most popular with Americans eating about 16 pounds compared to about 8 pounds of cantaloupe and honeydew. The avocado has become a major fruit, now consumed in various forms at the rate of 7 pounds or more per person a year. Other fruits that are more minor figures on the American table include mangoes, figs, dates, and exotics such as carambola (star fruit).

Berries have always had a place in America's kitchen and many are native to North America. Blueberries, blackberries, raspberries, and strawberries are the most commonly eaten berries, fresh and in bakery products, pies, jams, and jellies. Blueberries were a regional fruit until 1916, when highbush berries developed in New Jersey began to be grown and sold nationally. Modern cultivated strawberries are crossbreeds of American and

European varieties and consumed at 8 pounds a year are the most popular of all berries. Strawberry shortcake, for instance, is one of the oldest American baked desserts while strawberries and cream is an equally old springtime creation. Ninety percent of the nation's strawberries are grown in California and Florida, meaning that like most other fruits they are shipped thousands of miles to consumers across the nation.

Tree Nuts

At about 5 pounds per person, tree nuts are small but important parts of the American diet. Good sources of oils and proteins, Native Americans used them in many food preparations. Pecans, hickory nuts, pecans, filberts, black walnuts, and pine nuts were abundant in North American forests and readily used by European settlers. Old World species such as English walnuts, hazelnuts, chestnuts, almonds (in California), pistachios, Macadamia nuts (mainly in Hawaii), and cashews (not technically a nut, but a fruit) were introduced over the centuries. Of all native American nuts, only the pecan is commercially grown. Almonds have become the most popular of all nuts because of their perceived health benefits; almond milk is widely used as a dairy substitute. Nuts are usually sold shelled, either raw, or in the case of almonds toasted for eating out of hand as snacks. Nuts are also components of baked goods such as pies, cakes, tortes, muffins, and scones and are ingredients in candies.

Herbs and Spices

Herbs and spices are integral elements of not only American but worldwide cooking. Spices were among the first and most important trade items between the world's earliest civilizations and getting them was a rationale for Europeans to sail across the globe, beginning in the fifteenth century. American kitchens are almost always stocked with both pungent and sweet spices as well as a number of fresh and dried herbs. Processed foods also contain herbs and spices in large and small amounts. Most spices come from South and Southeast Asia, some from Central and South America, and many herbs are grown domestically, though they have European origins.

Mustard seed was an important flavoring in all Old World food preparations, not just ground into sauces but in cooking as well. Because mustards grow almost everywhere, their significance in human consumption is often overlooked. Historically, black pepper has always been the most important "hot" seasoning. Grown in southern India, it has been traded to Europe since the first millennium BCE and remains a major trade item.

Long Form Chili

Yield: Serves 6

Ingredients
1½ cups dry pinto beans, washed and sorted
4 cups water
1 clove garlic
1 Tbsp butter or cooking oil
2 pounds boneless beef short ribs; trim fat and slice thinly against grain
1 Tbsp butter or cooking oil
1 pound coarsely ground beef chuck, browned and drained
2 large onions, chopped
3 large green peppers, chopped
3 large red peppers, chopped
2 celery stalks, chopped
½ cup chopped fresh parsley
2 cloves garlic, crushed and chopped
2 bay leaves
2 Tbsp cumin
2 Tbsp chili powder
1 Tbsp oregano
2 tsp ground allspice
2 tsp ground cinnamon
2 dried red peppers, seeded and smashed
3 Tbsp salt
½ cup vinegar
1 can (12 ounces) V8 juice
1 can (28 ounces) ground Italian plum tomatoes with liquid
1 Tbsp sugar
1 ounce unsweetened chocolate, melted
2 15-ounce cans dark red kidney beans with liquid
2 chopped ripe tomatoes for color
1 can (12 ounces) of beer (1 to 2 cups depending on thickness desired)

1. Soak beans in water overnight. The next day, drain the beans. Place them in large, heavy pan with 4 cups water and 1 clove garlic. Set on stovetop, and bring to boil; reduce heat, cover, and simmer until beans are tender, about 2 hours. Drain and set aside. Reserve some of bean liquid.
2. Heat 1 Tbsp butter or cooking oil to a deep, heavy pan; add short rib slices and sauté until lightly browned.

3. While the rib meat is cooking, heat 1 Tbsp butter or cooking oil in the pan. Add ground chuck and sauté until they are slightly browned. Set aside.
4. To the heavy pan with the rib meat, add onions, peppers, celery, parsley, and garlic to the meat; sauté 2–3 minutes. Add bay leaves, cumin, chili powder, oregano, allspice, cinnamon, salt, and vinegar. Cook for 2 minutes. Stir in dried red peppers and cook for 2–3 minutes. Stir to prevent from burning. Pour in V8 juice, plum tomatoes, sugar, chocolate, and ground chuck. Bring to simmer, cover, and cook for 2 hours.
5. After 2 hours, stir in the cooked pinto beans. Adjust seasoning with salt or chili powder, cover, and simmer for 30 minutes.
6. At the end, stir in kidney beans and chopped fresh tomatoes. Add 1 can beer and allow to simmer until thickened to taste.

There is hardly a savory dish made that does not include a dose of ground black pepper. Hot pepper, originally from Central America, is the top selling hot spice. Much of it is cayenne pepper, but with Mexican, Indian, Thai, Vietnamese, Korean, and regional Chinese foods being popular, other kind of chilies are made into powders and sauces for home use. Certainly, Southwestern American chili could not be made without a spicy chili powder.

Cloves, nutmeg, and mace come from the famous Spice Islands of Indonesia, cinnamon from Sri Lanka, and cassia—a milder form of cinnamon sometimes mislabeled as cinnamon—from Southeast Asia. All of these are used in cooking, some in meat dishes, but especially in sweet baking. Cinnamon, cassia, allspice, nutmeg, and cloves are popular flavorings in cakes and pies, such as apple pie, and are used as a flavoring for hot beverages. With the rise in popularity of Indian cooking, these spices, along with cardamom, turmeric, and cumin, are utilized more frequently. Cumin is a main flavoring of Middle Eastern cookery, as well as an ingredient in a number of processed foods. Ginger is a special case because it is pungent-hot, especially if freshly ground or sliced, but is also used in many sweet baking dishes. Its antibacterial qualities have given it a wider use than just a culinary spice; the same for turmeric because of its apparent antioxidant powers.

Most of the culinary herbs regularly used in American kitchens were also imported from Europe. The popularity of Mediterranean cooking, especially Italian, has led to oregano, followed by basil and parsley, as the most popular fresh herbs. Older American cooking styles often called for thyme and sage, still the most used herbs in traditional holiday turkey dressings. Other popular herbs include rosemary (especially for poultry), marjoram (heavily used in Mexican cooking), dill (in East European and Scandinavian dishes), tarragon (French and Mediterranean food), cilantro (Mexican and South American dishes), mint, and summer savory. Fresh herbs grown in greenhouses and imported are now widely available for home cooking.

Sugar and Sweeteners

One of the most important ingredients in the American kitchen is among the least healthful: sugar. This sweet substance has been in American cookery from the earliest days and an important part of transatlantic trade. It was a leg of the infamous slave trade and the core of the Caribbean plantation system. Sugar was mainly eaten and drunk in baked products, as molasses, and as distilled into rum. The average consumption in the Colonial era was about 2 pounds a year. That figure increased dramatically as sugar became a commodity, cheaply produced in the Caribbean and on the Gulf Coast. With the development of other sweeteners, such as corn syrups, American consumption of sugar is about 130 pounds per person. White and brown sugars kept in kitchen pantries are used in baking and for sweetening beverages, but about half of American sugar intake comes from processed foods that use corn-based syrups such as high fructose corn syrup, dextrose, and glucose syrup. Other sweeteners include sorghum syrups and the healthier honey and maple syrup.

Other Ingredients

Some ingredients are not usually listed as "food" but are used in food preparation and preservation. Among these are salt, vinegars, and cooking oils. The world's oldest food preservation substance is also one of the most common of Earth's minerals—salt. Used in moderation, it enhances the flavors of bland food and so is the world's most common cooking ingredient. Salt is sold in several forms, ranging from finely ground plain table salt with or without iodine, sea salt with more minerals than plain ones, coarser salt usually called Kosher, to flavored salts. Vinegar, an acidic product, appears in more than twenty varieties, the most common being "distilled" and "white." Distilled is mildly acidic made from fermented fruits or grains while white usually comes from sugar cane and has more acid than the other kinds. Both of these vinegars are used in cooking, food preservation such as pickling, and as household cleaners. Other flavored vinegars are used for salads and cooking ethnic dishes. Red wine vinegar, balsamic vinegar (originally from Modena in Italy), rice wine vinegars (used in Chinese, Korean, Japanese, and Filipino dishes), and sherry vinegar (Spanish in origin) are found on supermarket and specialty store shelves in most of the country.

Cooking and eating oils are core ingredients in American cuisine. Since the arrival of dairy cattle in North America, butter was always the primary cooking medium and remains so for fine cookery. Animals fats—lard and suet—garnered from pigs and cattle were just as popular, though not nearly as widely used today as in the past. Cheaper substitutes made from hydrogenated oils, called margarine, were invented in the nineteenth century and are still popular in numerous forms. Cooking oils are the most popular of all substances used for frying and sautéing foods. Soybean oil, canola (from a Canadian-developed seed plant), sunflower, safflower (one the world's oldest food plants), and olive oils are all widely used. Olive oils, of various grades and national origins, are also a prime ingredient of salad dressings.

From pancakes to biscuits, breads, muffins, and cakes, Americans do a lot of baking using leavening agents. The oldest is yeast that is usually sold

---

Fruit Pancakes

Yield: Makes about 12 pancakes

Ingredients
2 cups flour, sifted
2 Tbsp sugar
1 Tbsp baking powder
1 tsp salt
2 eggs, beaten
1½ cups milk
¼ cup melted butter or oil
2 large apples (¾ pounds), peeled and finely chopped (or 1 pint strawberries, sliced, or equal amount of rhubarb, finely chopped and sprinkled with honey or sugar)
1 tsp ground cinnamon (if using apples or rhubarb)
Cooking oil

1. In a large bowl, combine flour, sugar, baking powder, salt, eggs, milk, and melted butter and beat together, leaving some lumps in the batter.
2. Add the fruit and cinnamon to the batter, mixing thoroughly.
3. Heat a griddle and coat with thin layer of cooking oil. Spoon batter into griddle and brown on both sides, about 3 minutes. Serve with syrup, honey, or fruit puree.

dried in packets but also in jars that require refrigeration. These types were developed in the nineteenth century, as were two other baking aids: baking soda and baking powder. Sodium bicarbonate derived from plants and later minerals had been used in baking since the 1830s and widely used as a cleaner and deodorant in homes. Baking powder, first patented in 1856, revolutionized American baking. Baking powder leavening dramatically shortens the time taken to raise, or leaven, flour-based products so all quick breads, biscuits, pancakes, muffins, scones, and more, use it.

Among the ingredients in America's processed foods are those largely hidden or listed in small print on package labels. Called food additives, these are mostly chemicals or naturally occurring substances used for preserving, coloring, and flavoring foods. Mono and diglycerides, tricalcium phosphate, citric acid, ascorbic acid, lecithin, sulfites, red 40, and other colorings are among those used in bakery products. All of these are considered to be safe for human consumption by the United States Department of Agriculture Food Safety and Inspection Service.

CHAPTER THREE

Appetizers and Side Dishes

Almost all the world's culinary customs have foods that are meant to stimulate diners' appetites for main meals or to serve as small accompaniments to social functions, especially those featuring beverages. Called appetizers, hors d'oeuvres, and starters, among other names, some of these also serve as side dishes at main meals. Small dishes can also become full meals when several or many are eaten together. Spanish tapas (meaning small plates) and Mexican antojitos (meaning little cravings) are two such traditional preparations that have become popular full-meal options in North America. Small appetizer-like dishes are flexible because they have many functions in American cuisine, from set meals to snacking, but mainly as accompaniments to other food and drink.

Appetizers are relative newcomers to the North American table, being a part of dining changes that took place in the nineteenth and twentieth centuries. From the earliest European settlements to the mid-nineteenth century, most meals consisted of one main dish accompanied by perhaps bread or biscuits and some kind of drink. A stew or roasted meat or fowl might be eaten, occasionally with side dishes served on separate plates such as starchy cooked foods or vegetables with perhaps a dessert to follow. Three or four-course meals were imported from Europe in the early nineteenth century by wealthier Americans who found French cooking and dining fashionable. Through fine dining restaurants, cookery books, newspaper articles, and cooking schools, these new ways of dining filtered downward to the middle-class restaurants and home cooking. By the twentieth century, a formal evening dinner began with an appetizer, followed by soup, then a main course, ending with dessert. Simpler meals might start with either an appetizer or a soup, often depending on the season, but either has the same function: to stimulate the diner's taste buds for what is to follow.

Side dishes are preparations that complement the main items on a dinner plate—usually a protein such as red meat, poultry, fish, or meat analogue—with some carbohydrate and a vegetable alongside it. In modern dining, side dishes might also be vegetables and carbohydrates but served in separate dishes. Casseroles, cooked cheese-based preparations, vegetables baked with other ingredients, poultry dressings, dumplings, relishes, sometimes raw salads or salads made of cooked vegetables, and many more are usually considered to be side dishes. Some of these kinds of foods might also be main dishes: macaroni and cheese is the most famous example.

Appetizers—Hors d'Oeuvres

Starters can be classified by type: party foods served before dinner, and appetizers served at the dinner table including soups. The first kinds are often called hors d'oeuvres from the French phrase meaning "outside of work" (there is no final "s" in the French original). The word implies eating outside of a formal meal, meaning small bites as warm ups for the main course. In the nineteenth century, when hors d'oeuvres migrated to North America, they were often the same as appetizers, simple foods served on the table just before or with the main meal. They might have been celery stalks, olives, slivered carrots, radishes, sliced hard-boiled eggs, or oysters. In fine dining situations, such as upscale restaurants or dinner parties among the wealthy, hors d'oeuvres on the tables were more complex preparations featuring pastries with bits of spiced meats or fish and delicacies such as caviar. By the twentieth century, the "appetizer" and hors d'oeuvre had separated into today's familiar types. Hors d'oeuvres came to be associated with cocktail hours, served before dinner, and usually compound preparations using crackers, small pieces of bread, or filled savory pastries. They are also found on banquet tables, especially self-service buffets. Appetizers remained on the dining table, many of them fairly simple, others taking more preparation. Raw vegetables such as celery stalks filled with flavored cream cheese is an example of a simple vegetable enhanced with an American favorite, cheese.

For some foods, the line between hors d'oeuvres and appetizers blurs with the same or similar dishes appearing in both predinner social gatherings and at the table. Popular from nineteenth century and into the first two decades of the twentieth century, raw oysters played that dual role. When they declined in popularity (largely because of sewage pollution in their East Coast beds) oysters were supplanted by shrimp. The small crustaceans from the Gulf Coast had been on American tables from the nineteenth century and when put together with piquant sauces it was called "shrimp cocktail." The phrase "cock-tail" dates to the early 1800s and meant something spicy to drink or eat. Cooked shrimp arranged around the rim of a stemmed glass or small bowl with sauce in the middle was popular in restaurants from the 1930s and by the 1960s had become a standard hors d'oeuvre at parties. Shrimp and a piquant dip remains a popular party food at home and at restaurant buffets. In fine dining restaurants, shrimp cocktail is considered to be old fashioned.

For many years, classic hors d'oeuvres were French in style with some English tea sandwiches (small crustless white bread sandwiches) usually in the mix. Hors d'oeuvres are either hot or cold with attention paid to visual presentation of the item itself and the way that they are presented. Cold types include smoked or marinated seafood, marinated vegetables either raw or cooked, charcuterie (smoked or salted meats such as ham, salami, and sliced sausages), small salads made of finely sliced or mini vegetables, and expensive caviars (eggs from fish of various species). Hot hors d'oeuvres are often pastries filled with soft cheeses, ground meats, or finely chopped vegetables that are called in French vol-au-vents, fritters, chopped meats that are battered and fried (rissoles), and croquettes, among others.

Chicken Liver Paté

Yield: Serves 6–8

Ingredients
1½ pounds chicken livers, cleaned
2 onions, sliced
1 cup water
¼ tsp dried thyme
¼ tsp ground black pepper
2 tsp salt
½ pound unsalted butter, softened
2 Tbsp whiskey, cognac, rum, or other liquor
0.75 ounce unflavored gelatin

1. Place livers and onions in a deep pan. Add water, thyme, pepper, and salt. Bring water to boil. Reduce heat and simmer, covered, for 15 minutes or until livers are done, that is, no longer pink inside.
2. Remove livers and drain, reserve liquid for gelatin. Place livers and onions in food processor or blender or use a hand mixer and add softened butter and liquor. Puree until creamy.
3. Have ready a buttered loaf mold. Place liver puree in it.
4. Strain reserved liquid. Add package of gelatin, allow to soften, and mix. Pour over livers. Refrigerate paté overnight.

One American variation of the pastry wrapped hors d'oeuvre might be the most popular of all: pigs in blankets, also called hot dog rolls. These are small sausages, often called Vienna or cocktail hot dogs when using that variety of sausage, wrapped in a pastry but leaving the ends exposed, usually baked. A modern variation is the bagel dog in which a bagel crust enwraps the small hot dog. Most of these tidbits are meant to be eaten by hand, by using toothpicks or small forks.

Of all French hors d'oeuvres, the canapé is the most popular type. Originating from the French word for "couch," it is a small piece of bread with a topping, like a person sitting on a couch. Canapé are hot or cold, the bread either a single square or round of white or whole wheat bread. Toppings vary from pickled fish such as sardines and anchovies, smoked fish like salmon, crab, and ham, to mushrooms, chopped eggs, and cheeses. Various sauces are standard for these preparations, especially flavored butters, bordelaise (red wine and bone marrow), and hollandaise (a kind of mayonnaise). Chefs trained in French techniques are schooled in making and setting out canapés in artful ways because they are thought of as party foods meant to go with lightly alcoholic aperitifs.

Mock Crab Canapés

Yield: Makes 8 canapés

Ingredients
½ cup grated mild cheese
4 Tbsp butter, softened
½ tsp salt
½ tsp paprika
½ tsp yellow mustard
1 tsp anchovy paste
1 tsp vinegar
2 Tbsp chopped olives

1. Place cheese in a mixing bowl. Add softened butter, salt, paprika, mustard, anchovy paste, vinegar, and chopped olives. Blend well.
2. Have ready 8 small rounds or squares of bread. Spread mixture on bread and serve.

Adapted from *Mrs. Curtis's Cookbook*, New York: The Success Company, 1909.

Hors d'oeuvres and appetizers were enhanced by additions from ethnic cuisines that become popular in the mid-twentieth century. One of these is the first course in an Italian meal, called antipasto, meaning before the pasta course. Popular in Italian restaurants, antipasto spilled over into party foods and has become standard forms of hors d'oeuvres. Typical antipasti trays will have bits of Italian fresh and hard cheeses, cured meats such as salami and prosciutto (cured thinly sliced ham), cooked cold calamari (squid), pepperoncini (small peppers pickled in olive oil and vinegar), olives, anchovies, artichokes, bruschetta (toasted breads covered in finely diced tomato mixtures), and Italian breads cut into small rounds. Also from the Mediterranean and related to Italian cuisine, Spanish dishes have entered the American food inventory. The best-known Spanish dishes are called tapas (also called pinchos in the northern part of the country). In Spain, these are served very much like hors d'oeuvres in taverns, bars, and parties to accompany alcoholic beverages, especially wine for which Spain is famed. Tapas bars and restaurants first became popular in North America in the 1980s; soon after, other restaurants and caterers began serving Spanish-inspired creations. Often served on small rounds of bread, as are canapés, popular tapas include bacalao (salted cod), morcilla (blood sausage), pickled peppers, small onions and other vegetables, calamares (batter dipped squid), chorizo (sausage), empanadillas (small turnovers filled with meat or vegetables), tortilla de patatas (potato-filled omelet cut into small squares), albóndigas (small meatballs), gambas (shrimp fried in olive oil), and many others. Tapas are often served with sauces of various kinds, some spicy, others more citrus-flavored as expected from a nation famed from its lemons and oranges.

American food preferences have been influenced by Asian cuisines, especially from the late 1960s onward. Since there are many Asian finger foods coming from popular street food traditions, it is only natural that some of them would transfer to American hors d'oeuvres. Dumplings of various kinds are now common in arrays of hors d'oeuvres. Chinese, Southeast Asian, and Korean steamed or boiled pot stickers are often served with soy or hot sauces. Fried dumplings of many types such as Chinese won ton and eggrolls, Korean *mandoo*, and Filipino *lumpia* are commonly served, also with sauces. Japanese cuisine also has dumplings but their best-known contribution to the hors d'oeuvres table is sushi. This is rice, wrapped in seaweed, and filled with wide arrays of fillings that range from fresh fish to meats and vegetables. The best-known American version is the California roll. Skewered bits of meat, especially the Vietnamese and Thai satays, are almost everywhere where hors d'oeuvres are served. One pseudo-Asian creation was once among the most popular appetizers/hors d'oeuvres in

America: rumaki. Rumaki is made by wrapping water chestnuts and cooked chicken liver in bacon, then marinating it in a sweet soy sauce mixture. It was invented in so-called Polynesian restaurants in the 1940s, like Trader Vic's, and was served at almost every reception, cocktail party, and in many restaurants into the 1980s, before it fell out of style.

Mexican cuisine has always had an important place in America, but from the 1970s onward, Mexican and some Latin American dishes have gained an ever-larger share of the American taste buds. Modern hors d'oeuvres include a number of Mexican or Mexican-inspired creations. Taquitos, small rolled tortillas filled with meat or cheese are as common as egg rolls, while mini-burritos are a wheat tortilla wrapped finger food. The most common hors d'oeuvres came from appetizers served in Mexican–American restaurants: tortilla chips and the related nachos. Tortilla chips are tortillas cut into wedges or strips, deep fried, and served with salsas. One of the most popular ways to use chips is with guacamole, made from mashed-up ripe avocado mixed with lime or lemon juice, chopped onion and tomato, and usually jalapeno peppers. Nachos, named for Ignacio "Nacho" Anaya, the restauranteur who invented them in Piedras Negras, Mexico, in 1943, are tortilla chips covered in melted cheese. Nachos, made with a gooey processed cheese mixture, have become a common street, ballpark, and fair food as well as a messy-to-eat hors d'oeuvre.

Guacamole is one example of foods that accompany hors d'oeuvres and appetizers: dips. Dips are liquids or semi-solid condiments used with solid foods as flavor and texture enhancers. In the case of guacamole and popular Middle Eastern foods such as hummus, the chip or bread wedge is used as an edible tool to get the condiments into one's mouth. Dips come in many forms from dairy-based preparations to emulsified sauces, and mashed beans and fruits such as avocados. Others are thin liquids such as spicy soy, vinegar-based, and hot pepper sauces for Asian foods. Sriracha is one example of a hot chili sauce that originated in Thailand and has become widely popular in North America. Chopped vegetables like Italian giardiniera are also forms of dips. Dairy-based products include sour cream (often laced with herbs such as dill), soft cheeses and processed cheese products, béchamel-based Mornay sauce, and yogurt. Mayonnaise and all of its derivatives such as seasoned aioli sauces are standard preparations. One of the most popular dairy mayonnaise-based dips is made with spinach. Both the Lipton and Knorr brands (both now owned by Unilever) created dips in the mid-twentieth century using dried onion or vegetables soup mixes with sour cream or mayonnaise and frozen spinach. Easy to make, inexpensive, and tasty with salt and fat, they remain American classics. Processed beans and pulses such as garbanzo, lentils, and black beans

---

Jan's Guacamole

Yield: Serves 4–6

Ingredients
2 large ripe avocados
½ small sweet onion, finely chopped
8–10 grape tomatoes, quartered
¼–½ jalapeno depending on its heat, finely chopped
2 tsp powdered cumin
1 tsp salt
Juice of ½ medium-sized lime
½ cup of cilantro leaves, coarsely chopped

1. Peel the avocados and remove pits.
2. Place avocados in a large bowl and mash into a rough paste.
3. Mix in the onion, tomatoes, and jalapeno. Add cumin, salt, and lime juice and mix well. Add the cilantro leaves and mix in gently. Serve on corn tortilla chips.

Courtesy of Jan Thompson.

---

are also widely used for dipping breads like pita and naan, raw vegetables, and chips. Raw vegetable-based dips are always popular and include giardiniera, relish (once called piccalilli), Mexican and Southwestern tomato and chili pepper-based salsas of all kinds and other tomato-based sauces for the ever-popular shrimp.

Table Appetizers

For many years during the twentieth century, restaurants placed relish trays on tables to serve as appetizers. Relish trays were also features of home meals such as a formal family Sunday dinner and could also serve as snacks while waiting to be seated for dinner. Most of these had simple ingredients such as celery stalks, sliced carrots, radishes, cucumber slices or rounds, small or sliced pickles, stuffed or plain olives, cauliflower florets, artichoke hearts, sliced green peppers, small tomatoes, and perhaps some cheese cubes. There might be a dip or not depending on the host's preferences. Relish trays have largely disappeared from restaurants but vegetables trays are common in home entertaining and at public functions such as parties.

Sausage as an Appetizer?

One food is rarely thought of as an appetizer: sausages. German restaurants were popular in nineteenth-century America and in the better ones, platters of fat sausages were brought to diners' tables to be eaten as appetizers before the usual heavy meal to follow. One of these restaurants was Charles Feltman's on the Coney Island boardwalk, founded in the 1870s. So popular were his sausages that he set up grills to serve customers outside the restaurant. Many other portable stands followed and helped create one of America's iconic foods, the hot dog.

Soups

In a formal three-course meal, soups serve as a kind of appetizer. In early American cookery, soups were one-pot dishes utilizing leftovers or items that could not be readily eaten. Animal bones are an example; cooking them in water is the best way to get nutrients from otherwise inedible items. Many such soups were thick, often something like a stew. These dense soups have always been part of American diets but soups served as first courses only became part of regular meals in the late nineteenth century. French food and dining habits became all the rage among America's upper classes, fancy hotels, and restaurants in the nineteenth century. By the end of that century, French styles had moved downward into middle-class home and restaurant dining so that cookery books and food and etiquette newspaper articles told ordinary Americans that soups were a necessary starter for all decent meals. The 1920s phrase "everything from soup to nuts" means a full meal from start to end and is still used today.

There are an endless variety of soups in American cuisine ranging from vegetable-based to legume and meat and poultry-based creations. Starter soups are usually more like broth, meaning the liquid produced by long cooking meat or vegetables over a long period and served either by itself or with some solids in it. French soups from which these descend are called pottages, but the most refined is the consommé. It is a clarified version, made by heating broth with a mixture of egg whites, ground meat, and finely diced vegetables to draw off impurities, leaving a clear, rich liquid. Consommé is not usually made at home, but the ingredients used in it are used in other kinds of soup.

Vegetables form the base of many soups and are often included when making soups from meats. Consommé calls for mirepoix, a mixture of diced carrots, onions, and celery and these, along with root vegetables such as potatoes, and sometimes turnips, parsnips, or rutabagas, are commonly used for pure vegetables soups. Tomatoes are also popular, especially in Mediterranean soups such as the Italian minestrone. Legumes are also widely used in soups, the best known being green and yellow pea, lentil, and soups using various beans such as navy and black. Black bean soup with lots of garlic is a famous Spanish–South American treat. Among African Americans who retain some traditional West African dishes, peanut (originally ground nut) soup is still eaten. The most common ingredients in soups are meats or meat bones. Beef broth was immensely popular in the nineteenth century because it was thought to strengthen people's bodies; today, beef bone broth is a descendant of the original. Chicken soup in all of its varieties might be the most popular soup of all. It was always on the American menu and became even more popular when French and Eastern European soups were introduced. Always said to be food for health, there is no more famous one than Jewish chicken soup, alias Jewish penicillin.

Basic soup ingredients are often mixed. Meat soups always have mirepoix, meaning diced mixed vegetables, along with herbs such as bay leaves, thyme, marjoram, tarragon, chervil, and parsley among others. Vegetable and legume soups are often made with meat broths for flavoring. Additions of dairy products form another class called "creamed" soups. Bisques are soups with milk or cream added, as in lobster bisque or clam chowder. Creamed vegetable soups are familiar on American tables and include potato, potato-leek, broccoli, cauliflower, and corn varieties. When served, soups often have additions to the basic ingredients from which they are made. Noodles of various sizes, many forms of dumplings, grains such as barley, pasta (as in the Italian pasta e fagioli (pasta and beans), rice, small cubes of toasted bread called croutons, and small round or hexagon shaped oyster crackers all appear in soups. The idea of these dishes is the same as appetizers, to encourage the diner's palate but not fill them up before the main course is served.

Salads

Salads composed of fresh greens, cooked cold vegetables, or combinations of these were well known in European cookery from the Roman period onward. Recipes for salads appear in printed cookbooks dating from the nineteenth century as healthy foods and are often thought of in the same way today. Lettuce and other greens-based salads were features of French tables in the nineteenth century where they were eaten between main courses and desserts as a kind of palate cleaner—used to remove the taste of richly sauced meats and fish so that equally rich desserts could be enjoyed. As wealthy Americans adapted French dining styles, they took up salads and that habit trickled down to middle-class homes and restaurants later in the century. Truck farmers in and around cities usually grew seasonal greens including lettuces, chards, mustard, and beet greens (kale was used mainly as cow food until the 1970s) for city markets. They also gathered wild greens such as dandelions for home consumption. By the 1870s, lettuces and greens were grown in urban greenhouses throughout the United States and when head lettuces were grown in California late in the century, they became popular because of their crunchy texture. Better known as iceberg, with crisp texture and dense heads, it was shipped fresh all over the country from the 1920s, and became the standard American salad at home and in restaurants. By the 1920s, lettuce salad was served at the beginning of the meal as a starter.

Iceberg lettuce dominated the salad world until the 1980s, when it declined in part because it has little nutritional value, but it made a comeback in restaurants in the early twenty-first century. It is usually served in wedges but also served as whole leaves as a base for other ingredients, or cut into strips. Because iceberg lettuce is flavorless, it is usually served with a lot of dressing. Usually, these were thick liquids made from mayonnaise, sour cream, buttermilk, vinegar, and oil, and often cheese. The most popular dressings are blue cheese, ranch (made with buttermilk), Thousand Island, French, Italian, and Caesar (this is usually made with romaine lettuce and croutons). High in calories, these dressings remain highly popular as a visit to the salad dressing section of any supermarket shows.

Leafy lettuces are now the most popular kinds served in restaurants and widely available in supermarket produce sections. Packaged prewashed greens such as romaine, spring mix, and mesclun are common, with specialties such as endive, radicchio, arugula (rocket), Swiss chard, kale, and shredded cabbages also available. Simple to prepare using bottled dressings, salads can also include small cherry or grape tomatoes, sliced tomatoes, cucumbers, radishes, mushrooms, onions, avocado, and even fruits such as grapes and strawberries, sliced hard-boiled eggs, and anchovies, among many others. Perhaps at no other time in American dining history have salads been eaten so widely.

Side Dishes

By definition, side dishes are foods served in smaller portions to accompany a main food item. Some side dishes are cold, others hot, some are on the plate with the main item, and some appear in separate dishes served family-style (meaning a large dish which is passed around the table from which diners take the amount that they want). Most side dishes are vegetables and starches that come from grains or root vegetables. They appear in many varieties, either as a single item such as plain green peas or string beans, or composed dishes made of several ingredients such as macaroni and cheese or potato salad.

Since humans began processing grains, long before agriculture began, breads have been the chief accompaniments to main dishes. In Western cookery, eating soup or a soupy stew without bread is unthinkable. Almost all breads are made from grain that has been ground, mixed with a liquid, leavened, or not, and baked. Starchy vegetables such as manioc (also called cassava and yuca in the Caribbean) that are made into bread-like cakes or patties serve similar functions to grain breads in West African and Caribbean cuisines, but these are not common in American cuisine. Wheats of various kinds, rye, and barley are the usual grains used in American loaf breads and many flatbreads of today, and corn is used in cornbread, a Native American creation.

Breads

Breads are usually leavened with yeast or chemicals such as baking soda and baking powder and then baked in ovens. Loaf breads using yeast take at least an hour or more to rise, but quick breads that use chemical leavening take much less time. Yeast breads are made in numerous styles ranging from soft white presliced loaf breads to crusty French and Italian styles, coarser textured whole grain and others in-between soft white and whole grain. Bread shapes also vary. While sliced bread is a standard—it makes a good sop for meat and vegetable juices—and baguettes have become popular as well. One of the most common bread forms is a small bread roll or bun called a dinner roll. These are made in many forms, either round or oblong and sometimes square, with crusts ranging from chewy to soft. They are usually set out in baskets or on plates before the main course along with butter patties and can be eaten beforehand or with the main dish. One of the most famous of these is the Parker House soft roll invented in Boston in the 1870s. It is made with milk and a little sugar and baked so that it has a slightly hard shell but a soft, somewhat sweet, interior. It and other softer rolls can be found ready for baking in frozen sections of grocery stores.

Quick breads are as old as American cuisine serving foods that accompany main dishes. Cornmeal-based breads leavened with baking powder and baking soda vary in size and shape. They range from many kinds of round Johnny cakes to cornbreads baked in sheets and then cut into squares. Cornbreads are associated with Southern cooking but are widespread throughout the United States. Even more widespread and better known are flour-based biscuits. Biscuits have always been made throughout the nation from Colonial times to the present: Bisquick is a national brand of premixed ingredients available everywhere. It is in Southern cookery that biscuits have the greatest presence and the largest variety of styles. Ingredients can vary from lard, vegetable shortening and butter mixed with milk, buttermilk, cream, egg whites, sesame or benne seeds, and flour made from soft wheats. Ways to make biscuits range from super-flaky beaten biscuits (using steel rollers, called a "biscuit brake," through which the dough is passed several times), to rolled doughs that are cut into shapes, to drop biscuits. Biscuits are served plain with butter or covered in cream or red eye (made from ham drippings) gravies. There are many other biscuit varieties, some that are regional such as Maryland or Virginia biscuits and others that are passed down generations within families.

There are some other baked accompaniments that came to mainstream American cooking from ethnic communities. Tortillas are the most widespread because of the rising popularity of Mexican and Central American foods. Tortillas are thin, flat pancakes made from dried corn that has been soaked in lime, dried, and then ground into a fine meal. Mixed with water, these are quickly baked on a comal, or flat griddle, until just cooked but still pliable. Tortillas are used as scoops for sauces or just torn into pieces and eaten with a main dish. In northern Mexico and the American southwest, wheat flour tortillas are also used the same way. Flatbreads are standard in North African, Middle Eastern, Indian, and East African culinary traditions. Among the best known are puffy yeast-raised breads called lavash, naan, and bazlama (Turkey), and non-raised chapati or roti (India and East Africa) and yufka (Turkey). All are used as wraps or torn into pieces as sops for main dishes. Most of these kinds of flatbreads are available in grocery or ethnic specialty stores throughout America.

Main Side Dishes

Cooked grains have always been used as side dishes in American cooking practice, though some have become popular only as ethnic cuisines have influenced standard cooking. Rice has been grown in North America since the seventeenth century when it was introduced from Africa into South Carolina. Fragrant Carolina "gold" rice is now rare, replaced by long and medium grain white rices and smaller quantities of short-grain rices. White rice is the central part of the grain from which the nutritious outer layers have been removed. Brown rice, which has most of the outer layer, is becoming more popular as Americans are more interested in healthy foods. Some specialty rices are now grown in America as East Asian and South Asian cuisines have entered the dining scene. Jasmine and basmati rice are now widely sold in grocery stores and so is sticky short-grain rice such as Italian Arborio (for making risotto). All these types of rice are boiled and then served plain or mixed with other ingredients, traditionally with butter, and with other seasonings depending on the style of dish being cooked. Seasoned and mixed rice dishes include fried rice (which migrated from Chinese restaurants to home kitchens), pilaf (from Middle Eastern/Turkish cookery), and rice and pasta mixtures, made famous by a commercial dried product introduced in 1958 called Rice-a-Roni.

Other grains used by Americans are bulgur wheat for North African couscous and Middle Eastern dishes, sorghum, buckwheat groats (in Eastern European cookery), and in recent years quinoa from the South American highlands. One American seed remains from pre-Columbian times as a specialty: wild rice. Grown in the upper Midwest, especially Minnesota's lakes region, wild-grown rice is collected by hand using canoes, but most commercially raised wild rice is domesticated. Expensive by itself, it is often mixed with plain rice for sale in grocery stores.

Before the 1970s, pastas were simply called macaroni, noodles, and spaghetti (originally called vermicelli, meaning little worms). Cooked macaroni served with grated hard cheese has been on the menu since Colonial times and in the nineteenth century, recipes for baking it with mixtures of softer melting cheeses became common. Today's macaroni and cheese is often served as a side dish. Flat noodles are just as old but became more prevalent with German and Eastern European immigrants who served them as side dishes and as bases on which to ladle stews and soups. Spaghetti, deriving from the word "strings" in Italian, really became popular at the end of the nineteenth century when it became either a side dish, a main dish when served with meatballs and heavy tomato sauce, or as ingredient for chili creations. Today, there are many other pastas that often appear as hot side dishes, usually with grated cheese or other dressings and as cold salads.

Vegetables and legumes are the most popular side dishes, especially potatoes; in the twenty-first century, Americans eat more potatoes than any other vegetable. Numerous varieties of potatoes of different textures can be found in today's markets, from thin-skinned white such as Yukon Gold to thick skinned Burbank Russets (used for baking and fries), to many small ones in multiple colors such as fingerlings. Considered to be a perfect accompaniment to meat and fish dishes, potatoes are made and served in scores of ways. They are boiled and served plain, mashed, baked, fried, roasted, hashed, and stewed. Within each potato cooking technique are variations in preparation. For instance, potatoes can be deep fried or pan fried/sautéed. Deep-fried potatoes may be cut into sticks of varied thickness, thin ones called "shoestring" or thicker ones known as French fries or *frites* in French. The sticks themselves might be peeled or have skins on or cut into crinkle shapes. Thin-cut deep-fried rounds, called potato chips, are widely consumed as a snack and lunch side dish. These, too, are made in various thicknesses and with different flavors. Pan-fried potatoes are usually cut into rounds and fried with onions, but when shredded and fried they are called hash browns. The most versatile of all vegetables, potatoes are also made into other kinds of side dishes such as pancakes, potato salad, puffed, stuffed, scalloped with cream, and soufflés.

Distantly related to the white potato, sweet potatoes are usually considered to be of the same culinary family. They are prepared in the same ways as their cousins: boiled, mashed, and baked. Sweet potatoes have become more popular in the twenty-first century because of their health benefits such as high in fiber and vitamins A and C and their anti-inflammatory qualities.

As plants, native to the Americas, beans of various kinds have always been on the American table. Developed into numerous varieties over the past two hundred years, fresh green beans, also called string beans, have always been staples on American tables. They are usually boiled until soft and then served plain with butter or a sauce such as hollandaise. They can be cooked with other ingredients such as bacon, garlic, and onions, but when made into casseroles they become an iconic American dish. Other fresh beans are also common, especially lima beans in several sizes and varieties.

Dried beans of many kinds are also common side dishes. Once soaked and cooked, dried beans are made into numerous styles of baked beans. Great Northern, kidney, pinto, and black beans are commonly used. Most baked bean preparations call for sugar, molasses, or syrups: vegetarian baked beans in tomato sauce or beans cooked with pork fat are the most common. Beans are almost always side dishes at barbecues and there are many canned varieties of these available on grocers' shelves. Black beans and pinto beans, either whole or "refried" (meaning mashed and fried in oil) are accompaniments to Mexican-style dishes as well as for barbecues. Cooked garbanzo beans (also known as chickpeas) appear in Italian cookery and when mashed and mixed with spices become hummus, also a side dish to many Middle Eastern-style main dishes.

Peas were a main protein source for European peasants into the nineteenth century but in America are considered a complimentary vegetable when eaten fresh. They grow in pods, so preparing them requires shelling and boiling until their outer skins become soft. Peas are usually served with butter, though are also popular when topped with creamed sauces made from butter, flour, and milk or cream. Like most other vegetables, a number of pea varieties have been developed over the past 200 years, the most common being small sweet or baby peas, larger regular peas, and a fat, mealy one called marrowfat that is popular in England and in some American kitchens. Today, most peas are sold already shelled, ready to use either frozen or in cans, though grocers sometimes sell whole peas and they are available in season in farmers markets. When mixed with diced or shredded carrots, peas are ubiquitous in grocery frozen food sections. Two fresh variations are also regularly consumed: snap peas and snow peas. These are eaten whole, pod and all, the latter widely used in East Asian cooking.

Sweet corn, distinct from corn used for meal and animal feeds, is an all-American side dish. It is served boiled or roasted on the cob, with salt and butter or, if doing it Mexican-style, with chili powder. Boiled corn kernels can be eaten plain or mixed with beans and peppers as in succotash and it also appears covered in creamed sauces, usually with some onion in it. Sweet corn is best if eaten straight from the field because the sugars in it do not have time to become starches. Since most Americans cannot get such corn unless in season and in places where it is available, they buy it either frozen for the freshest flavor, canned, or just eat corn ears from grocery stores that have become starchy with age.

Cabbages are cruciferous plants of the species *Brassica oleracea*, the same group as broccoli, cauliflower, and Brussels sprouts. Cabbages have been used in side dishes since Dutch settlers brought them to New Netherlands (now New York) in the seventeenth century. The Dutch name for cabbage, *kool*, is preserved in the name for a cold salad, coleslaw. Shredded cabbage preserved in vinegar, called sauerkraut, is a standard preparation that Dutch and German immigrants added to the American food store. Like coleslaw, it is a common side dish. Boiled cabbage was once widely used and still is when paired with corned beef, but since it gives off strong sulfurous odors, its usage waned in the twentieth century. Brussels sprouts, which look like really small cabbage heads, have far less odor and are prepared by boiling, roasting, or baking, often with melted cheese or a cheese sauce on them. On the other hand, Asian cabbage varieties such as bok choy, have risen as more and more Americans eat Asian dishes. Like sauerkraut, pickled Asian cabbage, namely versions of Korean kimchi, now have presences in many grocery stores across the nation.

Broccoli (an Italian word, meaning "little branches") and cauliflower are also vegetables in use since the Colonial period, but they did not become widespread until they were commercially grown in California in the 1920s. There are various colors of cauliflower, such as the lime-green Romanesco and purple and orange varieties, but the most common cauliflower in America is white—the large leaves covering the cauliflower head when growing do not allow it to become green. Packed with vitamins, minerals, and fiber, broccoli and cauliflower use boomed in the 1970s when they became known as healthy foods. Both broccoli and cauliflower are mainly cooked by steaming, gently boiling, and stir-frying. The best way to retain their vitamin content is by using the most advanced technological cooking technique: microwaving the florets as quickly as possible. In the early twenty-first century, cauliflower rice, meaning the florets broken into tiny bits, have become healthy substitutes for potatoes and even pizza crusts.

Greens of all kinds are frequent side dishes in an American meal. Spinach is the best known, largely because of farm industry advertising campaigns in the twentieth century: in 1931, the cartoon character Popeye became a kind of spokesperson for canned spinach. Since it is mostly water, spinach in its several varieties is low in calories but high in vitamins and fiber, hence its reputation as a healthy food. It is best when steamed, wilted in a frying pan, or very gently boiled and is often served plain or with drizzled lemon juice. One of the best-known variations is creamed spinach made in ways similar to other creamed vegetable recipes. Other popular greens side dishes include varieties of chards, especially Swiss chard and silverbeet, kales, beet greens, and—especially in Southern cooking— mustard and collard greens. Chards are delicate-leaved plants that require only slight boiling or poaching but because of bitter compounds in most kales they are usually soaked in water or parboiled before final poaching or sautéing. In Southern and Soul Food traditions, mustard and collard greens are often boiled with a smoked meat such as ham hock or turkey leg for flavoring with the juices, called "pot liquor," soaked up by cornbread.

Americans eat many types of cucurbits alongside their main dishes. This native American family includes squashes and pumpkins of both hard-shelled (winter) and soft-shelled varieties. The soft summer squashes are actually immature ones picked in the summer and include zucchini (an Italian name), pattypan, crookneck, and straightneck. They are prepared by slicing them in to sticks or rounds or in half and then boiling or sautéing with olive oil or butter and herbs. Zucchini are so prolific in household gardens that they are used in many other preparations such as stuffed recipes

Spaghetti Squash

Yield: Serves 4–6 as a side dish

Ingredients
1 3-pound spaghetti squash
4 Tbsp butter
½ Tbsp fresh ginger root, minced
½ tsp large pinch cinnamon
¼ tsp small pinch nutmeg
¼ cup white raisins
½ cup heavy cream
¼ tsp salt
¼ tsp white pepper

1. Preheat oven to 350°F. Bake squash whole for 1½ hours or until the inside is soft. Check this by poking a fork into the squash. When done, cut in half lengthwise. Scrape meat from the center and discard seeds.
2. Melt butter in skillet, add ginger, cinnamon, nutmeg, and white raisins and sauté for about 5 minutes.
3. Add heavy cream, salt, and pepper to mixture. Add squash and toss in pan to coat it. Cover pan, reduce heat to simmer, and cook for 10 minutes.

Serve as a side dish.

and in breads and cakes. Winter squashes number among them acorn, buttercup, hubbard, cushaw, and spaghetti varieties. Some, like acorn and hubbard, are cut in half, have the seeds scooped out, butter set in the middle of each concave half, and then baked until cooked through. Others such as spaghetti squash can be cut laterally, the numerous seeds removed, and then steamed or boiled until the meat, which looks like strands of spaghetti, are pulled out and then prepared with seasonings or sauces. Squash served with corn, beans, and peppers is authentically American food.

Mushrooms of various kinds are widely consumed as side dishes. Many are domesticated such as the standard white and its mature version called portobello, cremini, and baby bella, among other names. Since Asian cuisines became popular in America, mushrooms such as the Japanese Shiitake and small enoki varieties are widely available. Wild mushrooms are highly prized for their flavors, the best-known being morels, chanterelles, and porcini. The most prized and most expensive is the truffle. Mushrooms

---

Stuffed Mushrooms

Yield: Serves 8–16 as an appetizer

Ingredients
4 large mushroom caps
1 Tbsp olive oil
1 large green or red pepper, finely chopped
1 medium onion, finely chopped
8 cherry tomatoes, quartered
2 Tbsp fresh thyme leaves
½ tsp salt
4 ounces melting cheese of any kind, shredded

1. Preheat oven to 350°F. Clean mushrooms by peeling skin from the top and cleaning out the gills on the inside.
2. Heat olive oil in a frying pan; add green or red pepper, onion, cherry tomatoes, thyme leaves, and salt. Sauté until onion is translucent. Remove from heat and allow to cool. Mix cheese into the cooked vegetable mixture.
3. Place filling onto the inside of each mushroom cap. Set on a baking sheet in oven and bake for about 5 or more minutes until cheese melts and filling begins to brown. Remove from oven and cut into halves or quarters depending on how large the mushrooms are. Serves 8–16 as an appetizer.

Courtesy of Jan Thompson.

---

are usually sautéed in butter or oil, sometimes seasoned with herbs, or served plain.

There are numerous other vegetable side dishes, some seasonal, others cooked, or raw versions of staples such as carrots, onions, and green or red peppers. Tomatoes are made into various side dishes by frying, stewing, broiling, and stuffing. Asparagus is common, particularly in the spring when the plant is at its most tender. Asparagus is cooked by gentle boiling but more often steamed—there are special cylindrical pots for this task—and served with squirts of lemon juice, butter, or hollandaise sauce. Beets are usually boiled until soft, often served plain, while other root vegetables such as turnips, parsnips, kohlrabi, and rutabagas can be served in slices, seasoned with salt and pepper, glazed with brown sugar, or mashed like potatoes. Eggplants are also widespread in American cooking, though often associated with Mediterranean and Middle Eastern cooking as in baba ghanoush when mashed eggplant is mixed with tahini, olive oil, and herbs. Classic American eggplant preparations include baked recipes such as scalloping, stuffing, plain, and broiling with olive oil and herbs. Considering the variety of vegetables available to Americans, it is a nutritional shame that they do not eat more of them.

CHAPTER FOUR

Main Dishes

Probably coined in 1850s California, "square meal" has become a standard American phrase. The word "square" meaning honest, not deceptive, suggested a hearty and nourishing meal. Later, when a number was added to it, the idiom became "three square meals" or simply "three squares." That means filling, nutritious food served three times a day, something that most Americans now think of as standard eating practices. Three squares a day—breakfast, lunch, and dinner/supper—only became common by the later nineteenth century when major changes in the ways that Americans worked and lived created the now familiar pattern. Industrialization, the rise of cities and later large suburbs, along with a larger middle class and new fashions in cooking and dining led to the way that Americans came to think of meal traditions. Since cultural change is constant, and new ideas about food and nutrition arise, these three-substantial meals a day traditions have been changing. Meal composition is not exactly what it once was.

Before the majority of American lived in metropolitan areas, when most were farmers, what we now call lunch did not exist. Breakfast foods were not exactly the same, nor were evening meals. From earliest days, Americans thought of breakfast, literally breaking the fast after a night's sleep, as necessary to give them energy to start a work day. Before the industrialization of American food from the later nineteenth century onward, what that meal consisted of depended on region and social-economic class. In Colonial New England, corn boiled into mush or baked or steamed into breads with other grains (the famous "rye 'n injun") were often flavored with molasses or maple syrup. Fruit and savory pies were also popular and remained so up to recent times. In the Middle Atlantic states where English, Dutch, German, and Scandinavian settlers lived, wheat pancakes, waffles, doughnuts, and sweet buns became breakfast foods when served with increasingly popular coffee. Buckwheat pancakes were a regional specialty well into the twentieth century. Breakfasts in the South differed greatly between moneyed people such as plantation owners and poor folks including slaves.

In plantation big houses, the owners and their families ate eggs, meats—especially bacon and ham—milk and cream, biscuits and gravy, baked sweets, and corn cakes with butter and preserves of all kinds. Poor whites and African Americans made do with corn pone and hominy mush with some bits of pork, greens, and perhaps some eggs from their own chickens. The Southern city of New Orleans has always been a special food place because of its location and mixed ethnic population. There, French beignets (doughnuts), calas (fried rice cakes with sugar), French toast, and huge breakfasts featuring eggs, sausages, grits, cooked meats, and gravies were common. Such breakfasts spread to the rest of the country after New Orleans was acquired in the Louisiana Purchase of 1803.

As American farms extended across the continent, breakfasts became more substantial on the farms, while at the same time, hotels and restaurants in the growing cities also laid on New Orleans-style breakfasts for their newly moneyed clienteles. Farm families who arose at dawn might have had a small snack before their early chores such as milking followed by a more substantial meal. If the family had animals and income enough, breakfasts might include eggs, meats, breads, and often coffee, all prepared by the family women, eaten before the men did the hard work of plowing, planting, weeding, animal keeping, and much more. Women worked even harder processing and preparing food, gardening, dealing with domestic animals such as chickens, cleaning, and sewing, among other labors. They, too, ate large calorie-laden breakfasts. Dinner, not called lunch, was the day's main meal and was served at midday. Hearty fare with plenty of meat, carbohydrates, and sugary desserts such as pies were served because farm labor demanded lots of calories. What we now call dinner was usually referred to as supper and consisted of leftovers from the midday spread. It was always lighter in nature since bedtime was early and dawn was waking time when the toils began again.

Breakfasts began to change as the balance of America's population shifted from farm to city and as new ideas about healthy eating took root. Unlike farm work that started at dawn and ended at sundown, urban-based manufacturing and businesses lived by the timeclock. Work was usually done during a set number of hours and that led to changes in eating times and habits. People who commuted to work at a set time in the morning began to eat breakfasts faster than on farms, nor could most of them go home for a second large breakfast or midday dinner. Convenience and speed of food preparation grew in importance. At the same time, most Americans were concerned about eating healthier meals. Popularized by Sylvester Graham (1794–1851) among others, whole grain, coarsely ground grain was seen

Buttermilk Biscuits and Gravy

Yield: Serves 6

Buttermilk Biscuits
2 cups flour
2 tsp baking powder
½ tsp baking soda
½ tsp salt
1 tsp sugar
3 ounces butter, softened
¾ cup buttermilk, room temperature

1. Preheat oven to 425°F. Place flour, baking powder, baking soda, salt, and sugar in a large mixing bowl and blend thoroughly.
2. Cut butter into the flour mixture using a fork, pastry blender, or fingers until small pea-sized lumps are formed.
3. Add the buttermilk and mix until it is incorporated. Knead gently for a minute or two.
4. Have ready a board with flour spread on it. Lay the dough out on it and flatten it by hand or with a rolling pin until 1-inch thick. Using a 2-inch diameter glass or biscuit cutter with the edge dipped in flour, cut into 6 large biscuits.
5. Place biscuits on a greased baking sheet and bake for 10–15 minutes. The biscuit centers should be flaky. Remove from oven and serve.

Gravy
1 pound breakfast sausage, pork or chicken
5 Tbsp all-purpose flour
4 cups milk
¼ Tbsp salt
⅛ tsp poultry seasoning or powdered sage
½ tsp onion powder
¾ tsp ground black pepper

1. Place sausage in a large skillet over low heat and sauté until sausage browns. While cooking, break up the sausage into small pieces with a spatula.
2. When cooked and lightly browned, add flour; sauté for several minutes until the flour is incorporated. Add milk, salt, poultry seasoning or sage, onion powder, and black pepper. Bring to a boil, stirring constantly. Reduce

heat and simmer for 5 minutes. If the mixture becomes too thick, add some water or milk.

Serve hot over split, steaming-hot biscuits.

as a wholesome food that could prevent illness and build the body. Today, whole grains with lots of fiber are still recommended by nutritionists for a healthy diet. Milk was also another such food that, in the words of a twentieth century advertisement, helps build strong bones and is vital to good nutrition. When Dr. John Harvey Kellogg and his brother Will Keith Kellogg invented a whole grained flaked cereal at their Battle Creek, Michigan, sanitarium and marketed it as Toasted Corn Flakes in 1902, American breakfasts were transformed. It joined older cooked cereals like Quaker Oats and a flock of new ones such as Post Grape Nuts to become America's largest breakfast food category. Although cooked eggs, often with a meat, remains a breakfast standard, many other manufactured food products mean breakfast to Americans.

Lunch underwent an even greater transformation than breakfast in the nineteenth century. The word originally meant a snack, something small that could be eaten on the go between main meals. One driver of change was that people working in town and cities could not usually go home for the midday meal. New kinds of dining arose to serve these new workers. Unlike today, many factories were located in cities and neighborhoods grew up around them. Lunch could be brought to workers from home, often by women of the household, in pails—the ancestor of lunch boxes. Because the food had to be filling, it ranged from thick soups with bread to sandwiches and meat pies, often with an apple or a pie. The famous hoagie or submarine sandwich from the Philadelphia shipyards was one, the Cornish pasty among miners in Michigan and Wisconsin was another. For workers in businesses and services, ranging from shopkeepers, sales staffs, clerical workers, and many others, lunches came from street food vendors, moveable and later permanent dining cars, and small restaurants. Newly invented lunchrooms, cafeterias, and lunch counters appeared in cities across the country. Lunchrooms were created especially as safe and wholesome dining places for female clerical workers as opposed to male-only saloons and beer parlors. By the early twentieth century, lunch restaurants of all kinds served workers, shoppers, and families who came to the city for various activities. Cafeterias, for example, served lighter meals such as soups, salads, sandwiches, and entrees such as chopped beef, ham, or chicken in modest portions with vegetables at cheaper prices than full dinners. Lunch counters were almost strictly soup, salad, and sandwich places featuring items like grilled cheese, tuna fish, and egg salad sandwiches. Today's lunch eateries are really versions of the earlier types since they offer lighter quick service foods sandwiches—hamburgers, hot dogs, submarines, and pizza slices—and soups and salads.

Female customers helped shape lunch restaurants and also changed lunch eaten at home. Women of the new middle classes emulated upper-class fashions in preparing "luncheons" as forms of social gatherings. These featured nicely decorated tables, with flowers a common decoration, on which small plates of small sandwiches, light soups such as consommé, jellied sweets, ice creams, small cakes, and tea were served to guests.

Open-Faced Burgers

This recipe dates back to the 1950s when youth group leaders served them to hungry teenagers. Today, it is a quick dinner option.

Yield: Makes 8 open-faced burgers

Ingredients
1 pound ground sirloin
4 hamburger buns (8 halves)
Prepared mustard to spread
Salt and pepper, to taste
Hamburger pickles
Ketchup and preferred burger toppings

1. Have ready a heated broiler. Line broiler pan with foil. Open hamburger buns and place face up on pan. Spread mustard across each halved bun followed by a thin layer of ground sirloin reaching the edges of the bun. Salt and pepper to taste.
2. Place open-faced burgers under broiler and cook until hamburgers are browned and cooked through. Watch carefully; if edges brown to quickly, move to oven shelf below to finish.

Serve open-faced. Top with favorite burger toppings.

Courtesy of Deborah Lorentsen.

Etiquette and cookbooks from the late nineteenth century onward featured menus, recipes, and décor for such gatherings. Tea rooms, among other dining spots, served similar fare so that light lunches crossed the boundaries of home and public dining and helped create the modern idea of lunch.

Most Americans think of the evening meal, called dinner or supper, as a family meal eaten while sitting at a dining room table and consisting of a starter such as soup or salad, a main dish with perhaps some side dishes, followed by a sweet dessert. That was not what the day's last meal always was nor is it even so today. Early American dinners did not have courses, these not introduced into upper class dining until the early nineteenth century when French fashions became popular. Food courses were accompanied by the new kinds of dinnerware and utensils, namely numerous forks, spoons, and knives for each course. Fashionable plates, bowls, serving dishes, and glassware, many of them imported from Great Britain, France, and Germany, became important to proper dining. Rules for good eating manners were now to be observed by all diners. Each utensil had to be used properly, for instance, larger spoons for soups, small ones for desserts and stirring beverages, small forks for appetizers and salads, large forks and round-ended knives for main courses were among many. Americans learned to cut and eat their food in a new way: the fork was held in the left hand, the knife in the right for cutting food into small pieces. Once the piece was skewered on the fork, the diner then put down the knife, shifted the fork to the right hand and then carried the food to their mouth. This process was meant to slow down the speed of eating and to permit more conversation, just as the genteel classes in Europe did.

Knife and fork hand shifting became the fashion as dining style trends flowed downward to the middle classes. Good quality plates (often called china from porcelain dinnerware imported from Asia), tableware, and glassware became more common because of mass production. As depicted in television shows of the 1950s to the 1970s, when the American middle class was at its most prosperous, the nuclear family ate when the breadwinner arrived home from work in the early evening. The old farm suppers changed to the new pattern as many farm families shrank to only 2 percent of the population and farming became more mechanized and less manual labor intensive. Families could expect a filling main course of meat, poultry, or fish, served on a platter or separately plated surrounded by secondary foods. Much has changed since then as food tastes have altered and family dining transmuted by work, play, and convenience foods. One is just as likely to find sushi or pizza on the dinner table as a large roast beef.

Pot Roast

Yield: Serves 6 or more

Ingredients
3–4-pound pot roast (rolled or flat)
1½ cups flour
¼ cup olive oil
1½ cups red wine
2 tsp salt
½ tsp white pepper
2 tsp thyme
1 tsp rosemary, crushed
1 whole onion
4 cloves
3 bay leaves
2 turnips, quartered
2–3 carrots, cut in 2-inch pieces
2 cups beef broth, boiling
6 small red potatoes, scrubbed
6 carrots, halved
6 small onions
½ cup wine
¼–½ cup water

1. Preheat oven to 325°F. Dredge roast in flour. Heat oil in a deep Dutch oven on stovetop, add pot roast, and brown on all sides.
2. Remove Dutch oven from heat and add wine, stirring to loosen the meat scrapings and making a sauce. Return roast to pan and coat it with the sauce.
3. Add salt, white pepper, thyme, rosemary, whole onion, cloves, bay leaves, turnips, and 2-inch pieces of carrots. Cover with boiling beef broth.
4. Set Dutch oven in oven, cover, and cook for 2½–3 hours. Remove Dutch oven from oven and add red potatoes, halved carrots, and small onions. Return Dutch oven to oven, cover, and cook for 1 hour.
5. Remove Dutch oven from oven, remove pot roast and vegetables from pan, and set aside. Stir wine and then water into the remaining sauce. Serve sauce on side along with vegetables and sliced meat.

Breakfast

The Unites States Department of Agriculture (USDA), the government agency that oversees most aspects of America's food, regularly issues guidelines for healthy eating. School breakfasts and lunches are a special interest but education about nutrition in general is the ultimate goal. Recommended breakfasts include whole grain cereals, fruit juices, fruit, eggs, and milk. Calories and sodium intakes are supposed to be low because fats and sugars are kept to a minimum. For instance, a breakfast burrito with eggs, sausage, and cheese contains 681 calories, 8 milligrams of saturated fat, 480 milligrams of sodium, and 60 milligrams of sugar, while two corn tacos with eggs and black beans supply 356 calories, 3 milligrams of saturated fat, 92 milligrams of sodium, and 0 milligrams of sugar. The recommended low-calorie breakfast does not comport with another widely cited nutritional recommendation: breakfast is the day's most important meal so it should be substantial. Today's most common breakfasts are a hodgepodge of styles, from coffee and baked goods, to cereals and fruit, to eggs and meats accompanied by toasted breads.

Eggs have always been on American tables because they are a good protein source, inexpensive, and easy to cook. Despite health scares in the past concerning cholesterol levels, eggs remain on breakfast menus. Eggs can be made in myriad ways, fried and scrambled being the most common. Fried eggs are whole eggs placed in a frying pan with a fat such as butter, margarine, or cooking oil. They can be cooked until the yolk is hard or left runny—the better for dipping bread or toast in. Scrambled eggs are made by mixing the raw yolk and whites in a bowl, either plain or with a little milk or cream and seasoning such as salt and pepper. When frying, the eggs are stirred with a spoon or fork. The omelet is a form of scrambled eggs, only the egg mixture is not stirred so a kind of pancake is formed. Many omelets have other ingredients added such as cheese, bacon, ham, mushrooms, green or red peppers, onions, lobster or crab, or some combination of these. A jelly omelet is a plain one removed from the pan loaded with jelly or jam and then formed into a roll. It is eaten by cutting the roll into slices.

Other kinds of egg preparations are less common than fried, scrambled, and omelets, but often served. Boiling in the shell is the simplest method, producing both hard boiled and soft-boiled versions. The latter is usually served in a small egg cup, the top of the egg removed, and the yolk eaten with a small spoon. Poached eggs are made by breaking whole eggs into simmering water and allowing them to cook until the whites are set and a white film appears over the still soft yolks. Shirred eggs are similar, though not simmered but baked in an oven until they look like poached eggs. Both poached and shirred eggs are usually served with a sauce and other additions. The famous Eggs Benedict is composed of a toasted English muffin topped with a slice of grilled ham, a poached egg, and covered with a Hollandaise (mayonnaise-based) sauce. Other versions of poached eggs have cheese sauces such as Mornay, or au gratin, or cream sauces.

Historically, eggs have often been accompanied by meats. The Dr. Seuss story, *Green Eggs and Ham*, describes the classic American combination, save for the egg color. From earliest days, ham and eggs have been staples of home cooking and breakfasts at quick service places such as diners. McDonald's Egg McMuffin is one version of the dish. Ham and eggs with grits and red-eye (ham) gravy is a Southern specialty. Sausages or breakfast links and meat patties are also usual additions to the plate with eggs. Most sausages and patties are usually pork products, though poultry, beef, and meat substitutes are becoming more popular, with the most popular of all being bacon. American eat more than 900 million pounds of bacon each year, or about three pounds per person, so, "bacon and eggs" is as American as any on the breakfast table. Other meats normally eaten for breakfast include chicken livers, corned beef hash, and kidneys—usually in English-style breakfasts. Fish can also be a breakfast food, usually when smoked as in kippers (herring), chubs (a carp), whitefish, and thinly sliced smoked salmon in various forms, notably the Jewish version called lox.

Pancakes, also called hot cakes, griddle cakes, and flapjacks, are also iconic breakfast foods. So popular have pancakes been that a ready-mix product became the first personified brand (the brand picture or logo played as a real person): Aunt Jemima in 1893. Pancakes are also the basis of local and national restaurant chains such as The International House of Pancakes that began as a breakfast place. The most common pancakes are made by mixing white wheat flour, eggs, and milk, usually with a leavening agent, together into a batter and then cooking round cakes in a hot greased frying pan or griddle. They are usually served in stacks of at least two (called short stack), but often more with a pat of butter allowed to melt on top along with a coating of a sweet syrup. Syrups can be fruit flavored but maple syrup has always the most famous of its type. From the twentieth century onward, pancake syrups were transformed by the use of corn syrups, especially high fructose corn syrup. There are many brands using these corn products, many are simply called pancake syrup. Some are maple flavored, others with fruit tastes, but most are simply sweet. Pancakes with syrup or without are often accompanied by other ingredients such as bacon, sausage, and berries, or dusted with powdered sugar.

Other kinds of batter-based foods regularly appear on breakfast tables. Thin pancakes called crepes and Swedish pancakes are usually filled with jam, preserves, or fresh berries, rolled up, sprinkled with powdered sugar, and then cut into bite-sized pieces when eaten. Similar thin pancakes called blintzes are usually filled with dry cottage cheese, then rolled and eaten in pieces cut vertically. Potato pancakes are made with grated potatoes, onions, eggs, and a breadcrumb binder, or when done Jewish style and called latkes, matzo meal is used. Pancakes can also be puffy as in the German pancake made with more eggs and baked in an oven so that the pancake rises to overflow the pan in which it is set. German pancakes are typically served with syrups or fresh fruit and powdered sugar.

Waffles are another kind of batter-based cake commonly made for breakfast and the basis for restaurant chains. Waffles are made by pouring batter onto grid shaped iron pans and then baking on a stovetop or in an electric appliance specially made for them. There are many kinds of waffles including puffy Belgian varieties, but American waffles use batters similar to regular pancakes. In today's world of convenience foods, premade, usually frozen waffles that only require toasting, are widely available in grocery stores. Like pancakes, waffles are usually consumed with butter or margarine melting on top and syrups, but can also be served with fresh berries, cream cheese, or cooked meats such as ham or bacon on top.

Baked goods are almost always on breakfast tables, the simplest being toasted bread slices. Before the 1920s, toasting bread was often hit-or-miss because the bread had to be sliced by hand and even electric toasters (invented in 1909) required that the bread be flipped from one side facing heating elements to another. The popup toaster (1919) and sliced bread (1928) made toast easy to make and a breakfast staple, especially when it accompanies other foods such as eggs and meats. White bread is frequently used but there are lots of other kinds, from whole wheat, to multigrain, to raisin, cinnamon, and others. Toast is normally served with butter or margarine and preserves such as jellies and jams.

Other kinds of bread-like baked products can serve as breakfast meals alone. The original Continental breakfast consists of a croissant, jam, marmalade or jelly, alongside fruit juice and coffee or tea. Originally French, the croissant is a light butter-rich fat crescent-shaped roll that fairly melts in the mouth. Ideally made by individual bakeries, as in France, the croissant has become mass produced and sold for home use in most grocery stores. Perhaps the most common of the bread-type breakfast foods is the English muffin. This thick round mini-bread is usually prepared by slitting it horizontally then toasting each side and serving it with butter and preserves. Originating in urban Jewish quarters, the bagel has become a regular feature of American breakfasts. Where there are specialty bakeries, these can be bought warm from the oven, but mostly they are mass produced for grocery stores sold fresh or frozen. Bagels can be flavored with fruits and spices unlike the originals that are plain and often accompanied by cream cheese or lox (smoked salmon).

Sweet baked goods are frequent breakfast foods. Rolls, often called Danish pastries, are another European import that features in Continental-style breakfasts. Made with sugar, butter, and egg-based sweet doughs, these are usually made into rounds that are topped with sweet fruit fillings such as raspberry, cherry, or almonds, among others. They are similar to long rectangular coffee cakes, also served at breakfasts. Of all baked breakfast treats, muffins are the most American of all because they go back to the Colonial area. An American invention based on baking powder, muffins are sweet raised quick breads that are often laced with spices such as cinnamon and baked with a wide variety of berries and fruits. Blueberry and apple are favorite versions, but cranberry, raisin, and other dried fruit types are also eaten. Scones are relatives of cake-like muffins, only with more butter and more dense. Often called Scotch scones, they are commonly made with raisins or currents. Fruit pies were once very popular but today are mostly represented by premade toaster tarts invented by the Kellogg Company in 1964: Pop Tarts. Loaded with sugar, they are among the easiest breakfast-and snack-foods to make, requiring only a toaster or oven to prepare.

Other sweet products used for breakfasts include doughnuts that are available in many versions almost everywhere and are often purchased at doughnut chains such as Dunkin' Donuts. As Mexican cuisine has become more popular and panaderías (bakeries) appear in American cities and towns, so does pan dulce (sweet bread). The two most popular kinds are the *concha* or seashell, a soft, raised bun made with cinnamon and the *oreja*, an elephant ear. Other sweet breads such as Italian panettone, Polish paczki, and Danish kringles (a Wisconsin specialty) are more seasonal and specialized.

Cereals account for about 30 percent of American breakfast consumption. Hot cereals made from corn (the famous Southern grits) wheat, barley, rye, oats, or buckwheat were staples of most early American homes. Quickly-made oats became the breakfast food of choice during the late nineteenth century, and became even more popular in the late twentieth century when oatmeal was declared to be good for heart health. Hot cereal sections of grocery stores are overwhelmingly stocked with oatmeal, though other whole grain hot cereals can be found nearby. Since speed of cooking and convenience are major factors in modern American food, microwaveable cereals to be made and eaten from their containers are widely available. Since they began to be marketed around 1900 as convenient and healthy foods, cold cereals have accounted for three-quarters of all breakfast cereals. Originally, these were whole grain products such as corn flakes, wheat bran, rice and oat-based creations such as Cheerios. Preparation was and remains simple: add milk and one is ready to eat a fast and theoretically nutritious breakfast. In the 1950s, in order to attract more children to their products, manufacturers began to add more and more sugar to the point where nutritionists regularly condemn these cereals as not suitable for children. Nonetheless, the top selling cereals, such as Honey Nut Cheerios, Frosted Flakes, Froot Loops, and Lucky Charms, are well-sugared.

Dairy products are important elements of any breakfast because Americans think and have been told by food authorities that cows' milk helps made children's bodies strong and healthy. Milk is drunk straight from the glass, is poured on to cold cereals, and is used in coffee and teas. Because many people are fearful of excess weight-inducing fats, milk comes in several forms, whole (3.25 percent butter fat), 2 percent, 1 percent, and no-fat. Other kinds of cows' milk include lactose-free for people who cannot break down milk sugars in their digestive systems (actually, most of the world's adults are lactose intolerant), flavored milk such as chocolate, buttermilk (especially used in baking biscuits and quick breads), and creams that range in fat content from whipping to half and half (half whole milk and half heavy fat). Other animal milks, especially the very rich and strongly flavored goat milk, are often available in grocery and specialty whole food stores.

Other milk-based products include cheese, especially soft ones for spreading on bread such as bagels and raisin bread. Cream cheese, the best known being Kraft's Philadelphia Brand, in several forms of fat content, is common. Since the 1960s, when Americans first learned about its flavors and healthy qualities, they have come to eat a lot of yogurt for breakfast and lunch—about 14 pounds per person annually. Yogurts are sold in containers from small six-ounces to quarts with many flavorings and thicknesses. Fruits of all kinds are added to yogurt products, as are flavorings such as vanilla. The most popular kind of yogurt is called Greek yogurt, a thicker product made by draining water from the initial batches of yogurt.

When citrus fruits were made available to the national market in the late nineteenth century, oranges and grapefruits became cheap enough to serves as everyday foods. In the 1920s, Americans became, and still are, obsessed with getting more vitamins in their diets. Milk was one way, citrus fruits another. Half a grapefruit, the wedges cut from the peel, was a breakfast standard that has mostly disappeared. Orange and grapefruit juices have not and are widely sold either plain or with other fruits such as mango or berries in grocers' cold cases, as are frozen concentrated juices. Other kinds of juice stand alongside citrus, from apples to grape, pineapple, cranberry, tomato, and mixed vegetable and others. All are regular breakfast beverages usually drunk before eating the main breakfast food.

Lunch

Like all American meals, as society and the economy have changed from earlier forms, so has lunch. For many families when parents work away from home and during the school year when most children are at school, lunch is nothing like the old midday dinners on a working farm. Even when parents and children are at home, or in homes without children, lunches tend to be light repasts meant to keep one going until the final evening meal. There are three kinds of lunches: one eaten at home; packed lunches to be eaten away from home; and school lunches/canteen meals that substitute for home cooking.

Of the first two lunch types, sandwiches are chief among dishes. Among the most flexible dishes of all, sandwiches can be composed of almost anything but they must have bread, a roll, or wrapper of some kind to enclose the filling. Most Americans use presliced white bread because it is cheap, easy to use, and has the soft texture that Americans like. From the later twentieth century onward, whole grain breads became increasingly popular for health reasons. They are made in many versions, some with grains and seeds such as wheat berries, oats, flax, barley, rye, kamut, quinoa, and chia, and almost all have whole grain wheat as the base. No matter what the bread is, perhaps the most popular filling is peanut butter along with jelly or jam. Peanut butter is a product dating to the nineteenth century that became an American standard sold in several incarnations. The most common and cheapest commercial peanut butters are thick, smooth products made with some sugar and salt. Natural peanut butter, made from finely ground peanuts alone or with salt, has no sugar. Chunky products have pieces of peanut added to the slurry. One specialty peanut butter that is always found on grocers shelves is mixed with swirls of jelly already in the jar. Peanut butter is a cheap way to get protein into a diet, jelly and jam less so. Other kinds of nut butters such as almond and cashew have gained a larger share of the market because of their health benefits.

A whole category of packaged meats called "lunch meats" exists in grocers' cold cases. Sliced meats including turkey, chicken, ham, roasted beef, and salami are ready made for sandwiches as is one of the oldest forms of processed meats, bologna. Cheap and flexible because it can be eaten cold or heated, bologna has inspired famous brand jingles and food folklore. Similar in taste and texture to bologna, hot dogs are also popular lunch meats because they are quick and easy to prepare. Sandwiches usually require not only bread but condiments such as mayonnaise, mustard, lettuce, ketchup, and sometimes tomatoes and pickles. If meats are not the central protein in a lunch sandwich then cheese—usually packaged in presliced blocks or individually packaged slices, along or layered with lunch meat—is a prevalent ingredient. Nothing is more American than a ham and cheese or grilled cheese sandwich. Sandwiches are often accompanied by chips, usually made from potatoes but also from processed corn products.

Sandwiches are consumed at home or taken out for lunch at work and school. Home lunch is a regular meal for retired people living at home,

---

Tuna-Noodle Casserole

This is a version of a lunchtime dish but can also be served at dinnertime.

Yield: Serves 2

Ingredients
6 ounces elbow macaroni
2 Tbsp butter
1 green pepper, diced
1 small onion, diced
2 tomatoes, chopped
1 stalk celery, chopped
½ pound broccoli florets
1 6-ounce can tuna fish, broken into flakes
4 ounces cheddar cheese, shredded
Salt and pepper to taste

1. Preheat oven to 350°F. Boil macaroni according to package directions for about 8 minutes. When tender, drain and set aside.
2. Place butter in a frying pan and melt over medium heat. Add green pepper and onion and sauté until soft. Add remaining vegetables and sauté until soft.
3. Place macaroni in an oven-proof casserole dish. Mix in the vegetables and tuna fish. Sprinkle with cheese. Place in oven and bake for 25 minutes or until cheese is melted and bubbly.

---

parents who remain or work at home, and among families on weekends. Home lunches are often leftovers from an evening meal and can be almost anything from meats to casseroles. Soups are a common lunch, either accompanied by a sandwich or salad of by itself but almost always with bread or crackers such as saltines. Canned soups are an early convenience food later joined by prepackaged salads and dishes made from packages such as the ubiquitous and much-loved macaroni and cheese. And, of course, the possibly most popular food of all often appears, pizza. Pizza can be delivered premade or frozen to be baked or microwaved at home.

School lunches are a special category that bridge public dining, eating out, and home cooking. For a number of students coming from low-income backgrounds, school lunches (and breakfasts) might be the first or main meals of the day. School lunches have changed over time going from cheap high-carbohydrate foods in the 1930s to calorie and nutrient-conscious meals of today. Federal rules require that lunches have vegetables and fruits, whole grains, milk, and less-saturated fat proteins such as turkey frank-furters. Nonetheless, school lunches often include cheese fries, chicken strips, tacos, pizza, and chips of various kinds. Students and school staffs can also buy food from vending machines, many of which are filled with sugar and processed carbohydrates. With many choices, school lunches can resemble ones eaten at home.

Dinner

The evening meal, called dinner of supper, is usually the day's largest and most culturally significant. Since the latter part of the nineteenth century, the evening meal has been seen by most Americans as a time when family members gathered together to reinforce family solidarity. Authorities on culture and etiquette urged families who increasingly lived in urban areas to dine together at least once a day, just like farm families had always done. City and suburban houses were now built with a special room for it in imitation of the upper classes, the dining room. A family sitting around a dining room table has been an image seen in American popular culture, from movies and television to print advertising, for generations. Although most Americans eat dinner with family or companions, modern families have undergone changes in structure and activities. Today, only about half of Americans eat dinner together four or five times a week, and many do so only three times a week. This trend has led to different kinds of foods and ways of preparation being eaten for the evening meal. Dinners have become more casual, the older order of service with specialized plates for salads, appetizers, and breads having been whittled down to one small plate. The dinner plate remains large enough to hold a substantial amount of food but for everyday dining is likely to be affordable stoneware or even plastic such as melamine and not fine china. Utensils have also become simplified, just fork, knife, and teaspoon or soup spoon on the table. And with some dishes such as pizza and some fried chicken, eating from one's hands is acceptable. Still, no matter the simplification of the service, the family meal remains the ideal with families of all kinds trying to eat together.

The main dish at dinner has traditionally been a large piece of animal protein in the middle with vegetables and starch surrounding it accompanied by a sauce or gravy. The old image often portrayed in illustrations, film, and television of the father of a family craving a roast and serving it remains

---

Fettucine Italiana

Yield: Serves 4–6

Ingredients
½ pound egg noodles
½ pound spinach noodles
½ cup olive oil
10–12 broccoli florets, blanched in water for about 5 minutes, or micro-
    waved for 2–3 minutes
12 medium shrimp, deveined, shelled, and boiled for 5 minutes
2 cloves garlic, cut in half
Salt and pepper to taste

1. Prepare noodles as directed on package. Should take about 8 minutes in lightly salted water. Drain at once and set in a warm pan.
2. Heat oil in large deep skillet. Add broccoli, shrimp, and garlic and sauté 3 to 4 minutes until garlic is light brown. Add salt and pepper to taste.
3. Place pasta on each dinner plate and pour on the vegetable-shrimp mixture. Remove garlic cloves before eating.

To blanch vegetables: Boil large pan of lightly salted water. Add vegetables and cook vigorously for no more than 5 minutes. Drain in colander under cold running water, or plunge at once in ice water to prevent further cooking. Veggies should be crisp. Alternatively, place broccoli in a microwave dish and cook on high heat for 2–3 minutes, until tender-crisp.

To cook shrimp: Follow vegetable directions.

in American cultural memory. Roasted, grilled, or fried meats, especially beef, pork, or poultry, have always been the most popular. Lamb and veal have always been eaten but often thought of as ethnic specialties. Chicken has become America's most popular meat, overtaking beef in 2000 and eaten at almost double the amount of beef by 2019: roast, fried, and broiled chicken is now the meat most expected on the dinner table. Fish has also been a main course, only in much smaller amounts than meats. Catholics who follow the old religious dietary rules of meatless Fridays are among the nation's main fish consumers, though others who think of fish as healthier protein than red meats eat fish once or more times a week.

What is considered a main course is now varied for several reasons. One is the influence of ethnic foods, another is convenience of food preparation and related to that is sourcing of main dishes. Italian food became popular in the early twentieth century, especially pasta dishes such as spaghetti, ravioli, and lasagna. Accommodating to abundant meat, something scarce in southern Italy where these pasta dishes originated, and American tastes, Italian American cooks created spaghetti with large and plentiful meatballs served with lots of tomato sauce and grated hard cheese. It became a popular main dinner with many spin-offs such as pasta a la Bolognese and fettucine Alfredo among many others. Raviolis and other stuffed pastas, also with plenty of sauce, remain as main courses, as does lasagna—wide noodles layered with meat and cheese, covered in tomato sauce and baked. Dinner dishes might now be Chinese or Southeast Asian stir-fry or rice-based dishes, Latin American rice and bean preparations, or Indian curries. And with the rise of vegetarian and vegan dishes—made entirely from plants, such as potatoes, eggplants, beans, and peas—vegetables and

Convenience Foods

Two kinds of food have had major influences on American's dining habits: convenience foods and ethnic foods. Canning was the earliest kind of convenience food and Italian-inspired spaghetti was subjected to it when a French chef named Alphonse Biardot opened a successful canned soup and canned spaghetti plant in Jersey City in 1886. Today's can of SpaghettiOs is a direct descendant. Canned Chinese-based chop suey and chow mein is also found canned on grocers' shelves. That began in 1922 when a Korean, Dr. Ilhan New, and his friend Wally Smith, an American grocer, founded the La Choy Company in Detroit, Michigan. La Choy remains a major brand of not-exactly-authentic Chinese cuisine.

legumes are the basis of several popular meat alternatives that are now common as main dinner dishes.

Convenience of food preparation in the form of premade dinner dishes has been part of American life since the nineteenth century. Canned meats such as corned beef and canned tuna fish were among the first of the ready-to-eat foods. In 1928, Chef Boyardee began selling canned pasta preparations and in the 1930s, prepared stews such as Dinty Moore made by George A. Hormel & Company were sold. In the 1940s, canned chow mein became immensely popular followed by frozen dishes such as pizza and pizza rolls that could be microwaved. Frozen entrees took off after World War II, made famous and widespread as TV dinners produced by C.A. Swanson & Sons. Although the company did not invent such meals, its brand became the market standard. Placed in a compartmented foil tray, a typical TV dinner was a meat portion—turkey and Salisbury steak the most common—with a side of mashed potato and a green vegetable such as peas and a gravy. Heated in an oven, they were ready for eating while presumably the diner sat in front of a television set. Actually, these were ideal for working families who did not have time to cook meals from scratch. Other kinds of frozen dinners have remained popular and are found in every grocery store, especially those that come in microwaveable packaging. Among the largest consumers of these kinds of meals are senior citizens, some of whom live alone, and single people who often eat at home alone. As people have become more health conscious, varieties of vegetarian foods are increasingly sold, as are a wide variety of ethnic dishes ranging from Asian to Latin American.

Take-out food has become larger part of home dining since 2000. There are several forms of such cuisine: dishes prepared by restaurants, by food

Microwave Ovens

What is the most important modern kitchen tool, aside from stoves, pots, pans, and manual utensils, ever invented? Many argue that it is the microwave oven. Microwave ovens began as World War II radar equipment. Scientists at Raytheon, the company that made radar, noticed that things got hot when near the rays emitted by the radar. In 1947, the company sold the first oven for $3,000 ($35,000 in 2019 U.S. dollars). By the 1970s, prices dropped and microwave sales zoomed, so did food products made to be cooked in them. Today, 90 percent of homes have them, as do almost every restaurant, cafeteria, school, hospital, vending place, even hotel rooms.

stores, and by companies that sell pre-portioned, ready-to-cook ingredients. Chinese food and pizza have traditionally been the most popular foods for home delivery. Since 2010, preferences have changed to chicken, mostly fried, accounting for 20 percent of all deliveries, followed by Chinese, pizza, sushi, Mexican, hamburgers, and pasta. Even these favorites are changing as restaurant delivery services have linked to a greater variety of restaurants to meet diners' more varied tastes. One service reported that poke bowls, bean burritos, chicken sliders (chicken sandwich), cauliflower rice bowl, and buffalo cauliflower were among the most popular dishes ordered.

Food stores have moved into the prepared food market in the twenty-first century, especially with roasted chicken. The warehouse stores chain COSTCO has sold so many that they now operate their own chicken-raising and processing facilities. Prepared green, vegetable, and pasta salads, meat, pasta, and rice dishes can be found in almost all stores as whole areas are now devoted to making meals to be taken home. Several major chains are now offering home delivery as well as store pick-up meals.

A newer kind of home service is one where preportioned ingredients are delivered in packages ready for quick and easy cooking at home. Most of them offer dishes to accommodate varied diets such as vegetarian, vegan, paleo, keto, gluten free, diabetic, and "kid-friendly" dishes. Many make international dishes that might not be made at home, such as Moroccan chicken with harissa sauce and tagine vegetables and chicken, chicken tikka masala, and many others including old fashioned beef dishes. Like other kinds of delivered foods, these are meant to be eaten in a family setting or with groups of friends sitting together, as is the American tradition. No matter what the circumstances, roughly 80 percent of all American evening meals are consumed at home.

CHAPTER FIVE

Desserts

Hardly any American dinners are complete, meaning fully satisfying to the diner, without a sweet course at the end. Before the nineteenth century, sugary desserts that are common today hardly existed; fresh and dried fruits and nuts were often served after dinner parties or in wealthier homes along with tea or coffee. Cheap sugar largely produced on slave-worked plantations in the Caribbean entered Europe and its colonies in the later seventeenth century and revolutionized sweet cookery. A number of main dishes had sugar added to them or were served with sweetened condiments: lamb with mint sauce and turkey with cranberry sauce are two that remain on American menus. Pies that were once mainly savory, such as meat pot pies, became sweet ones that were reserved for dessert. As with other parts of meals, French styles greatly influenced the English-speaking world including America. The word dessert comes from a seventeenth century French *dessirvir* that means "to remove what has been served" implying that something will be served after the main meal. While fruits and nuts and cheese remained on menus, French chefs developed sugar-based treats such as iced cakes, macaroons, meringues, ice creams, tarts, and various custards, among others. Along with other elements of the meal, these were adopted by Americans in the early nineteenth century.

So sweet is the American palate that some people are accused of only eating a meal in order to get to the dessert; for generations, parents have admonished children that unless they eat their vegetables, they won't get dessert. Over the same generations, home cooks have taken special pains to create desserts. Anyone opening one of the thousands of community cookbooks printed since they began in the 1860s will see that a significant portion of the recipes are desserts. Most of these are baked goods, pies, cakes, and cookies being dominant, but there are plenty of custards, ice creams, and gelatin treats as well. One reason for desserts' overwhelming presence in community cookbooks—and in family recipe collections—is that in the past, most American main meals were fairly plain and did not need elaborate recipes; baking did and still does. Making good pies, cakes, and cookies is a way for cooks to show their skills and to be appreciated by those who eat them and by fellow bakers. Bakers like to experiment and share recipes, so the many variations of baked goods made their ways into home collections and local cookbooks. Also, recipes created by company test kitchens to go with their easy-to-make products are conventional in recipe collections; though some of them are adapted by the cooks who submitted them. Ways to make gelatin desserts, for example, proliferated with the appearance of easy-to-prepare Jell-O around 1900 and other brands in the twentieth century. Cake, cookie, and other baking mixes helped make for even more varieties of desserts for sweet-loving Americans.

Tastes in desserts and in the ways that they are served have changed over time. In fancy dinner parties of nineteenth century, men and women would leave the table after the main courses and retire to separate parlors or perhaps onto a patio on warm evenings where they took desserts, together with coffee or tea. Delicate cakes with creamy fillings or toppings and ice creams were thought to be more feminine, thus served to "ladies." Ladyfingers, a type of light sponge cake baked into long, slim forms, are a reminder of these distinctions among desserts. Heartier pies, mainly with fruit fillings, were thought to be more suitable to men in early days and were always on farm tables for hard working men and women. Pies were regular features of diners, and also associated in popular culture with working-class men who ate slices and drank black coffee while seated at dining counters. By the twentieth century, and the rise of the middle classes, views of desserts changed so that a cake made from a boxed mix with frosting from a can, or a gelatin creation, or ice cream from a grocer's freezer case might be served at the dining room table right after the dinner dishes had been cleared. The aristocratic cakes of famed chefs have thus been democratized just as sugar became a food of the masses.

Baked Desserts

Pies and Tarts

Americans have always loved sweet pies, expressed in the phrase dating to the early twentieth century, "as American as apple pie." Fruit filled pies are the best known, but pies are made with many ingredients and come in various forms. Most American pies are made from a pastry shell formed in a round rimmed baking pan, filled with a filling of choice, then covered with another pastry topping and then baked until the pie is cooked through and golden brown on top. Called shortcrust, the pastry ingredients are simple, usually wheat flour with a fat cut into it and with cold water mixed in to form a paste. This is rolled out and cut to form the bottom, sides, and top of the pie. Ingredients for pie pastry vary from lard to vegetable shortening or butter. Fats determine how flaky the crust will be, though some bakers add baking powder to achieve this effect. Other kinds of pie, such as tarts and flans, are open faced, the pastry used only to line the bottom and sides of the baking pan. Some single-crust pies are made with crushed Graham crackers and ground nuts mixed with butter. Though it seems a simple process, making pie pastry takes skill that comes from considerable experience and home bakers take pride in making them well. Pies are always best served warm from the oven, but leftovers can be safely microwaved, and can appear on breakfast and lunch tables.

Apples are so widespread and well-loved throughout North America that it is not surprising they are the most popular fruit used in pies. Because Americans prefer certain flavors and consistency in their pies, particular apples are preferred and other ingredients are added to sweeten and thicken pie fillings. Tart apples with less water in them are considered the best for baking: Granny Smith (an Australian variety), Winesap, Gravenstein, Rome Beauty, Jonathan, and varieties of Greenings, among others. These are sliced before baking, mixed with sugar, usually cinnamon for flavoring, and cornstarch or tapioca as thickening agents. Sometimes, lemon juice is added for further tartness and raisins as a complementary fruit. When baked in double-crusted pie, the apple juices form a thick, sweet sauce that makes for the desired pie filling. Preprepared thickened apple slices are sold canned and frozen. When baked, a typical 8-inch pie is sliced into eight wedges and served plain, with whipped cream or ice cream (pie á la mode) or even with cheese slices. Other versions of apple pie include Dutch apple usually made with cinnamon, nutmeg, brown sugar, and topped with a streusel consisting of brown sugar, cinnamon, and butter mixed together and baked on top. Glazing the top crust with a mixture of melted confectioner's sugar and cream is also a well-liked way to prepare apple pie.

A number of other fruit and berry pies are made in similar ways and enjoyed as much as apple. Some are seasonal such as rhubarb—not technically a fruit but often mixed with other berries—cloudberries, lingonberries, wild or local strawberries, huckleberries, and American persimmons. All fruits are seasonal but in America's industrial food production system, fruits and berries are available year-round fresh, canned, or frozen. Cherries are among the most liked for pies, but not all varieties are suitable. Sour or tart cherries are the favorite fruits because, like apples, they provide a tart-sweet taste. Most of America's tart cherries are grown in northern Michigan where Traverse City is called the cherry capital of the world. Since tart cherries are seasonal and regional, canned or frozen products are usually used in pie-making. Spices are not always combined with cherries in pies, only sugar and thickening agents to give them a more natural flavor. Cherry pies are served plain, á la mode, with whipped cream or perhaps warm heavy cream.

As one of America's most popular fruits, peaches are also a major ingredient of American pies. Brought to the American South in the early years of European settlement, peaches became associated with Southern states such as Georgia, though they are grown in northern states such as Illinois and Michigan. They appear in early New England cookbooks as seasonal fruits with recipes for preserving them. Peaches are now shipped fresh, if not exactly ripe, almost all year round from California or South America and are canned or frozen, so peach pie fillings are easily available. Ripe peaches are juicier and sweeter than apples so that making pies requires more thickening agents to get the proper consistency. Mace, cinnamon, and lemon are the usual additions and less sugar than berries or apples is needed to make this famous American sweet pie.

Strawberry, blueberry, blackberry, and raspberry pies are also familiar fillings for sweet pies. Traditionally, strawberries are a springtime berry in North America and pies made with it are still more or less seasonal. Strawberries are often mixed with rhubarb because it, too, is a springtime plant, though with an extremely tart flavor. Strawberry pie is often accompanied by a dairy product such as ice cream or whipped cream, likely because plain strawberries and cream have been a springtime treat since the Middle Ages. Before the early twentieth century, blueberries were eaten in the eastern and northern United States since that is where the wild low-bush berries—also called huckleberries—and high-bush berries are native. In 1916, cultivated highbush berries were commercialized and began to be grown in many parts of the country. As a result, blueberries became prized for baked goods and also because they are beneficial to healthy diets. Blackberries and raspberries were imported to America by early European colonists and became wild across the continent where they were picked and eaten locally, especially by people living in the country. Cultivated varieties were grown all over the United States, so both berries are available year-round and are frequently used in pies and other baked goods. Their sweet and tart flavors, especially raspberries, contrast well with sugary pies, muffins, and other baked goods.

Single-crusted pies are just as popular as double crusted and, depending on the filling, easier to make. There are several types of single crust sweet pie fillings: fruit, vegetable, nut, custard, cream, and meringue, among others. Any of the double-crusted fruit pies can be made as single-crust

Almond Torte

Yield: Serves 8

Ingredients
¾ cup butter, softened
½ cup sugar
1 egg, beaten
2 Tbsp rum
½ tsp ground cinnamon
1 cup ground almonds
1¼ cup flour
1 cup or more blackberry jam
Fresh blackberries (optional)

1. Preheat oven to 425°F. Place butter and sugar in a bowl and beat by hand or with an electric mixer until fluffy. Mix in the egg, rum, cinnamon, and almonds. When liquid is thoroughly mixed, blend in the flour, mixing thoroughly.
2. Turn dough into a ball and place in refrigerator to cool for about 1 hour.
3. Turn dough onto a floured board. Take 2/3 of dough and flatten it so that it fits a 10-inch springform pan. Grease pan and set dough into it. If it comes apart in places, patch it with extra dough.
4. Spread jam on the crust. If you have fresh berries, dot them on the top.
5. Place the remaining 1/3 of the dough on a floured board and roll it out to about a 10-inch circumference. It will be thin. Cut the dough into strips and lay them crosswise in lattice form across the torte.
6. Place in preheated oven and bake 40 minutes until lattice is browned. Remove and serve plain or with vanilla ice cream or whipped cream.

Note: Cold torte makes a good breakfast treat.

ones, though many of them are classified as tarts or tortes. Because they are iconic holiday desserts, the best-known single-crust pie is pumpkin. This is actually a pumpkin custard because the gourd's pulp is mixed with eggs and milk, together with heavy doses of cinnamon, nutmeg, cloves, and ginger that are set into the shell and baked. Some cooks make their own pumpkin pulp by splitting a fresh pumpkin and steaming it until the pulp becomes soft. Most people buy canned pulp along with premixed spices for their pies. Whipped cream is a delicious topping for such a spicy pie. Other vegetables are used in similar ways to pumpkin. Sweet potato pie and bean pies, both using mashed ingredients made into custards, are often thought of as Southern cuisine, African American in particular.

Flavored custards and creams by themselves are used as pie fillings and there are many of them. Perhaps the most famous American version and the most basic is the chess pie. It consists of eggs, butter, and sugar beaten together and baked until golden. Variations of chess pie include lemon, vanilla, buttermilk, coconut, chocolate, and nuts. Coconut custard or cream pie is made by placing grated coconut on the bottom pie shell, covering it with custard, and then topping the pie with more coconut. The coconut on top should be browned or toasted by baking. Banana cream pie is made similarly, while chocolate pie has chocolate added to the custard, and French Silk Pie is a lighter chocolate mousse-like variation. Often, pudding mixes are substituted for fresh ingredients as time savers. Whipped cream is a usual topping for these kinds of pie. Another kind of custard pie uses meringue as a topping: lemon meringue pie. A favorite American version is called Key lime pie. The basic ingredients for lemon meringue are egg yolks, lemon juice, and lemon zest (shavings from the yellow rind), along with cornstarch to make the filling very stiff. The ingredients are mixed together in a saucepan over low heat to cook and thicken it. Once in the pie shell, the mixture is topped with meringue, a mixture of egg whites, sugar, and cream of tartar, beaten together into peaks. The pie is baked for only a few minutes until the meringue is just beginning to brown. Key lime pie was invented in the nineteenth century in the Florida Keys where small sour limes grew wild. The filling used eggs, Key lime juice and grated peel, and condensed milk. This filling is topped with meringue and baked in the same way as lemon meringue pie.

Meringue is also the base of another kind of single-crust dessert: chiffon pie. The filling for this pie is whipped egg whites folded into a flavored gelatin mix. The result is a lighter textured pie than a custard or mousse filled one. The egg whites are usually mixed with sugar and heated to prevent bacterial growth and the gelatin can be flavored in a variety of ways. The most common flavors are chocolate, lemon, lime, pineapple, and raspberry. Chiffon pies can be made at home using prepared mixes but most are brought at bakeries and chain pie stores.

Tarts are similar to single-crust pies but they are usually made with firm butter-based doughs called pâté brisée in French baking traditions. Tarts have more solid fillings and are baked in straight-side pans rather than slope-side pie pans. The word "tart" is French but these kinds of creations are found in all European and American baking traditions in either sweet or savory variations. An English favorite called treacle tart was transferred

Butterscotch Cream Pie

Yield: Serves 6

Pie Crust
1 cup flour
⅛ Tbsp salt
¼ cup butter, vegetable shortening, or lard, cut into pieces
2–3 Tbsp cold water

1. Preheat oven to 350°F. Place flour in a large bowl and mix in salt. Cut butter into the flour quickly using a pastry blender, fork, or fingers until small pea-sized lumps form. Blend in cold water, one tablespoon at a time, until a firm dough is formed. Form into a ball and refrigerate for 30 minutes before using.
2. Roll out pie crust on a floured board to the shape of an 8-inch pie pan. Line the pan with as much dough on the sides as you have dough.
3. Set in oven and bake for 20 minutes or until the crust is browned. Remove from oven and allow to cool in the pie plate.

Filling
2 cups milk or 1 can evaporated milk (13–14 ounces)
1 Tbsp cornstarch
2 Tbsp butter, softened
2 cups dark brown sugar
3 eggs, separated
1 tsp vanilla
2 Tbsp powdered sugar

1. Prepare pie crust and permit to cool.
2. Place milk, cornstarch, brown sugar, and butter in a bowl and beat together by hand or with an electric mixer on medium.
3. Place mixture in a heavy saucepan, heat to medium, and cook until the sugar melts.
4. Beat egg yolks separately and add to mixture in the saucepan. Add vanilla to pan. Cook over the lowest possible heat until mixture becomes thick.
5. Pour into pie shell and refrigerate until quite chilled.

To make a meringue topping:

1. Place egg whites in a bowl and whip until very stiff; add two tablespoons powdered sugar and whip again until thoroughly mixed.
2. Spread over pie. Set in a preheated 350°F oven and bake pie for 2–3 minutes until meringue is brown. Use meringue topping while pie is still warm, then chill.

Instead of meringue, one variation is to top pie with whipped cream.

to America where it takes several forms. Molasses, the product of sugar refining, is the liquid left when sugar has been removed from the sugar cane juice. Molasses can be made from other plants such as sorghum, sugar beets, maple, and corn. The original sugar cane molasses or treacle is a thick, dark, strongly flavored confection that is made into large tarts or small tartlets either plain or mixed with nuts. In the nineteenth century, refiners created lighter versions of molasses called golden syrup and, in America, corn syrup. Both are the bases for a number of tarts or pies such as sugar pie (the official Indiana state pie), shoofly pie (a famous Pennsylvania Dutch treat), butter cream pie, and the most American pie of all, pecan pie. The pecan, an Algonquin word, is a native American nut that grows widely in the American South and was eaten plain or made into tarts and pies. Most modern pecan pies use corn syrup, especially the Karo brand that created the standard recipe. There are many variations of corn-syrup pies and tarts, the best-known being maple syrup to butterscotch (using browned sugar). All of these are made at home and served as after dinner desserts and often at gatherings such as parties and luncheons.

Quick Breads

There are two other kinds of easily made home-cooked desserts that are almost universal in American kitchens, cobblers and quick breads. Cobblers are a Colonial dish and remain popular because they are easy to make, especially with refrigerated biscuit doughs. The basic recipe is chopped fruit mixed with sugar that is placed in a baking dish, covered in soft dough and baked for 40–50 minutes until the fruit is cooked through and the crust is browned. Bakers making their own dough put sugar in it, but many use the original recipe for plain biscuits. There are numerous variations of the cobbler with different names: crisps, brown Betty, and pandowdy among them. Crisps, sometimes called crumbles in British usage, are chopped fruit fillings topped with streusel (butter, flour, and sugar formed into small crumbs) or more often oatmeal combined with brown sugar and cinnamon. These toppings are sprinkled over the fruit in a baking dish and then baked. Brown Betty is composed of alternating layers of chopped fruit with streusel of oatmeal-brown sugar mixtures, also baked in a baking dish. Pandowdy is a nineteenth-century New England dessert that was often flavored with maple syrup. It is made like a pie but during cooking the crust is broken into pieces, or "dowdied" so that they are submerged into the thickened fruit liquid. When made with biscuit doughs, the pandowdy resembles cobblers except that the crust is filled with cooked fruit syrup. All of these desserts are frequently served with ice cream, whipped cream, or—if the family follows British customs—with a warm custard.

Quick breads are universal in American kitchens, especially during late summer when zucchini overruns home gardens and are cheap in farmers markets and grocery stores. Because America was the world leader in the nineteenth century development of baking powder and baking soda, the baking technique is particularly American. There are several types of quick breads, some made with leavenings other than eggs or yeasts, others using eggs plus fats. All quick breads are basically mixtures of flour and baking powder and baking soda that are mixed together with sugar and some salt in a bowl. Then pulps made by mashing fruits or vegetables or liquids are added to form a wet batter. If eggs and shortening or butter are used, these are beaten together with the other wet ingredients. This mixture is usually put into a loaf pan and baked until done, but it is also the basis for muffins and scones. In fact, cakes and even pancakes can be considered quick breads. However, the term usually means the goods baked into loaves. The best-known quick breads are banana (made with overripe bananas), zucchini that uses the mashed interior of various soft squashes, applesauce, carrot, pumpkin, strawberry usually with nuts, poppy seed, date-nut, and even beer, among many others. All these breads can be mixed with berries and nuts and topped with sugar glazes or not. Muffins are made with similar batters that are poured into cup-shaped pans that are lined with paper and then baked. They come in numerous varieties, perhaps the most familiar being blueberry, cranberry, cinnamon, and chocolate. Drier and denser scones that are native to Britain are also widely available in America. These, too, are usually made with berries but also with dried currants, raisins, and nuts. Quick breads are eaten as desserts but also as snacks during the day, but muffins and scones are most often seen as breakfast foods.

Cakes

The cake family is one of America's favorite dessert forms. For many generations, making cakes has been something of a family activity. Home bakers, traditionally women, made cakes with the help of the family's children and by doing so passed on recipes, techniques, and love of baking down the generations. Many Americans of older generations can remember having to beat cake ingredients by hand in large bowls using wooden spoons and when electric mixers became widely used in the mid-twentieth century, they learned how to use them. Licking leftover batter from the bowl is a fond childhood memory (though eating raw eggs should be discouraged) and an even greater pleasure was frosting a cake and eating all the remaining sugary frosting. It is no wonder that cake making ingredients, pans, and preparation devices remain integral to family life.

Though any thick, usually round or rectangular product, is referred to as a "cake" as in a cake of soap, the word usually means sweet baked goods made from batters that are baked and then topped, layered, or coated with a sweet frosting. Cakes are usually made from eight ingredients: flour, sugar, eggs, shortening (butter, hydrogenated oils, lard or cooking oil), baking powder, liquid such as milk, salt, and a flavoring. However, not all ingredients are the same since some cakes are made with yeast and others created without flour, while flours differ from standard all-purpose to heavily sifted and bleached soft wheat flours called "cake flour." Since the 1930s, when they were invented by a Pittsburgh, Pennsylvania, baking company, cake mixes have become staples of American kitchens. Major brands such as Duncan Hines, Pillsbury, and Betty Crocker, and smaller brands, fill grocers' shelves because the mixes are more convenient than making cakes from scratch: just add water and/or oil and eggs, stir, and the batter is ready. Cake mixes come in flavors ranging from plain vanilla to lemon, chocolate (Devil's Food), and spice, among many others. And the mixes can be supplemented with other flavorings or ingredients such as nuts.

Cakes can be categorized into a half dozen or more basic types but there are endless variations within each category because bakers' imaginations run wild when it comes to creating and decorating these delicious treats. Among the most prevalent types are layer cakes. Made from flour, sugar, butter or its substitutes, eggs, and liquid (or cake mixes), these ingredients are beaten well in order to aerate the eggs and flour into batters that are poured into two or three baking pans and then cooked. The resulting layers are then cooled and stacked with filling between each layer and the whole coated with a frosting of various kinds. Yellow (using whole eggs), white (using egg whites), and chocolate (with cocoa or melted chocolate) cakes are the most common kinds. Sometimes, the term vanilla cake is used for non-chocolate cakes but all of them use vanilla extract as an important flavoring ingredient. Devil's Food, a more dense chocolate cake traditionally using melted chocolate rather than cocoa powder, is a well-loved chocolate variation. A related chocolate cake called Red Velvet has become even more widespread, partly because the cake itself has a red tint with contrasting white cream cheese or buttercream frostings (originally, the cake was slightly red from acidic reactions to buttermilk or vinegar mixed into the batter). A hybrid, marble cake, is made by layering white or yellow cake with chocolate cake batter. Other usual layer cakes include walnut spice, lemon custard, Boston cream pie (a two-layer pie with a chocolate icing), several kinds of coconut cakes, Lady Baltimore cake (flavored with rosewater, made with meringue frosting and, raisins, nuts, and candied orange peel), and German chocolate cake (invented by an American baker named Samuel German), among numerous others. Layer cakes are made for all kinds of celebrations.

Icings or frostings are important elements of all kinds of cakes. The most usual is buttercream frosting. As the name says, this is made of softened butter mixed with powdered or extra fine sugar, vanilla extract or other flavors such as lemon, orange, or almond extracts, and cream. Melted chocolate is also a frequent ingredient for these frostings. Beaten together, they form a soft texture that can be used as fillings between cake layers and a covering for the whole cake. Decorations using this frosting mixed with food coloring can be piped on using a pastry bag with an appropriately shaped tip. Fondant is another customary frosting especially used on fancy cakes. It is made from sugar and water mixed with gelatin or another liquid stabilizing agent with perhaps a flavoring such as lemon in two forms, poured and rolled, both thick and workable, into sculptured forms such

Southern Little Layer Cake

Most layer cakes have two or three decks but the Lane Cake from Alabama has four or more and the Southern Little Layer Cake, or stack cake, has anywhere from eight to twenty layers. Made up of thin layers cooked separately, the individual cake discs are immediately frosted when they are laid on top of each other, and then the whole cake is frosted again. Smith Island Cake, the official state cake of Maryland, is also a cake with multiple layers. The idea of multiple thin layers comes from European tortes and a special German cake called *Schichttorte* where the layers are actually cooked on a grill.

as flowers. Royal frosting is another regular form of cake icing, this one made with beaten egg whites and powdered sugar plus flavorings. Melted chocolate, lemon, orange, mocha (with coffee mixed in), and coconut are all regular icings. Chocolate mixed with corn syrup makes for a shiny, glazed cake topping. Cake fillings can be buttercream but fruits and berries are widely used. These are usually mashed and heated together with sugar and cornstarch to make a thick sweet product that Americans love in their cakes. In the modern era, home bakers do not have to make frosting and fillings from scratch since these are readily available premade on grocer's shelves.

Another kind of cake is made with the same ingredients as layer cakes, only they are made into other shapes such as single layer, loaves, or cupcakes. The simplest kinds of single-layer cakes are upside down or dump cakes. To make these, cooked or fresh fruits are set in a baking dish, the batter put on top, and then baked. Of right-side up cakes, among the best known of the single-layer cake is carrot cake. Usually made in round or square forms, it is then coated in a cream cheese-based frosting. Cake brownies are also in this category, though very dense, fudge-like, and coated with chocolate icing. Brownies are made in square pans and, aside from their texture, fall in the class of sheet cakes. These are commonly made both at home and for parties because of their simple preparation: batter is poured into a greased pan and, when done, simply frosted or not depending on the occasion. Bundt cakes became popular in the 1960s when a chocolate swirl version of it called the "Tunnel of Chocolate" won a prize at the Pillsbury Bakeoff competition. Bundt cake is made in a special pan that is round, fluted on the inside, with a large tube in the center. It descends from European yeast-based cakes called *kugelhupf* or *bundkuchen* in German, but modern American versions are made with regular cakes batters made from scratch or from specially formulated cake mixes sold by the major brands. One of the most familiar recipes for such cakes is the "1–2–3–4" method that is also used in many pound cakes. The name comes from the ingredients: one cup of butter, two cups of granulated sugar, three cups of flour, and four eggs (along with some vanilla extract). Creaming the butter, sugar, and then eggs makes for a lighter cake because air remains incorporated. Bundt cakes can be made in many flavors and are often drizzled with a vanilla cream icing.

Cupcakes are another style made from ordinary cake batters. Poured into pans with cylindrical molds in them, cupcakes come out of the oven looking like thick mushrooms. Cupcakes come in many flavors, chocolate and vanilla the most widely eaten. They are normally topped with variously flavored icings. One of the ways that Americans get cupcakes is by buying them freshly made in bakeries or bakery sections of grocery stores, and maybe the most prevalent of all, packaged and sold in stores by national

Chocolate Chip Brownies

Yield: Makes 8

Ingredients
½ cup butter or margarine, melted
¾ cup light brown sugar
1 egg
½ cup milk
1 cup all-purpose flour
¼ tsp baking soda
½ tsp salt
1¼ cups quick oats
6 ounce package semi-sweet chocolate pieces
½ cup sugar
3 Tbsp orange juice
1 tsp grated orange rind

1. Preheat oven to 375°F. In a large bowl, mix butter, brown sugar, and egg thoroughly. Stir in milk.
2. Sift flour, baking soda, and salt together.
3. Stir flour mixture into liquid and mix to form a batter. Add oats and chocolate pieces; blend well.
4. Grease a 9-inch square pan. Spread batter in pan and set in oven. Bake 30 minutes.
5. While brownies are baking, mix sugar and orange juice in a small pan. Bring to boil. Stir in orange rind and cook until a syrup forms.
6. Just before brownie is done, pour hot syrup over hot baked brownie. Cool and cut into 8 wedges.

Serve with vanilla ice cream or whipped cream.

baking companies. Famous brands include Hostess, Tastycake, and Little Debbie, all of whose chocolate cupcakes have fluffy vanilla cream fillings and white squiggles as decoration on top.

Sponge cakes have been widely used since they were perfected for home kitchens in the eighteenth century. These light-textured cakes are made by beating the fats, sugar, and eggs the same way as in the Bundt cake recipes mentioned above. When baking powder was added in the mid-nineteenth century, the modern sponge cake was born. Versions of the cake appear in small shell-shaped cakes called madeleines in French and in ladyfingers,

Berry Shortcake

This is the classic way to make berry shortcake. Any berries will do.

Yield: Serves 5 or 6

Biscuits
2 cups flour
3 Tbsp sugar
½ tsp salt
1 Tbsp baking powder
1 cup heavy cream
½ tsp vanilla extract
Melted butter for brushing on top of the biscuits
Additional sugar for sprinkling on top of the biscuits

1. Preheat oven to 425°F. Place flour, sugar, salt, and baking powder in a large bowl and blend well.
2. In a separate bowl, mix cream and vanilla extract. Mix this liquid into the flour mixture and stir. Only mix long enough to form a dough—the less handling, the lighter the biscuit will be.
3. Place the dough on a lightly floured board. Gently flatten the dough evenly to about 1-inch thickness.
4. Using a 2½-inch cookie cutter or a glass with the edge dipped in flour, cut out 4–5 rounds. Recombine the dough, stretch it out, and cut it similarly. There should be 5–6 biscuits in all.
5. Place the biscuits on a greased sheet tray. Brush the tops with melted butter and sprinkle with additional sugar. Bake for 12 minutes or until a golden brown.

Filling
1½ cups heavy whipping cream
2 Tbsp sugar
2 cups strawberries washed, hulled, quartered, and dried
1 cup blueberries, washed and dried

1. In a stainless steel bowl, whip the cream with a whisk or electric mixer until soft peaks form. Add the sugar and whip for about 10 more seconds. The whipped cream should remain soft.

To assemble:

1. Separate the still-warm biscuits in half. Place the bottom of the biscuit on a plate or in large individual portion bowl. Place some of the berries on the biscuit bottom.
2. Spoon the whipped cream on top of the berries. Place the remaining berries on top of cream. It is alright if the cakes appear messy.
3. Place the top of the biscuits on top of the berries and serve immediately.

long narrow cakes that are used in many confections. The most famous one, Charlotte Russe, is made by setting ladyfingers around a mold and filling it with rich custard topped with fruit, fruit sauces, or chocolate sauce. Small round sponge cakes with depressions in the tops are what most Americans think of as the base for strawberry shortcakes. The original shortcake is really more like a sweet biscuit, but when large commercial bakeries began selling the small sponge cakes, they became the preferred type for such fruit-topped and filled confections. Ultralight angel food cake made using only whipped egg whites, cream of tartar, finely granulated sugar, and cake flour is often used as a base for fruits and cream fillings and toppings. It is usually available premade in grocery stores. The most widely consumed sponge cakes are likely the many commercial versions, notably Twinkies invented by a Chicago bakery in 1930.

Cakes made without one or more usual cake ingredient forms another class. One of these is the flourless cake, the best known of which are cheesecakes and flourless chocolate cakes. Ancient Greek and Roman cooks made cheesecakes but the modern versions came about in the nineteenth and twentieth centuries. The basic recipe calls for eggs, sugar, cream cheese or a fresh cheese such as ricotta, mixed together, placed on a crust of crushed graham crackers or other sweetened crumbs and then carefully baked; many a homemade cheesecake has fallen flat if the oven is opened before the filling is fully set. It is likely that most cheesecakes eaten at home were purchased from a bakery or in frozen form. Of these there are two main types. One, from New York, is a dense product made with sour cream or has a sour cream topping; the other identified with Chicago is a lighter cake that is more amenable to freezing. Cheesecakes come in various flavors and with many toppings such as fruit. Flourless chocolate cake is made by mixing beaten eggs, butter, and sugar with melted chocolate. It is usually glazed with a ganache made of melted semi-sweet chocolate and heavy cream.

Eggless cakes are another kind of baked dessert in this category. The usual recipe is for vinegar and baking soda to replace eggs as a leavening agent, the acid and alkaline mixed together result in a foaming action that raises the flour and sugar body of the cake. Called Depression and War cakes, these were commonplace during hard times when ingredients were scarce or rationed. Such cakes are still made today because of dietary restriction among some dessert lovers and the ease of making them.

Fruit cakes are a different order of dessert creations and as old as the first civilizations four millennia ago. They have many forms ranging from sweetened breads with dried fruits, to baked cakes and steamed cakes such as plum puddings. Since most of these desserts are made and consumed around holiday times, they will be discussed in more detail in Chapter 7: Holidays and Special Occasions. However, sweet breads such as Italian panettone are sold year round as a breakfast treat. Since steamed puddings are kept for many months, they can be eaten at other times of the year; in Great Britain, they eat them with warm vanilla custard sauce.

Pastries

Puff and flaky pastries are other types of desserts that are loved in America. Puff, or choux pastry, is composed of water or milk, butter, flour, and eggs. The liquid is heated, then mixed well with butter and flour. Eggs, while still warm, are then beaten into it. The result is soft dough that is either placed in a pastry bag for piping or spooned in small mounds onto a metal sheet for baking. The extruded pastries can be fried into the classic New Orleans beignet and into Latin American churros, among others. One thick oblong-shaped type called an éclair is filled with a flavored custard cream or even whipped cream and coated with chocolate. The éclair is served cold, as are the round puff pastries that are also filled with custards and whipped creams: cream puffs and profiteroles. Puff pastries are easy to make at home, but most of the desserts made with them are bought from bakeries for eating at home.

Flaky pastries are made with many layers of ultrathin dough that are layered and filled before or after baking. Called *pâté feuilletée* in French, the pastry consists only of butter, flour, and salt. Making it at home is arduous because the pastry must be rolled out, folded in certain ways, and rolled out again and again, all the while keeping the butter in the dough cold. Home cooks usually buy the dough frozen, thawing it out for use. Millefeuille, or "thousand leaves," is used in a large number of desserts including the Napoleon. Named for the city of Naples in Italy, not the French emperor, the dessert is made with multiple layers of pastry leaves interspersed with custard and then topped with a chocolate, chocolate and lemon, or vanilla glaze. Popular all over the world, Napoleons are made in various ways and flavors but always with flaky pastry. Two other versions of *pâte feuilletée* are also used in desserts: baklava and strudel. Baklava is a common Turkish and Middle Eastern dessert using phyllo—thin sheets of dough but drier and less puffy than the French kind. Phyllo leaves are wrapped around nut mixtures and then covered in sweet syrup or honey. Baklava can be found in most grocery stores, either fresh or frozen. Strudel is also made with dough stretched as thinly as the baker can make it. Coming from Central and Eastern Europe, strudel came to the United States in the nineteenth century with the large numbers of immigrants and has remained part of the American dessert inventory ever since. Made with many fillings and flavors, the best known is *Apfelstrudel*, or apple strudel, though nut strudels are almost as widespread. Strudels are not hard to make at home, once one knows how to handle thin doughs, but most are purchased from bakeries or bakery sections of grocery stores where they usually sit next to coffee cakes and Danish pastries.

Cookies

One special kind of baked dessert crosses into the snack category: cookies. Small cakes that range from flat and hard to soft and chewy (such as the snickerdoodle), cookies can be made in many ways. Drop, rolled, rolled and cut into shapes, pressed into molds, bars, filled with small cakes, filled with fried fruits or chocolate chips, cookies come in every shape and flavor one can imagine. Cookies are often made at home either from scratch or from packaged ingredients. These are either dry cookie mixes or premade refrigerated doughs that are sliced and baked. The Tollhouse chocolate chip cookie invented in 1936 is probably the most famous cookie still made at home. The recipe is on the back of every package of Nestlé's semi-sweet chocolate chips. Most cookies today are store bought, some made by local bakeries, but most by large baking companies. Companies such as Keebler (with its elves advertising), Nabisco, Pepperidge Farm, Pillsbury, Gamesa (Mexican cookies now widely available), Lance, Mrs. Field's, and Famous Amos are among the best-known brands. Likely the most famous of all cookies, aside from chocolate chip, is the Oreo made by Nabisco. The original, made to rival Sunshine Biscuit's Hydrox cookie in 1912, is composed of two discs of chocolate cookie sandwiching a layer of thick cream filling. Almost five billion Oreo cookies in several flavor versions have been sold since then. These and other cookies regular serve as snack foods and a dessert, especially when they accompany items such as ice cream.

Brown Cookies

Yield: Makes 24

Ingredients
½ cup sugar
½ cup lard or butter or margarine
1¾ cup flour
½ tsp baking soda
½ tsp baking powder
½ tsp ground cinnamon
¼ tsp salt
1 large egg
2 Tbsp dark molasses
¼ cup whole milk

1. Preheat oven to 350°F. Place sugar and lard/butter/margarine in a large bowl and beat together by hand or with an electric mixer on high until fluffy.
2. Sift together flour, soda, powder, cinnamon, and salt in a mixing bowl. Add egg and molasses and mix together by hand or with an electric mixer until uniform.
3. Alternating between flour and milk, combine all ingredients to make a smooth batter. If using an electric mixer, set it low. Cover with plastic wrap, set in refrigerator, and chill 1 hour.
4. Use a tablespoon to scoop about 2 tablespoon portions. Roll into a ball shape and place on a parchment-lined sheet pan. Bake approximately 12–15 minutes or until dark brown on top and bottom. Chill on a cookie cooling rack.

Courtesy of Gustav Lundquist and Benjamin Lundquist Johnson.

Other Desserts

Custards are among the oldest American desserts, having been imported from several European countries by early immigrants. Basic custard is milk and sugar mixed with eggs (yolks are preferred) heated together until thick and then allowed to cool. Thickness depends on how many eggs are used and if thickeners such as cornstarch are added. Custards are made in numerous forms ranging from banana to Italian *zabaglione* (made with sweet wine), crème brûlée (flamed with a lighter before serving), caramel cream, leche flan, and its more famous relative *flan de tres leches* (made with whole milk, condensed, and evaporated milks). Thick custard called pastry cream is widely used in filling the pastries mentioned above. When custard is thickened with starch, it becomes pudding. In British usage, puddings can be savory such as the batter and meat drippings creation, the Yorkshire pudding, but in American cuisine, puddings are sweet. Blancmange is the original plain vanilla-flavored pudding but the most popular are chocolate and butterscotch. Most puddings are made from packaged mixes that can be found on grocers' shelves everywhere. One special kind of pudding, though, is always made from scratch, bread pudding. Stale bread is cut into squares, sometimes coated in fruit jam, mixed with custard and dried fruits such as raisins, and then baked until firm. Bread pudding is best when served with *crème anglias*, a thin custard sauce.

Gelatin desserts have been popular in America since the eighteenth century. Early gelatins, called jelly, are collagen that came from boiling calf or pig feet, the velvet from young deer, or the swim bladders of fish. The thick liquid is then used on cold meats and also sweetened for desserts. Americans used to eat jellied cold meats but these have fallen out of favor; today, sweet gelatins are the overwhelming favorite kinds. Gelatins are still mainly made from animal parts (unless using vegetarian kinds that use vegetable-based gelling substances), but are powdered and packaged; the most famous brand being the century-old Jell-O. Now owned by the Heinz-Kraft company, Jell-O is made in more than sixty flavors, mostly fruit, the most popular being strawberry and lime. The company makes a variety of products that simplify classic dessert recipes that use gelatin in them. Bavarian cream, coconut cream, butterscotch pudding and pie filling, chocolate pudding, lemon meringue, and flan are but a few of them. Starch-based puddings are also used in pudding cakes that are easy to make at home and commonly sold in grocery stores. Gelatins are also used in cakes, the most famous being Jell-O Poke Cake, so called because holes are poked into a sheet cake, warm Jell-O of whatever flavor is desired poured over it, and then the cake is cooled until the gelatin is set. This American invention is a favorite picnic cake.

Iced Desserts

In surveys of American dessert preferences, ice cream comes out at the top of the list. Iced desserts became popular in North America in the eighteenth century: presidents George Washington and Thomas Jefferson, and James Madison's famous hostess wife, Dolly, served vanilla ice cream at dinner parties. Hard to make and expensive to buy from confectioners, ice cream did not become popular until the mid-nineteenth century. When an American inventor named Nancy Johnson patented the first hand-cranked ice cream churn in 1843, the revolution in ice cream consumption began. Using ice and salt for freezing, ice cream could be made cheaply at home. Commercial production began in the 1850s and ice cream consumption rose steadily to today's annual ingestion of roughly twenty quarts per person.

Ice cream and related frozen confections come in many flavors and are served in many ways. Ice cream contains from between ten to sixteen percent fat, but other frozen confections do not. Gelato is low fat, while sherbets are made with milk and fruit juice, sorbets have no milk nor do granite (flavored granulated ice) or shaved ices. The richest ice creams have custard bases, meaning that they are made with eggs, but most do not—butterfat levels make up for the "mouth feel" of custard. A once-popular old recipe for homemade ice cream called for sweetened condensed milk to be frozen in refrigerator ice trays. Today, most ice creams are bought from grocery stores or ice cream shops. The most popular flavors are chocolate, vanilla, cookies and cream, and cookie dough. Of the fruit flavored ice creams, strawberry has always been the most favored.

At home, ice cream is usually scooped from its container and served in a dish. It is not uncommon for fans of rich ice creams to buy pints and eat the creamy treat straight from the carton. Ice cream can be eaten plain or topped with warm chocolate, fudge, or fruit toppings. It is also a frequent accompaniment to warm pies (called "pie á la mode"), Brown Bettys and crumbles, or even made into dishes invented in soda fountains: banana splits and sundaes. Much ice cream is still eaten out of the home, either as street food or in shops. About a third of all ice cream is served in cones made from wafers or thin waffles. Invented around 1900, two kinds of cones came to dominate the handheld service: flat bottomed wafer and cylindrical waffle cones. Ice cream on a stick, such as Popsicles, appeared in the 1920s and have remained staples of the American food scene ever since. Americans can choose from several kinds of frozen treats sold by local or chain shops. Soft serve is, as the name says, a lower-fat soft ice cream that is swirled from a special machine into cones or dishes. It was invented in the 1930s and has been popular ever since. Dairy Queen, Carvel, and Mr. Softee are the best-known brands. Dense, thick frozen custard is also a popular version, especially in the Midwest. Several chains specialize in it, especially Culvers, and one famous shop, Ted Drewes in St. Louis, makes a type so thick that it is called "concrete." A number of other shops have regular ice creams that vary in fat content and toppings.

CHAPTER SIX

Beverages

All organisms need water to maintain life. For most life forms, plain water is all that they drink or live in, but being interested in flavors of all kinds, human beings have invented many ways to transform water into a vast array of beverages. In the United States, the liquid refreshment industry amounted to 34 billion gallons worth 180 billion dollars per year in 2018. Of these refreshments, Americans drink 88 gallons of coffee, 34 gallons of tea, about 40 gallons of soft drinks, 34 gallons of bottled water, 20 gallons of beer, 9 gallons of fruit juice, 2.6 gallons of wine, and 1.6 gallons of spirits or liquors each year. Each of these beverages appears in many versions ranging from mixtures with other liquids to different flavors. Milk consumption, on the other hand, has been declining from 28 gallons (about a glass per day) to 17 gallons per person annually. Americans eat a lot of dairy products in the form of cheese but liquid milk has lost popularity at the same time that plant-based milk consumption has risen dramatically. Plain tap water accounts for roughly 146 gallons, or about 1.5 quarts per capita day, and it is thought that an average family uses about 10 gallons water for drinking, cooking, and dishwashing. Clean tap water is one of the nation's greatest public health success stories and the basis for all of America's food consumed at home and in public.

Water

One of the things that early European colonists of North America marveled at was the abundance of fresh, clean water. In their home countries, especially in cities like London, water for drinking, cooking, and washing often came from polluted rivers and wells. People before the mid-nineteenth century did not understand the germ theory of disease but they did know that "dirty" water was bad for health. North America was largely rural until the nineteenth century so clean water was rarely a problem, but with the growth of city populations and poor sanitation methods, water-borne diseases such as dysentery and cholera became common. To fix these problems, city planners built reservoirs in the countryside, piping clean water to individual homes, factories, and public buildings. They also built sewer lines to carry waste away, constructed filtration systems, used chemicals such as chlorine to disinfect water, and constructed large water treatment plants. In recent years, some urban areas such as Flint, Michigan, discovered that when chlorine levels were raised to combat coliform bacteria, it increased lead levels in water from the old lead pipes to toxic levels. However, Americans now take it for granted that they can turn on a faucet and have potable water ready to consume.

Any region or city's water will taste and have different characteristics from others because of natural mineral content. "Soft" water from sandy areas tends to be more heavily filtered with fewer minerals and little taste. Most of the United States has hard water because of the limestone that underlies most of the continent. According to New York bagel bakers, the reason theirs are the best in America is because calcium and magnesium in their water strengthens the gluten in bread dough thus giving the bagels their requisite chewiness and hard exteriors. Chlorine affects the taste of water more than any other substance so to remove its "swimming pool" odor and flavor, many Americas use filters. There are many filters ranging from whole house types that remove heavy metals and particulate matter, to under counter models, countertop pitchers, and faucet add-ons. The internet is filled with products and advice showing that Americans are keenly interested in wholesome water with neutral flavors for drinking plain and for making brewed beverages such as coffee and tea.

Desire for water purity has led to a large market for bottled water. Spring water was the first popular "healthy" water to be bottled and sold in the United States. In the nineteenth century, natural springs around the country, beginning with Saratoga Springs in New York State, were tapped and marketed as curatives for all sorts of ailments. Most of the claims were debunked, but waters from places like Poland Springs in Maine, Deer Park in Maryland, and Shasta Springs in California remained viable businesses up to the present day. One of the main ways to distribute clean water began in 1906, the water dispenser or water cooler. Originally a large brass container with a spigot, the dispenser evolved over time into a replaceable five-gallon plastic or glass container set onto a metal stand with a tap in front. Sold and serviced by many local companies across the nation, the water cooler is a staple of businesses where the name has become shorthand for meetings and discussions by workers. Water dispensers were also used in private homes but have largely been replaced by water bottled in smaller containers. Grocery stores have shelves specifically for plastic gallon jugs of various kinds of water and even more shelf space for liter, quart, and pint bottles of water. Multiple packs are commonly sold for home use where, to a large extent, bottled water supplements tap water, though at a much higher price.

There are numerous types and brands of bottled water sold today. The United States Food and Drug Administration recognizes seven basic water varieties including spring water, artesian water, mineral water, sparkling bottled water, and purified water. All but purified water must come from natural sources and have the same mineral and natural carbonation as they have in the ground. Purified waters are those that have all bacteria and solid matter or minerals removed by various processes. Treated water is often

---

Rosemary and Berry Spritzer

Yield: 1 serving

Ingredients
5–6 blueberries
4–5 blackberries
1 tsp fresh rosemary leaves
1 ounce honey simple syrup (see below)*
1 ounce lemon juice
4 dashes plum bitters
3–4 ounces club soda

1. Mash together berries, rosemary leaves, and honey syrup in the bottom of a cocktail shaker.
2. Add lemon juice, bitters, and ice; shake vigorously.
3. Strain through a mesh strainer into a highball glass of ice.
4. Add club soda to taste—less soda for a stronger flavor, more soda for a lighter, refreshing flavor.

Simple Honey Syrup
½ ounce hot water
¾ ounce honey

1. Heat water in a small pan until hot but not boiling. Stir until honey dissolves.

Courtesy of Ryan Tippit.

sold as "drinking water" or "baby water" and is usually as plain as tap water. The most refined processes are reverse osmosis, meaning highly filtered, and distillation, where the water is boiled, turned into a vapor, and then cooled to its liquid state. Much of the plain water sold by major companies such as Nestlé (Poland Springs and Deer Park), PepsiCo (Aquafina), and The Coca-Cola Company (Dasani) is actually tap water from public municipalities that is re-treated before bottling. New variations on the standard waters have appeared in recent years. Bottlers have added flavors such as berries and fruits, vitamins, and minerals that help electrolyte levels in efforts to widen their markets. Whether they have greater health benefits than regular water is still under study.

One kind of bottled product that has proven to be healthful is mineral water. Most of the mineral water drunk in the United States comes from Europe where the spas from which it was drawn were popular health resorts. Though almost all water types, unless purified, have minerals in them, the term "mineral water" means higher mineral content than most others. Calcium, magnesium, and potassium are the major beneficial content, but brands differ in the amounts because of the geology of their sources. Some, such as the famous Vichy, have higher sodium content than others, such as the popular San Pellegrino, Gerolsteiner, Perrier (the most popular brand). Most of these waters are naturally carbonated (they contain carbon dioxide), a substance that binds minerals to the waters. Worldwide, there are around 4,000 different mineral or spring (usually with less mineral content) waters and Americans import about 130 million gallons of it each year. Of all waters, naturally carbonated mineral water is thought to be the most healthful of all.

Carbonated Soft Drinks, Soda, and Juice

Americans have liked carbonated beverages since the late eighteenth century, when scientists such as Joseph Priestly founds ways to make plain water fizzy by injecting carbon dioxide into it. People liked the sensation of little bubbles in one's mouth, the slightly sour flavor, and the fact that carbonated water seemed colder than the plain, or still, original. Over time, the processes for making it were refined so that by the mid-nineteenth century, soda water was sold by the glass mainly in pharmacies because it was considered to be medicinal. Pharmacists flavored carbonated water with lemon, ginger, birch, sarsaparilla, sassafras, or other plants and roots to make the still popular ginger ale and root beer. Cola beverages were also medicinal, some originally containing coca leaves (from which cocaine is made) and caffeine containing African kola nuts. The most famous brand, Coca-Cola, removed the coca leaves but the drink was still sold as a nonalcoholic tonic for many years after its invention in 1886. From the late nineteenth to the mid-twentieth century, drug stores featured soda fountains where customers bought soda, or pop, made by mixing flavored syrups with carbonated water added from countertop taps. They were consumed by the glass, which cost five cents until the mid-twentieth century, or plain carbonated water, also called seltzer, for two cents. Flavored sodas were also mixed at fountains with ice cream to make ice cream sodas and "floats" (soda with a scoop of ice cream on top). By the late nineteenth century, sodas had moved from healthful tonics to sugar-laden sweet drinks. Still, plain carbonated water was delivered to homes in dispenser bottles and in recent years, home carbonation devices such as Soda Stream have become popular once again.

Sodas of all kinds entered homes when they were bottled in the early twentieth century. After mid-century sodas were canned and after the invention of new plastic bottles in 1972, these became the most common ways of selling soft drinks. There is hardly a household today that does not keep soft drinks, sweetened sodas among them, in their refrigerator. They are not only drunk as pick-me-ups during the day but also accompany snacks and quick meals such as pizza. Soda flavors of all kinds are readily available in

---

Marjorie Fechtig's Punch

Yield: Serves 20–25

Ingredients
2 cups sugar
1 cups water
2 cans (12 ounces) frozen orange juice
1 can (12 ounces) frozen lemonade
1 large can (46 ounces) pineapple juice
1 quart ginger ale
1 quart orange sherbet

1. Place sugar and water in a pan and heat over medium temperature, stirring, until a thin syrup forms. Remove from heat and allow to cool.
2. In a large punch bowl, mix the syrup, orange juice, lemonade, pineapple juice, ginger ale, and sherbet. When mixing together, allow the sherbet to remain in small lumps.

Courtesy of Marjorie Fechtig.

stores. Grape, orange, lemon, lime (Green River), lemon-lime (7-Up the best known), vanilla (cream soda), and cherry joined root beer and ginger (as in ginger ale) flavored sodas as popular drinks. Chicago's Filbert's Root Beer Company makes twenty-five different flavors including watermelon, blueberry, and green apple. None of these flavors matches the popularity of colas, which contain not only cola nuts but citrus, cinnamon, and vanilla. Soda flavors are also mixed, the best loved being cherry coke. Although almost every state in the union has its own local soda such as Moxie in the Northeast, Vernor's in Detroit, and Dr. Brown's in New York City, most carbonated beverages are made by large national brands. PepsiCo, The Coca-Cola Company, and Dr Pepper Snapple Group are the largest, each of them selling different versions of cola and various brands of soda and bottled water. Grocery chains also have their own house-soda brands made by private label companies such as Cott, the world's largest such company.

What is in sodas has changed over the decades since they were introduced for home use. Before the 1980s, most sodas used cane or beet sugars, but in the 1980s, high fructose corn syrup (HFC) became the sweetener of choice because it was cheaper for manufacturers. Consumers in the United States did not seem to notice the difference but those in Latin America did and their sodas are still made mainly with cane sugar. High fructose corn syrup is controversial because it may contribute to obesity somewhat more than cane and beet sugars, though all sodas exist under that health issue cloud. As early as the 1950s, soda companies produced sugar-free products. Usually labelled diet sodas, low, or zero calorie, these contain artificial sweeteners such as aspartame and stevia and are a large percentage of the roughly 39 gallons of soft drinks per person each year consumed in the United States. Soda companies have diversified even these ingredients by mixing sugar and HFC with other products and selling them as "half the calorie" drinks. Carbonated sweetened soft drinks have been losing ground to water as a go-to beverage at home since 2010 and the trend does not seem to be reversing soon.

Not all soft drinks are carbonated and among the most popular of the non-fizzy products are powdered mixes. The most famous and still popular of these is Kool Aid. Invented by Edwin Perkins in 1927, the powdered flavoring was based on the Jell-O idea and came in cherry, grape, lemon-lime, orange, raspberry, and strawberry; dozens of other flavors followed. Kool Aid is simple to use sugar and water added to the flavored mix makes a quart pitcher full and it is cheap. Heavily marketed toward children from the 1930s onward, it is often made as a family-style beverage for drinking during the day and at children's parties. The proverbial children's lemonade stand often features Kool Aid and similar powdered drinks for sale.

Sparkling Lemonade (from Scratch)

Yield: Serves 12–16

Ingredients
Juice of 18 lemons
1½ pounds sugar
3 oranges, peeled and thinly sliced
1 pineapple, peeled and thinly sliced (shredded would be better)
1 pound strawberries, chopped
2 quarts sparkling soda water (seltzer), cold
Ice cubes

1. Juice lemons and place in a large bowl. Add sugar and stir until dissolved. Add oranges and pineapple. Stir well or, better, process with a hand mixer until fairly smooth.
2. Mix in the strawberries. Add the soda water and mix together.
3. Place in a punch bowl and add as many ice cubes as will fit. Serve in 4-ounce glasses. Makes about 3 quarts.

Adapted from *Mrs. Curtis's Cookbook*, New York: The Success Company, 1909.

Powdered "instant" beverages of all kinds became popular for similar reasons during the twentieth century. Some like Kool Aid were not particularly nutritious but mixes that promoted heath are commonplace in stores. Lemonade has been an American standard drink since Colonial times, so when General Foods introduced instant Country Time lemonade (in various flavors) it was an immediate success. A number of other brands are now available including the sugarless Crystal Light introduced in 1982. One of the most famous powdered beverages became famous when it was sent on America's first manned space flight in 1962. Orange flavored Tang had been invented in 1957 but did not sell well until it went into space. Based on marketing as a modern "space" beverage, and its convenience, Tang in several flavors sits on many household pantry shelves alongside other powdered drinks.

Most, but not all, of the carbonated and non-carbonated beverages consumed at home have either real fruit in them or are fruit flavored. Juices pressed from fruits are among the oldest of American beverages. Of all the fruits used from the Colonial period onward, grapes, oranges and lemons (in the old Spanish colonies of Florida and California), and especially apples were used. Apples, imported from Europe, flourished in America but less for eating than for turning into cider. The trees that John Chapman, alias Johnny Appleseed, spread from the East Coast to the Midwest were mainly sour apples best used for beverages. Americans migrating westward brought apple presses to make cider, a lot of which was not sweet but allowed to ferment into an alcoholic beverage, hard cider. Modern methods of pressing, straining, and pasteurization have made most ciders nonalcoholic, hard cider becoming a specialty drink. Grapes are used to make wines but pasteurized nonalcoholic grape juice was pioneered by the Welch's Grape Juice in the mid-nineteenth century and remains a major brand today. The bottled citrus juice industry began in California with a farmers' cooperative called Sunkist in 1907. Advertised as having lots of vitamin C, it became a household staple but competed with oranges and grapefruits freshly squeezed in home presses. Florida citrus growers followed suit but really took off when a frozen juice called Minute Maid appeared in 1948. Today, almost any home has fruit juices in its pantry either in bottles, single-serve packs, or frozen concentrates. Despite the fact that many are laden with sugar, they are generally considered to be healthier than soft drinks.

Cider Eggnog

Yield: Serves 6

Ingredients
1 quart apple cider
2 tsp grated nutmeg, divided
4 eggs, separated
1–2 Tbsp sugar

1. Heat cider with 1 tsp nutmeg in a deep pan until hot, but not boiling.
2. Place egg yolks and sugar in a bowl and beat by hand or with an electric mixer until they look like thick cream.
3. In a separate bowl, beat egg whites until they are stiff.
4. Add beaten egg yolks and sugar to cider mixture. Gently fold in the egg whites. Pour into a punch bowl, top with rest of the egg whites, and sprinkle 1 tsp grated nutmeg on top.

Adapted from *Mrs. Curtis's Cookbook*, New York: The Success Company, 1909.

Vegetable juices are also widely consumed as healthy beverages. Apart from tomatoes, vegetables were difficult to press at home because fibers and pulp were hard to remove, so the home juice industry was commercial from the start. The most famous juice is Campbell's V8, first put on the market in 1933. It is composed mainly of tomato juice with beets, celery, carrots, lettuce, parsley, watercress, and spinach. It has always been promoted as a healthy breakfast beverage. Other companies vary the ingredients slightly but the basic formula is the same for pure vegetable juice. In response to new tastes and declining sales, vegetable juice companies have expanded their ingredients to include fruits and other vegetables. Blends using banana, strawberries, cranberries, acai berries, blueberries, grapes, cherries, and sweet potatoes among others are widely available and attract people who want the perceived health benefits of various berries and fruits. This category of drinks crosses over into smoothies. These are thick liquids made from various ingredients that range from raw vegetables such as spinach, kale, broccoli, and Swiss chard, and other foods such as nuts, fruits, yogurt, nut milks, wheat grass, protein powders, and many more. Smoothies could not be made at home before the introduction of countertop food processers, blenders, and more recently powerful high-speed blenders that can process high-fiber foods and nuts. Health food stores have long made smoothies and they resemble *liquados*, highly blended fruit drinks that are common as street food in Latin American countries. Smoothies are not only home-made but are now made by beverage companies, large and small.

Milk

Since the late nineteenth century, milk (specifically cow's milk) has been considered to be the perfect food. Goat and sheep milk are even more nutritious but because of limited production and their strong flavors they are not widely used by Americans. Milk producers and government agencies concerned with nutrition have promoted milk as good for children because its calcium content promotes bone growth, it is filled with vitamins, and is relatively cheap. Also, milk was thought to be pure, thus fit for women as well as children. Through much of the twentieth century, milk was advertised with images of healthy boys and girls being served by their mothers. Pasteurization, enforced by law from 1909, greatly aided the idea of milk as the best possible beverage for families. Federal government guidelines made dairy products one of the four main food groups and recommended that children drink four glasses of milk per day. Though ideas about nutrition have changed over the past fifty years, USDA still recommends that people consume three glasses of milk each day, albeit a reduced or no-fat type. Milk is such an integral part of American culinary culture that, for the past century, the children's ritual of eating cookies after school without it was inconceivable; many adults think the same. And no one would consider eating cold cereal for breakfast without it swimming in a puddle of milk.

Milk comes in several versions and is sold in various ways. Before waxed and plastic containers, milk was sold in bottles, many of them brought to homes by milkmen using delivery wagons or trucks. Putting out empty milk bottles at night for pick up the next day was a family routine for decades. The first paper fiber-based milk cartons were patented in 1915, but it was not until the 1950s that cartons became the container of choice and, in the 1960s, plastic jugs appeared. Today, most milk is sold from refrigerated sections of grocery stores in gallon, half gallon, quart, and pint containers. Few home refrigerators are without a container of milk. At about the same rate that milk containers changed, so did milk types. The old bottled milk was rarely homogenized, meaning that the fat globules in it rose to the top in the form of cream. In homogenization, as most milk is today, fat is broken up and incorporated into the body of the liquid with no separation. However, as Americans became worried about caloric intake, milk producers responded by removing amounts of milkfat from their products. Modern dairy cases have milk ranging from non-fat to one percent, two percent, and whole milk. When heavy cream that is usually 35 percent fat is mixed with lower fat milk it becomes 11–18 percent half and half. Heavy cream is used for whipped cream and sauces and half and half is usually a coffee or tea creamer. Since a number of people cannot digest lactose, a sugar in milk, lactose-free milk is also sold by almost every grocery store. Buttermilk is a variety that was once very popular because it was thought to be a health-giving beverage. Its sharp taste that comes from fermentation— like yogurt—is not much favored now for drinking but it is used in baking products such as pancakes and buttermilk biscuits,

Milks have also been amenable to added nutrients and flavorings. The oldest and most popular is chocolate. Invented in the eighteenth century, chocolate milk is now made by adding a sweet chocolate-flavored syrup or sweet cocoa to a glass or container of milk, which is then served cold. Some mixes, such as Swiss Miss, have powdered milk in the packets and only require water for mixing. Premade chocolate milk using similar ingredients is usually available in grocery stores. This is different from hot cocoa and hot chocolate. These two drinks came from Pre-Columbian Mexico in the sixteenth century and evolved into two products. Hot chocolate is made by heating milk, adding pieces of high butterfat chocolate and then mixing it all together. Cocoa is a chocolate powder with most of the fat removed and processed so that it dissolves quickly in heated milk. Hot cocoa is a standard American comfort beverage with numerous brands available on the market. As well as sugared milk additions, there are others that were created to be health-giving. The best known is Ovaltine, invented in Switzerland in 1904, but made in America and a favorite staple throughout the twentieth century. The original version was made with milk, eggs, malted barley (sprouted and roasted grains), and cocoa, but modern ones have sugar as the number one ingredient. Malted milk remains truer to its origins as a healthier product. Using malted barley as the base, along with milk malts, became popular in soda shops and at home. Although the original brand, Horlick's made in Chicago in the 1880s, is now a British product, other companies such as Carnation make mixes for home use. Sweet malted milkshakes with ice cream are still popular and easily made if not very healthful.

The United States Department of Agriculture reports show that milk consumption in the United States has been steadily dropping in the twenty-first century. In 1946, per capita consumption was 267 pounds (milk is reckoned by weight not fluid measure) but in 2010, it was down to 146 pounds. Health concerns and also the growing interest in vegetarianism and veganism along with concerns about the effects of dairy farming on the environment have led to a rise in plant-based "milks." Soy, almond, coconut, flax, rice, and cashew milks are all found side by side in dairy cases across the country and have found places in home refrigerators. Americans will always want some kind of milk for their breakfast cereals, coffee, and homemade blended beverages. Plant milks can be substituted for any dairy milk, though the flavors are not exactly the same. If flavored then the differences are much diminished. So popular are plant-based milks that they now represent about 15–20 percent of the market.

Caffeinated Drinks

Coffee

Americans have loved caffeinated beverages in the form of coffee and tea from Colonial times to the present. In 2018, 64 percent of Americans over 18 years of age drank at least one cup of coffee every day. Because making and drinking morning coffee is routine in average households, one might think that most coffee is consumed at that time of the day, but with coffee shops and major coffee chains everywhere from cities to suburbs and small towns, a great deal of the dark liquid is also taken throughout the day as a pick-me-up. The average American coffee drinker downs about three and a half cups per day, though that is far less than half of what Scandinavians (especially Finns), Dutch, and Belgians swallow each day. Following European tastes and habits along with newer brewing technologies, American tastes in coffee have changed over recent decades. For instance, Italian espresso—a strong version put through special brewing machines and served in very small cups—has become a large seller in the United States.

When England ruled North America, tea was the favored morning beverage; the American Revolution, partly inspired by a tea tax, made the American colonists turn to coffee as a patriotic act. Coffee beans grown in Central and South America were sold green, buyers having to carefully roast them on a stove because they could easily burn and then grind them in hand-cranked coffee mills. The grounds were then placed in water and boiled to the desired consistency. The coffee made on chuck wagons for cowboys and pioneers travelling west was notoriously thick because it remained in the heated pot for long periods. Preroasted coffee beans sold in bags were invented in the 1860s and major brands appeared later in the century. Maxwell House, Folger's, Hills Brothers, and Eight O'Clock were among the leading coffee companies. These roasters learned to vacuum pack preground coffee in cans after 1900, giving birth to an icon of home handiwork projects: coffee cans were used all sorts of things including for baking cylindrical shaped breads. The first widely used instant coffees were marketed in 1910; the most widely used type called Nescafé was developed in 1938 and remains one of the world's leading brands. Later packaging innovations now keep high-quality roasted beans fresh for long periods of time so that people at home can make "gourmet" coffee as well as any coffee shop.

The kinds of coffee people buy and the ways that it is prepared has changed the family kitchen and cooking. There are numerous upscale coffees from which to choose, not only in specialty stores but in supermarkets as well. All of them use arabica beans for flavor, but much depends on where the beans were grown and how they are roasted. Coffee is grown around the world, each region's soil and climate lending different tastes to the beans. Some beans come from specific villages or estates; however, many roasters blend beans from different parts of the world. Depending on how coffee is to be made, beans can be ground at home, usually in electric grinders, or as in the past, bought already ground. Brewing is done is several ways, among them percolators, drip coffee makers, presses, and pod brewing. Originally made for stovetops and later in electric versions, percolators have a basket with grounds fastened to a hollow tube, the apparatus set within a pot with a cover. The water boils, moves up the tube, penetrates, and soaks the coffee grounds and then flows down to the bottom of the pot as drinkable coffee. Percolators remain popular but have been surpassed by manual or electric drip coffee makers. In these, ground coffee is put into a paper or mesh-lined basket set over a pot and boiling water is poured over it. Widely used in institutional coffee machines today, about 40 percent of home coffee making is done in electric drip makers that use either paper baskets or prepacked coffee packets. Long popular in Europe and now widely used in the United States, pressed coffee devices are cylindrical heat-proof glass cylinders with a mesh bottomed plunger. Ground coffee is put in the pot, boiling water added, and then the plunger set into the top; after about five minutes, the plunger is pushed to the bottom with the grounds and the coffee is ready. Most people think that this is the way to make the best tasting coffee. In the early 2000s, the Keurig company (now Keurig Dr Pepper) introduced an electric coffee maker using prefilled plastic pods. Because they are so convenient to use, pod and capsule coffee makers have become household standard appliances with many coffee companies making pods in many flavors—caramel, hazelnut, vanilla, cinnamon, chocolate, mocha, and maple among them. Unfortunately, unless the pods are recyclable, they add to the world's growing plastic disposal crisis.

Tea

Making morning coffee is an important American ritual but tea was once even more important and it retains a lot of its ceremonial elements. Tea came to America from China with Dutch and British colonists. Because tea was so expensive, serving it was confined to the richest colonists, especially for guests and other social events. Expensive tea services, meaning cups, plates, pots, milk and sugar jars, and strainers were imported from Europe at high costs. But as prices dropped in the eighteenth century, tea drinking moved to the middle classes and then to rural and urban working-class people. With Americans switching to coffee for their caffeine fixes after the American Revolution, tea consumption among ordinary folks dropped but it remained as an important beverage among the upper classes. Tea parties, afternoon teas, tea rooms, all of which were promoted as women's social events, all remained as elements of America's social life.

In the late nineteenth century, tea once again became popular with the introduction of cheap black tea from India and Sri Lanka and heavy marketing by tea companies. The Lipton Tea Company (still the largest in the world) used the term "orange pekoe" as a kind of brand name for the black teas that sold.

Teabags, invented in the early twentieth century, made brewing tea much easier and Lipton's "flow-through" tea bag introduced in 1952 is the industry standard. Today, Americans consume 3.8 billion gallons of tea a year,

Orange Pekoe

Tea drinkers have likely seen the name Orange Pekoe on the tea box and thought that it is a special variety or part of a brand. In fact, Pekoe is a Western term, likely a corruption of a Chinese word for *pai hao*, white fur on young tea leaves at the tip of the plant. Orange does not mean orange flavor or a plant color but refers to the Netherlands' royal house of Orange-Nassau, when Dutch merchants first brought tea to Europe in the seventeenth century. The name Orange Pekoe was invented by the tea tycoon, Sir Thomas Lipton (as in the tea brand) in the 1890s. Like many products, the brand name stands for a whole class of products.

about 80 percent of it not hot, like coffee, but iced. Iced tea drinking seems to have begun in the South and Northeast in the 1870s and has grown in popularity ever since. In the hot southern parts of the country, iced tea has always been a welcoming refreshment for visitors, mirroring tea's original social function. Most iced tea is served with some sugar and often with lemon but the South's famous sweet tea, the universal beverage, has double the sugar contained in another famous Southern creation, Coca-Cola. Iced teas can be made from scratch at home but just as often comes from powdered or liquid mixes made by beverage companies. Iced tea plain or mixed with fruit flavors is also widely sold in individual serve bottles in supermarkets and convenience stores and is often found in home refrigerators.

Alcoholic Beverages

Beer

When European settlers first arrived in North America, they brought their favorite alcoholic beverages with them. The Spanish in Florida and the Southwest planted grapes to make wine. English colonists in Virginia made beer, so did the Puritans in Massachusetts. One of the first things the Dutch founders of New Amsterdam (now New York) did was to set up a brewery. In northern Europe, beer was the standard beverage for everyone not only because they liked the flavor but because the water supply in their communities was impure. Most of the beers or ales, called "small beer," were made from whatever grains were available, were low alcoholic and not effervescent, but they remained popular until more modern brewing methods were introduced. Beer making was always local, usually done by specialists, but all that changed when German and Czech immigrants arrived with their traditional beer-drinking food cultures in the middle of the nineteenth century. They created a light clean-tasting beer called "lager," meaning laid down, that was aged before drinking. It is a refreshing beverage with a somewhat sour flavor that is best served cold. Breweries arose in cities and towns where the new immigrants settled and famous brands still bear German and Czech names such as Budweiser, Anheuser-Busch, and Pabst, among many others. Beer was not bottled until the system of capping was perfected in the 1890s, so beer was usually sold from kegs and if taken home was carried in pails, called "growlers." Bottling, and later canning invented in 1935 and later transformed into aluminum ring-tab cans, made beer easy to transport and a take home product.

Beer has been associated with professional sports, especially baseball, since its earliest days. Several beer companies have owned baseball teams—the St. Louis Cardinals and New York Yankees—and other companies have always advertised heavily with teams and special events. The beer sold had less alcohol than others and this kind of "light beer" has remained popular, not only because more of it can be consumed without becoming inebriated but because it has fewer calories than more traditional beers and ales. Beer remains a popular beverage when people gather in homes for barbecues and to watch sporting events on television: no Super Bowl is ever without beer commercials. But not all beers taken at home are lightly alcoholic drinks. Beer brewing began to change in the 1980s, when younger people became interested in craft beers. These are usually more highly-flavored beers, usually with lots of bitter hops, often with higher alcohol levels, and sometimes using more unusual ingredients than light-style national brands. Most of them are made in smaller, local breweries and microbreweries. Favorites include India Pale Ale (IPA), porters, stouts, and Belgian and German-style wheat beers, among others. There are hundreds of craft beers made in the United States and sales represent about 25 percent of the beer market.

Wine

Like beer, wine has been a favorite alcoholic beverage since Colonial days. Wine can be made from any fruit, though grapes are preferred by most vintners. Fruit wines were routinely made on farms throughout America's history because it is easy to ferment sweet fruits and wines were thought to be medicinal. Dandelions, elderberries, blackberries, raspberries, cherries, and rose hips were familiar types that are still made by some wineries. Certain kinds of grape from the Old World called *Vitis vinifera* are the most

prized. These grapes produce many of the best-known wines such as char-
donnay, sauvignon blanc, Riesling, pinot grigio, merlot, pinot noir, caber-
net sauvignon, shiraz, and zinfandel, among many others. American wines
are actually hybrids of European and native American grapes and are now
grown in every state in the union; the United States is the world's fourth-
leading wine producer with California as the top wine maker. Wine is a
social beverage commonly drunk with meals, as a light refresher at parties,
accompanying appetizers at parties, and often as an evening post-meal beverage. Sherry, port, and muscatel wines are the best known of these later
evening drinks. Sparkling wines, such as French Champagne, Spanish cava,
and Italian prosecco, and New York State Catawba are almost always served
at weddings, anniversaries, holiday parties—famously New Year's Eve—and
have been since the nineteenth century. In the past, wine was thought to
be of higher status than beer because of its European, especially French,
connotations, but wine has become democratized so that Americans consume about three gallons of it per person every year.

For most of American wine history, people liked sweet wines and still
do but in the 1960s, tastes began to change toward drier (meaning less
sugar content) and more complex wines. California wines labelled Chablis
(white) and burgundy (red) and rosé (wines with only some coloring from
grape skins) from large vineyards such as Gallo and Almadén were marketed to younger drinkers often in large bottles, or jugs. These are still large
sellers, though also sold in boxes—California's Franzia is the most popular—
as well as bottles. Once customers became educated in the complex flavors
of wines, such as berries in reds and citruses in whites, they began to drink
the varietals mentioned above. Today, more than 40 percent of Americans
routinely drink wine in every price range, under $8.00 a bottle accounting

George Washington's Whiskey

George Washington is known as the father of his country, but he was also a
father of the liquor business. Washington was chronically in debt so he turned
to the most profitable farm product he could produce from the grains that
his farm produced, whiskey. Washington's farm manager was James Anderson, a Scot who knew a good deal about distillation. Anderson supervised
the construction of stills at Washington's estate, Mount Vernon, that produced
nearly 11,000 gallons a year and had 270 regular customers. Whiskey mixed
with water became an everyday drink for Americans who, in the early nineteenth century, consumed 7 gallons per person compared to 2 gallon today.

for 60 percent of sales. Competition is intense with wine stores and some chain grocers like Trader Joe's marketing their wines as good quality at very low prices. Among wine consumers, searching out bargains is something of a household game.

Distilled Spirits

Europeans brought distillation to the Americas in order to make high alcohol content or "hard" liquors that they consumed at home. There are many kinds of spirits, as liquors are also known, from across the world: gin from the Netherlands and Great Britain, brandy from France, German schnapps, Eastern European vodka, British rum, Mexican tequila and mescal, Chinese shaojiu, and many others. The American kinds are generally called whiskey and, depending on the grain used, corn liquor, bourbon, and rye. The word whiskey came from the Scottish and Scotch-Irish immigrants whose food culture had long included it. When under British control, rum made from molasses was the spirit of choice except for people in the back country who made their whiskey from corn. The most famous of the whiskey producing areas is Bourbon County, Kentucky for which the liquor is named. Tennessee whiskey is much the same, but local and usually illegal

---

Anjou New York

Yield: 1 serving

Ingredients
1½ ounce bourbon
½ ounce sweet (red) vermouth
1 ounce pear nectar
Splash of triple sec
4 drops aromatic bitters

1. Combine all ingredients in a cocktail shaker with ice and shake well until thoroughly mixed.
2. Serve with ice in a rocks glass.

Optional: lemon peel for garnish.

Courtesy of Ryan Tippet.

corn whiskey made in the Appalachian Mountain areas is often called "moonshine." Hard liquors are usually sipping drinks served mixed with other liquids or unmixed, or "neat." From the early 20th Century they have been traditional pre-dinner time beverages for adults, especially in the form of cocktails, hence the term "cocktail hour" the time between the end of the workday and before a meal. Hard liquors have traditionally functioned as lubricants for social functions such as post-meal drinking and smoking relaxation. Though this kind of gathering has largely disappeared from home life, it is still observed in social clubs and can be seen in many old movies. Hard liquors are also common at celebratory and holiday meals— for instance, ouzo is common in Greek American celebrations and vodka in Russian and Polish American festivals at Easter. Of course, hard liquor is also the fastest way for people to become inebriated and that can be a personal health and public health problem.

In recent decades, two aspects of distilled spirits have become popular: mixed drinks and high-quality craft liquors. Mixed drinks using soda water, fruit juices, and bitters (intensely distilled liquids made with roots or fruits) go back to the nineteenth century; the first book to describe them dating to 1862. The modern tequila or mescal-based margarita is an example. Of these, the best known is the cocktail, a word now used for most mixed drinks. Cocktails became popular in the late nineteenth century and especially in the 1920s when women freed themselves of all kinds of social restrictions, including drinking habits. The best-known cocktails were martinis (made with bitters), Manhattan, Sidecar, Mint Julep, Whiskey Sour, Daiquiri, Bloody Mary (with tomato juice), Mai Tai, and Tom Collins, among many others. Cocktails have become even more popular in the twenty-first century as young people experiment with different ingredients to produce new flavors. A number of bars and restaurants have sprung up with specialist "mixologists" making a wide variety of new creations. At the same time as the boom in cocktails appeared, so did appreciation of craft liquors. Single malt and single location Scotches, bourbons, rye whiskeys, vodkas and tequila are now sought after and now available in many retail outlets, usually at premium prices. Hard liquors are only a small segment of the total alcoholic beverage market, but they have an important place in American food and drink history.

Holidays and Special Occasions

Official Holidays

Human beings will use any excuse to have a celebration in which food and drink play major roles. Often, the food and drinks are special to the event and almost always the occasion calls for serving lots of both. That is, people like to have feasts. Some of these events observe seasonal cycles such as midwinter and midsummer solstices. Others are natural to societies that depend on agriculture: harvest or planting festivals. Some mark observances particular to a religion, while others are secular, usually based on a political happening such as the traditional signing of the Declaration of Independence on July 4, 1776. All festivals are meant to bring communities together, food and drink serving as a social bond. The same bonding holds for special occasions such as weddings and birthdays, only these are for family members and close friends. Some of these cross categories as the world has become more secular and commercialized; Christmas being a good example. Americans call the larger festivals "holidays" from the word "holy," meaning religious rituals, but in the modern world, especially a multiethnic and multireligious one, the word really means celebration.

Like other world nations, the United States has official holidays when public offices are closed and workers in governments and school are given a day off. Technically, there are no federal holidays because each of the fifty states controls holidays, but they all recognize the same national days and so they are national. The days, in order of the year in which they were adopted, are: Independence Day (Fourth of July), Thanksgiving Day, Christmas Day, President's Day (Washington's Birthday), Memorial Day, Labor Day, Columbus Day, Veteran's Day (Armistice Day), and Martin Luther King, Jr. Day. A number of these national holidays began as local or state celebrations—Independence Day the most prominent—that became popular across the country before becoming official. Others, like Thanksgiving, were regional and were adopted as symbols of national unity. Yet other holidays were recognized to honor a particular group within American society: Columbus Day and Martin Luther King, Jr. Day are examples. The same can be said for many official state holidays around the nation such as Casimir Pulaski Day in Cook County (Chicago) to honor its large Polish community or Patriot's Day in Massachusetts and Maine.

Some holidays are held indoors because of the season and others are outdoor fests. Of the latter, none are more important than Independence Day,

---

Mrs. Rose Wilhelm's Kolache

Yield: Makes about 12

Ingredients
4 cups flour
4 tsp baking powder
¾ tsp salt
¾ pound butter or margarine, softened to room temperature
4 egg yolks
1 cup milk
1 cup sugar
¾ cup apricot, strawberry, raspberry, or blackberry jam

1. Preheat oven to 350°F. In a large bowl, mix together the flour, baking powder, and salt. Cut the butter into the flour mixture using a dough blender, fork, or fingers until pea-sized balls are formed.
2. In a separate bowl, beat together egg yolks, milk, and sugar with an electric mixer, hand blender, or by hand with a large spoon until the mixture forms a thick ribbon.
3. Pour the liquid mixture into the dry mixture and blend until a smooth dough forms. Shape into a ball and refrigerate for 30 minutes.
4. Roll out dough on a floured pastry board until it is ¼-inch thick. Have ready a 2–2½-inch diameter glass or cookie cutter. Dip end of glass in flour and cut rounds from the dough.
5. Top each round with a tablespoon or more of jam. Place kolache on a greased (you can use a baking spray) baking sheet and set in preheated oven for 10–15 minutes, or until lightly browned.
6. When baked top each kolache with apricot, strawberry, raspberry, or blackberry jam.

Courtesy of Rose Wihelm's granddaughter, Eleanor Hanson.

the Fourth of July. Parades, fireworks, ball games, and family cookouts at picnic sites, backyards, and porches across the nation make for the most active of all the holidays: the smoke arising from countless grills mixed with those from fireworks must surely impact global warming. Independence celebrations began in the Revolutionary War period and were local holidays until 1870, when Congress passed a law making the day an official one. Since then, the Fourth of July has been a major event across the nation from Washington DC to the smallest village, all of them serving now traditional foods. In the American South, the earliest Independence Day feasts were barbecues—whole roasted pig accompanied by hard liquor. Barbecues reached New England by the 1830s and became a standard way of preparing meats for family and community eating. In modern times, barbecues vary from smoking meats to cooking them in closed grills or ovens, and in some Hispanic communities where the original method exists, cooking them in pits dug into the ground. What is cooked varies from pork—most commonly ribs—to beef and now chicken, since it has overtaken all other meats in popularity. The secret of a good barbecue is in the sauces or marinades slathered on the meat before, during, and after cooking. Sauces vary from region to region, sweet in some places, vinegary in others, and always with some hot peppers. There are many bottled sauces on the market but a good number of sauces are made at home, sometimes using combinations of bottled versions mixed with other ingredients that are family "secrets." Since the nineteenth century, barbecuing, along with sauces, has usually been thought of as men's cooking, just as backyard and picnic area grilling are. Salads and baked goods are still considered to be women's jobs, just as they were in regular home cooking.

Grilled meats are the other great American Fourth of July food. Hamburgers, cheeseburgers, and steaks are among the most popular items cooked but the most historic, best-loved food is the hot dog. About 150 million hot dogs are eaten by American on this day alone, some of them gobbled down by competitive eaters at the Nathan's Famous Hot Dog Eating Contest held at New York's Coney Island. In total, about 7 billion hot dogs are consumed during the outdoor festival high season, from Memorial Day to Labor Day. Hot dogs can be prepared in many ways but done at home or at picnics, they are usually grilled over open flames. Hot dogs are almost always eaten on buns with mustard, often onions, sometimes ketchup, coleslaw, relish, and/or chopped tomatoes. In some parts of the country such as Wisconsin and other historically German areas, bratwurst is the preferred sausage. Sometimes "brats" are boiled in beer before grilling, other times not. They are always served with mustard, preferably a spicier kind, and onions on a bun.

Since Fourth of July dishes are much the same as picnic foods, cold dishes are also set out. If chicken is not grilled then it is fried and served cold. Like potato salad, coleslaw, devilled eggs, and baked beans (if made from scratch), and battered, breaded, and fried chicken is usually best made the night before. Fresh salads and boiled or grilled corn on the cob are made just before serving as are breads and rolls if they are baked fresh. Some desserts are made the day before, others like cobblers and pies should be served warm from the oven. From early days, special cakes have been part of the celebrations. Mainly, these are yellow or white sheet cakes elaborately decorated with icings in the form of stars and stripes or other red, white, and blue forms. Lemonade is a traditional beverage, though beer is even more likely to be downed since it is usually thought to go better with grilled meats than nonalcoholic beverages.

Memorial Day at the end of May and Labor Day in early September are the other major outdoor festivals that include lots of picnic-type foods. The foods served are much the same as the Fourth of July. President's Day, Columbus Day, Veteran's Day (Armistice Day), and Martin Luther King, Jr. Day are not especially known as feast days, though Dr. King's favorite dishes such as southern fried chicken, macaroni and cheese, and pecan pie might be served at commemorative dinners. Of the national holidays, two are serious eating days: Thanksgiving and Christmas. Both are perhaps the most important family gathering times and both entail a lot of meal planning and preparation involving family members.

Thanksgiving was not legally an official holiday until 1870, though it was declared one by President Abraham Lincoln in 1863 and by every president afterward. There are several origin stories about the current Thanksgiving celebration, its date, and what is eaten at the feast. Some of them are based in fact and some are not. Thanksgivings in the English colonies of North America began in Virginia and New England in the seventeenth century as religious observances to honor their survival in hostile environments. They were also harvest festivals in the style of their European homelands. The modern idea of a Thanksgiving celebration and the kind of meal eaten was created by an influential magazine editor and author Sarah Josepha Hale who used some local New England traditions as a model. She proposed a national day to reconcile a nation divided by the question of slavery, eventually convincing President Abraham Lincoln to declare a national day of Thanksgiving after the Union victory at Gettysburg in July, 1863 (and Vicksburg on the same day). Some of the old religious elements entered the celebration and remain today: people gathering around the table holding hands and giving thanks for everything that they have and wish to have. Hale described the dinner itself in her 1827 novel, *Northwoods*, as featuring a roasted turkey with savory stuffing, sirloin of beef, leg of pork, a joint of mutton, many bowls of gravy, vegetables, side dishes of goose and ducklings, chicken pie, pickles and preserved vegetables, bread, wine, pumpkin pie, plum pudding, custards, cakes, candies, currant wine, cider, and ginger beer. No sensible person today would even think of making such a monstrous banquet, but some elements remain: turkey and stuffing, gravy and sauces, vegetables, breads, and pumpkin pie.

Turkey is the centerpiece of modern Thanksgiving with about 46 million sold at Thanksgiving time each year. Most of them are large birds specially developed in the twentieth century for their large breasts; Americans prefer white poultry meat to dark. Because white meat is dry, turkeys are often pumped by processing companies with broth, amounting to about ten percent liquid. The overwhelming majority of turkeys are sold frozen, so home cooks have to thaw them out before roasting. Heirloom turkeys, older breeds that are raised on small farms, often organically, are a small portion of the turkey market. People who prize better flavor and humane animal rearing techniques—home cooks and chefs alike—buy these in increasing numbers. Preparing and cooking the turkey is a household ritual that often involves several people. Many cooks prepare their birds by marinating them in a salt solution, or brining them, the night before cooking. This makes for plumper, moister meat and if herbs are added, more flavor infused. Once ready to roast, the turkey might be stuffed or dressed. Turkey dressing means either a side dish or stuffing usually made from toasted bread mixed with herbs such as sage and thyme, butter or margarine, and often enhanced with giblets, nuts, or even dried fruits. Although health authorities say that dressings should be cooked separately, traditional stuffing of the main turkey body cavity and neck skin is often preferred. Dressings can be made at home but most are purchased in packages that require only butter and a liquid added. Once cooked, the next ritual is making gravy. Like stuffing, gravy can be bought premade but the best are prepared from scratch. Juices left in the roasting pan after the turkey is removed are skimmed of much of the fats, mixed with flour, salt, and pepper, and put in a pan and gently heated to form a roux. Once properly browned, turkey or chicken stock is slowly added then stirred and heated until the proper consistency is achieved.

Gravy is a critical addition to carved turkey, especially drier white meat and the mashed potatoes, or more healthy sweet potatoes that necessarily sit on the plate alongside the meat and cooked green vegetable. Mashing potatoes has often been a younger family member's job. Cranberry sauce is the other essential dish on a Thanksgiving table. It is not difficult to make from whole cranberries (it is often made as an elementary and middle school

Stuffed Turkey Lombard Style

Yield: Serves 8

Ingredients
1 8-pound turkey
Freshly ground pepper and salt to taste

Stuffing
8 ounces veal, finely chopped
4 ounces lean pork, finely chopped
4 ounces beef, finely chopped
7 ounces Italian sausage, skinned and chopped
3 eggs
4 Tbsp grated Parmesan cheese
4 ounces prunes, stoned and chopped
2 cooking apples, diced
15 chestnuts, boiled, peeled, and chopped
3 Tbsp butter, softened, mixed with ¼ tsp sage and ¼ tsp rosemary
4 slices prosciutto ham
4 cups dry white wine

1. Preheat oven to 350°F. Clean turkey and sprinkle salt and pepper in the main cavity.
2. Combine veal, pork, beef, Italian sausage, eggs, Parmesan cheese, prunes, apples, and chestnuts. Place in turkey cavity and fasten it shut with flaps of skin surrounding it.
2. Place turkey in roasting pan, dot with herb butter, and cover with slices of prosciutto and 2 cups white wine. Set in oven and roast for 2½ hours, basting every half hour or so.
3. Remove prosciutto from turkey top and continue to roast the turkey for another 20–30 minutes to brown the skin.
4. Remove turkey from pan and place pan on top of stove. Skim fat from pan, add 2 cups white wine, and bring to boil briefly to make a gravy. Place gravy in a dish and serve with dressing.

Note: To boil chestnuts, slit each one down the center and boil in enough water to cover for about 20–25 minutes.

cooking project) but like other meal elements, cranberry sauce is often bought in cans. The traditional American dessert is pumpkin pie. It can be made from scratch by cutting a fresh whole pumpkin in half or into pieces, roasting it, and using the cooked pulp for the pie filling. Mixed with eggs, milk or cream, and cinnamon, nutmeg, ginger, allspice, and cloves, the final result is really a custard pie. Beverages are commonly wine, cider, and if observing the original English settlers, beer and ale. One regional addition to the meal is macaroni and cheese. It is a Southern tradition brought to other parts of the United States mainly by African Americans who migrated in large numbers from the South in the twentieth century and among whom "mac and cheese" is a standard festive dish. In Hispanic American kitchens, other food elements are added, ranging from tamales (always made by all the women in a family or group), to pork roasts, rice and beans, flan for dessert, and in Puerto Rican communities, a rum drink called coquito. Thanksgiving is a flexible feast well able to take on new elements.

Christmas is the second major American feasting holiday. Like Thanksgiving, it was not widely celebrated until the middle of the nineteenth century when German immigrants brought their holiday habits, such as their ancestors' Christmas trees, cakes, and cookies. Christmas was also made popular by the publication of Charles Dickens' *A Christmas Carol* in 1843. In that short book, Dickens highlights a Christmas turkey and a banquet set out by the Ghost of Christmas Present. The book was so popular that roasted turkey with potatoes and gravy became a necessity for Christmas dinner. Dickens' dessert was a steamed plum pudding that was once

Puritan's Christmas

American Thanksgiving has been associated with English Puritans holding a harvest festival with their Native American friends at Plimoth Plantation in 1621. Naturally, Americans also think of Puritans celebrating other important winter and spring holidays as well. Not so. In fact, Puritans were a Protestant movement that considered almost all standard religious holidays to be pagan in origin and, worse according to them, invented by the Roman Catholic Church. They thought that merriment during "holy days" detracted from proper religious discipline. In 1659, the Massachusetts Bay Colony actually banned Christmas and fined people who did celebrate. Puritans did not celebrate Easter or any other such frivolous customs. As for the first Thanksgiving, the Puritans thanked God for saving the colony while feasting to excess and drinking their favorite beverage, ale.

popular but has been replaced by baked fruitcakes, Christmas cookies, cakes, and ice creams. Aside from plum pudding, Christmas meals look like Thanksgiving, cooked and served the same way: someone at the head of the festive table standing to carve the turkey serving each diner the piece that they want, the rest of the dishes served "family style" from bowls passed around the table, each person taking what they want from each. Also, like Thanksgiving, there are variations in the meal. Italian American traditions call for seafood, especially *baccala*, dried cod that is soaked and then cooked, often with pasta. In the South, barbecue might appear and in Mexican American households, tamales. After the meal, everyone can sit in front of a television and watch some of the many filmed versions of the beloved *A Christmas Carol*, perhaps while munching on cookies or candies.

Perhaps the main difference between Thanksgiving and Christmas cooking is the amount and variety of baking. The recipes go well back into the Middle Ages when heavily spiced foods were marks of fine dining and fancy baking. When spices became cheap in the sixteenth and seventeenth centuries, ordinary people used them for holiday cakes and cookies. Some home bakers still make traditional plum puddings, though to be true to English traditions, they must be prepared several weeks in advance. To make them, dried fruits such as currants, raisins, dates, and chopped apples, and citrus peel or zest, nutmeg, cloves, cinnamon, eggs, breadcrumbs, flour, brown sugar or molasses, suet or butter or margarine, and brandy or wine are used. The ingredients are mixed together, put in a cloth or a special pan, set over boiling water, and steamed for several hours. Once done, the pudding is drizzled with brandy or wine, wrapped up in a cloth, and set in a cool place until the day it is served. More brandy or wine is poured over it to keep it moist. When served, it can be flamed or severed in slices with a hard sauce made from sugar and brandy. Nowadays, fruitcakes made with dried fruits but baked are far more common. One kind is really an Italian yeast-raised sweetbread called panettone that can be made at home but is widely available in stores during the holiday season. Stollen, a German marzipan (ground almonds) and dried fruits filled cake is another special cake of the season that can me homemade but usually bought in store. Of the numerous special cakes, *Bouche de Noelle*, or Yule log, a rolled cake filled with cream and covered in chocolate is a classic, as are eggnog cakes made with a favorite holiday-time beverage.

The most popular sweet baked products, and the ones in which the family participates in making, are cookies. So popular among children is licking the mixing bowl of leftover cookie dough that cookie dough has become a regular ice cream flavor. Sugar cookies are the most common and easy to make of all cookies. The cookie dough is made from flour, sugar,

Aunt Angie's Black Fruit Cake

Yield: Makes 1 large cake for 8 or more servings

Ingredients
3⅓ cups flour
2 cups granulated sugar
1½ cups butter, softened
12 eggs
2 cups dark molasses
8 ounces brandy
6 ounces red wine
1 Tbsp ground cinnamon
1 tsp ground cloves
1 tsp mace
4 tsp ground nutmeg
2 tsp baking powder
2 pounds raisins
2 pounds currants
½ pound of citron

1. Preheat oven to 350°F. Spread flour on a baking sheet, set in oven, and allow the flour to brown. Do not burn. Remove from oven and allow flour to cool.
2. Place sugar and butter in a large bowl and beat together by hand or electric mixer until fluffy. Add eggs and molasses and beat gently until incorporated. Add brandy, wine, cinnamon, cloves, mace, and nutmeg and stir in well.
3. Sift together the browned flour and baking powder and beat gently into the batter until well incorporated.
4. Stir in the fruits and mix well.
5. Turn into a large greased baking dish. Set in oven and bake for 2 hours. Check center of cake with clean knife. If it comes out dry, the cake is done, if not, bake longer, checking every 15 minutes.

Adapted from *The Illinois Cookbook*, Paris, Illinois, 1883.

baking powder, shortening or butter, eggs, milk, and vanilla for flavoring. Once made, the dough is rolled out and cut into shapes appropriate to the season such as Christmas trees. After baking, they are usually decorated with sprinkles, icing, sugar dots, and more. Everyone knows that these are the best because they are left out on Christmas Eve as snacks for Santa Claus. Ginger is a major Christmas ingredient in cookies, especially when shaped into gingerbread men and also made into gingerbread houses. Since some major elements of Christmas are German in origin, some favorite cookies from that country are still made. Springerle are like sugar cookies only flavored with anise, giving them a licorice flavor. The dough is rolled out and then pressed into specially carved wooden molds or rolled over with carved rolling pins that leave pictures or designs on them. Some families of German origin pass the molds down the generations as a way of remembering their identities. Flavored with ginger, Pfeffernüsse or pepper nut is a must in German home baking. These drop cookies are made with ginger, allspice, cloves, cinnamon, and cardamom, giving them a spiced aroma and flavor. Swedish cardamom cookies are similar but they have more of this Indian spice.

Religious Holidays

Religious holidays have always been occasions in which food plays an important role. Spring festivals that celebrate the beginning of the agricultural year are very old in cultures around the world. In Christian traditions, Easter, not Christmas, is actually the most important holiday because it represents Jesus' death and resurrection. It also falls at the same time of the year as Passover, a Jewish holiday that Jesus probably observed. Easter has never been as important a food holiday as Thanksgiving and Christmas but there are foods and food events related to it. The holiday ends the forty-day Lent, or fasting season, one that begins with a festival called carnival (literally goodbye to meat) and Mardi Gras (Fat Tuesday in French). Carnival meant eating and drinking to excess but now is a party celebrated by parades such as in the old French cities of New Orleans and St. Louis. Two sweets are associated with these events. One is the New Orleans King Cake, a large round filled sweet bread decorated in multicolored sugar frosting and with a small baby figure hidden inside it. The other is the Polish *paczki* (pronounced *pon-schki*) a rich deep-fried pastry, like a Bismarck, that is filled with various flavored jellies or cream. Both have become more mainstream American dishes and can be found in bakeries throughout the United States in season.

Because rabbits—the famous Easter Bunny—baby chickens, and lambs are the symbols of Easter, decorated hard-boiled eggs, candy eggs, candy chicks such as marshmallow Peeps, jelly beans, chocolate lambs, and Easter baskets are either made at home or purchased in stores. Decorated eggs are the oldest of the foods and a venerable home crafts for children and for adults. They can be dyed in single colors, decorated with transfers or paints and, in Ukrainian and Russian traditions, elaborately painted in designs that go back to prehistoric Europe. Unless the eggs are refrigerated, they should not be eaten after two hours at room temperature. Candies last a lot longer so Easter baskets are usually filled with them.

Despite rabbits and chicks being prominent Easter characters, neither are prominent ingredients of holiday meals. Roasted lamb is, along with baked ham prepared in several ways, and adult chicken. Also on menus are various egg preparations such as devilled, along with potatoes, asparagus, and young peas. For dessert, lamb cake, made in the shape of a lamb with a white sugar-based or cream cheese frosting, is common. For both desserts and snacks, hot cross buns—sweetened bread with currants or raisins with an icing cross on each of them—are ubiquitous. Since interest in ethnic foods have become widespread, large dried fruit-laced sweet breads such as Polish babka, Russian kulich and paskha (a kind of cheesecake in pyramidal form), and rich desserts such as Mexican honey and spiced bread pudding called capirotada are made at home or purchased. Since Easter dining is both a family affair and often associated with members attending church, many a meal is served as a buffet with friends and community members attending.

Passover (Pesach) is a Jewish holiday that centers on a highly symbolic meal, as do other Jewish observances. It celebrates the biblical story of the Exodus of Hebrew peoples from captivity in Egypt more than 3,000 years ago. Though many Jews do not strictly observe biblical dietary laws (kosher) and rituals, most adhere to some for the Passover meal. One forbids fermented foods or beverages so the breads served are cracker-like matzo. Cakes or dumplings eaten in soups are also made from matzo. In many cases, any meats are processed and prepared according to kosher rules. The dinner (seder) is family centered and is often communal because guests are encouraged to attend. Meal preparation itself usually involves all members of family from cooking to ritual cleaning of the home, dishes, and cooking utensils, to setting and decorating the table. There is a set meal order starting with a bitter herb such as horseradish, a bone, a roasted egg, a sweet herb, and a thick sauce made from honey, apples, almonds, spices, and wine (haroset). Each dish represents a part of the Exodus story. Since most American Jews came from Eastern Europe, the meal itself is in that style: soup with dumplings, meat roasted with vegetables, a stewed sweet vegetable dish using sweet potatoes, carrots, prunes, and other root vegetables called *tzimmes*, and at the end, *afikomen* (a cake made with matzo meal). If Passover is the most important of ritualized Jewish dinners, Hanukkah has a greater variety of dishes. This eight-day long festival remembers when the Second temple in Jerusalem was rededicated and eight candles miraculously burned for eight days. In America, foods served include potato pancakes (latkes) usually with applesauce or sour cream, slow-cooked beef brisket, roasted chicken, sweetened noodle pudding (kugel), a braided sweetened bread (challah), jelly doughnuts (*sufganiyot*), and a cream cheese-based pastry filled with dried fruits and nuts (rugelach). A number of Jewish holiday foods have spilled over into regular American fare; matzo, for example, can be found in almost any grocery store and has become a snack cracker.

Besides Christian and Jewish festivals, Islamic and Hindu holidays are also observed with feasting. Although smaller in numbers in the United States, but not worldwide, many Muslims and Hindus maintain holiday traditions. In Islam, Eid Al-Fitr marks the end of Ramadan, the ninth month of the Islamic calendar during which devout Muslims fast during daylight hours. During Ramadan, Muslims eat a large breakfast called suhoor before sunrise and a meal after sundown. Breakfasts usually consist of spice flatbreads, halal meats often made into kebabs, and even hot dogs, pancakes, doughnuts, yogurt, and more. Evening meals are more modest, perhaps breads, cheeses, and salads. Eid Al-Adha is the celebration at the end of the Hajj, or pilgrimage to the holy city of Mecca. Each of these involves families, especially the women who are expert cooks, spending days preparing for the great feast. Islamic food traditions vary widely from country to country but some main dishes are roasted lamb, spiced lamb stews, kebabs such as shami kebabs (spiced meatballs), roasted chicken with flatbreads, *maqluba* (a Middle Eastern dish of layered meats, vegetables, and rice), tabbouleh (a bulgur wheat salad), lentil stews, and many other Middle Eastern and South Asian dishes. Sweets are especially important for these celebrations. Among the most widely eaten desserts are baklava (honey and nut cakes baked in filo pastry), lokum, a candy also called Turkish Delight, and from the Indian Subcontinent *sheer kurma* a sweetened milk with vermicelli, dates, raisins, pistachios, cashews, almonds, rosewater, saffron, and cardamom. Of the many Hindu festivals, Holi is the one that is best known in America. It is a springtime celebration of the new agricultural year marked by brightly colored clothing, colored powders, and waters that are sprayed on celebrants. Foods and drinks taken during this event are often based on milk. They include *thandai* (thickened milk with nuts and many spices), *gujiya* (a crisp fried pastry stuffed with nuts and dried fruits or coconut), *rasmalai* (fresh cheese balls in sweetened and spiced milk), chana (chickpea) masala, *dahi-vada* (lentils or potato fritters covered in highly spiced yogurt), and saffron rice, among many others.

Non- and Quasi-Religious Holidays

There are a number of non- or quasi-religious holidays observed in the United States. Some were invented to celebrate important events or groups of people, some to honor the family, and many minor ones are purely mercantile made to sell greeting cards or some classes of products. Mother's Day and Father's Day began in the early twentieth century as ways to honor senior family members. Neither have signature foods apart from a mother's and father's favorites made at home or eaten in restaurants. Since Father's Day is in June and considering men's traditional role in outdoor grilling, that kind of cookery is more likely to be done. Commercial interests have created a vast number of "special days," at least one for every day of the year, such as Secretaries Day, Bosses Day, Doughnut Day, Deep Dish Pizza Day, Empanada Day, and many others.

Halloween and Valentine's Day are actually rooted in ancient folk custom, Halloween was a millennia-old pagan European festival that honors the death of the agricultural year at the end of October. On the last night of the month, spirits of the dead arise and evil spirits emerge to cause mischief. To propitiate them, food and drink was left out for them. Today's trick-or-treating is a remembrance of those old rites; evidently the spirits like sweets because Halloween is among the biggest candy selling seasons of the year. The early Catholic Church changed this celebration into All Saint's Day and All Soul's Day and these are still important parts of cultural traditions in many countries, especially Latin America. Days of the Dead in Mexico is a major holiday when family members near and far return home to honor departed ancestors. Elaborate decorations and food preparations are made for the night of October 31 when families gather in graveyards waiting for them to return at midnight. Women spend a day or more making food, especially tamales, that they bring for the living and dead to enjoy. Days of the Dead has moved to the United States, mixing with Halloween at least in costumes and decorations. There are no traditional European foods in America for Halloween but the season calls for pumpkin pies and pumpkin spice-flavored drinks. Halloween cakes and cookies appropriately decorated are made at home and widely sold in stores. Valentine's Day also began as a pagan festival in honor of early spring, but was appropriated by the Christian Church in the early Middle Ages. In modern times, the day celebrates romantic love, thus hearts and flowers are the dominant decorative motifs in gifts, greeting cards, candies, and baked goods. Aside from cakes, such as red velvet cake, and candies there are no particular foods associated with Valentine's Day though it is a day when people take their most significant other out to dinner.

Other festivals honor major groups within America, though they are not official public holidays. St. Patrick's Day is the occasion of parades in cities with large Irish American populations and dishes such as corned beef and cabbage, potato dishes, and Irish soda bread are made at home or bought in stores. Columbus Day honors the Italian contribution to America, though Italian American dishes are so common that there is no special dish associated with it. A number of Native Americans have mounted counter Columbus Day celebrations, since they do not see Christopher Columbus in a favorable light, with a number of foods indigenous to North America. One Italian festival has no such objections: the Feast of San Gennaro in New York's Little Italy. Southern Italian in origin, it features a parade, street food such as sausages and peppers, meatballs, calzone, deep-fried rice balls, zeppole (deep fried dough), canoles, and an almond cake called torta di mandorle. Many of these are made at home by women who have kept the old cooking traditions.

California professor Dr. Maulana Karenga conceived of Kwanzaa in 1966 as a way to bring together African Americans. The name meaning "first fruits" comes from Swahili and is thus a kind of harvest festival centered in families and community. Food plays an important role in the holiday's events drawing on the rich traditions of the African diaspora. Festive tables feature fruits and vegetables such as bananas, okra, yams, squash, and ears of corn. Foods served are likely to be African American classics such as gumbo, jambalaya, Hoppin' John, jerk chicken, barbecue, catfish, black-eyed peas, collard greens, and plenty of Southern-style pies and cakes. Cinco de Mayo (Fifth of May) is not a national holiday in Mexico but it has become one among Mexican Americans and now among Americans in general. The Fifth of May is a holiday in the state of Puebla marking a victory by a Mexican army over a much larger and better equipped army of French would-be conquerors in 1862. In Puebla, there are parades and food events featuring the state's signature dish, *mole poblano*, and others such as *chiles en nogada* (poblano pepper stuffed with ground meat and covered in a walnut-cream sauce with pomegranate seeds), *chalupas* (a thick tortilla with shredded meats and salsa), and *camotes Poblanos*, a candy made with sweet potatoes. In the United States, some Mexican American families make traditional foods but for the general public, Cinco de Mayo has been commercialized into tacos, guacamole, salsa, chips, and lots of alcoholic beverages such as margaritas and beer. The lunar New Year, often called Chinese New Year, is a major festival in Asian countries. Apart from famous public dragon parades and fireworks, food plays a large role in the day's events. Families gather to share meals in which foods symbolizing good fortune are served. Whole fish is a centerpiece because it means prosperity,

---

Irish Soda Bread

Yield: Makes 1 loaf; serves 8

Ingredients
3 cups flour
4 tsp baking powder
½ tsp salt
¾ cup sugar
⅓ cup butter
⅔ cup raisins
2 Tbsp caraway seeds, crushed
2 eggs, beaten
1 cup sour cream
⅔ cup buttermilk

1. Preheat oven to 350°F. Sift together flour, baking soda, salt, and sugar in a large bowl. Cut the butter in with a fork, pastry blender, or fingers until texture of cornmeal. Mix in raisins and caraway seeds.
2. Beat eggs in a separate bowl until smooth; mix in sour cream until well blended. Mix in buttermilk.
3. Stir liquid mixture into dry ingredients and stir thoroughly until a smooth batter forms. If it is too dry, add a little more buttermilk.
4. Butter the inside of a large loaf pan, 11×6 inches. Pour batter into pan and set in oven. Bake for 1 hour or until knife inserted into middle comes out clean.

---

dumplings and spring rolls are for wealth, noodles are served because they bring long life, and sweet rice balls bring families together. All Asian food traditions are complex so many varied foods will be served on this auspicious day.

Special Occasions

Food is a central element of any family special occasion. Some, such as weddings, wedding showers, bar and bat mitzvahs, and funerals, are often catered, anniversaries are often celebrated by dining out, while birthdays, christenings, and Quinceañera can be observed at home or as catered events and parties, such as Super Bowl gatherings served with home cooked or store-bought prepared foods. Some weddings are small affairs with food made at home or store bought, but most weddings are large and elaborate because immediate and extended family members are usually invitees along with family friends. Wedding showers are parties that precede a wedding by a couple of weeks or more. Family and friends who will attend the wedding gather to give the wedding couple gifts for their home and to eat and drink. Because a shower is not a sit down dinner, the foods served are usually party foods such as appetizers, canapés helped down by drinks such as sparkling wine, white wine, and mixed drinks: these are adult parties. There can be three food elements of a wedding. A dinner or party held the day before the wedding rehearsal, a wedding reception after the wedding ceremony, and perhaps a breakfast for close family and friends the next morning after the wedding. Of these, only a wedding reception is really obligatory. The reception can be a full sit-down dinner or it can be a buffet, either of which is usually accompanied by sparkling wine used for toasts and lots of other alcoholic beverages. Depending on the wedding couple's preferences, reception meals can be anything from vegan to vegetarian to traditional meat dishes. Traditional catered reception meals will have an appetizer or two, salad, a fish dish such as lobster, and a meat dish such as beef filet mignon along with potatoes, a cooked vegetable, and breads. Dessert is where a wedding differs from any other celebratory food, the wedding cake. For those who follow British traditions, a wedding cake is made like a plum pudding, very dense and filled with candied or dried fruits and nuts. When sliced, the wedding couple is presented with a large slice that is wrapped up and kept in cold storage for a year as a good luck charm. In America, cakes come in many forms, from sheet cakes to multitiered ones frosted with a rich fondant. The colors and flavors can be anything that the wedding couple want, but typically they are white with decorations such as flowers on them. Cakes are not cheap so having an elaborate cake is a major expense but one borne by millions of families.

Birthdays are anniversaries, yearly celebrations of milestones in a person's life. Cake is a must at these events, though not as elaborate and expensive as the wedding varieties. Birthday parties are generally held for children in the family and are joyous events, at least until cleanup time. Alongside party hats and favors, the food served is "kid-friendly" including pizza, tacos, small sandwiches, hamburgers, hot dogs, fruits, ice cream, and birthday cake. Birthday cakes can be of any variety but the most popular for children's parties are white or yellow sponge with white or chocolate frosting and candles marking the honoree's age. A cake is also required for adult birthday parties, though these can be more varied than a child's confection. Adult party foods are also as varied as the celebrant's tastes but appetizers and buffet-style dishes are the most common for larger numbers

Maine Disgusting Cake

Yield: Serves 6 or more

Cake
2½ cups sifted flour
2½ tsp baking powder
1½ cups sugar
½ cup butter, melted
1 cup milk, room temperature
1 tsp vanilla
2 eggs, beaten

1. Preheat oven to 350°F. Sift together flour, baking powder, and sugar into a large bowl. Mix in butter with a fork or pastry blender. Stir in milk, vanilla, and eggs. Beat together by hand or with an electric mixer until the batter is smooth for about 2 minutes.
2. Pour batter into two round 8-inch cake pans that have been greased and dusted with flour.
3. Set in oven and bake for 30–35 minutes. When done, remove from oven, allow to cool for 5 minutes, and turn onto cake cooling racks. Place in refrigerator and allow to become cold; this allows the filling and frosting to adhere.

Richmond Chocolate Frosting
½ cup sugar
1½ Tbsp cornstarch
1 ounce (1 square) unsweetened chocolate, grated
½ cup boiling water
1½ Tbsp butter
½ tsp vanilla

1. Have ready a double boiler with water boiling in bottom pan. Mix sugar and cornsarch in top of double boiler. Do not place top over boling water until next ingredients are added. Add grated chocolate. Stir in ½ cup boiling water and mix well. Place top of boiler pan over boiling water in bottom half and cook mixture until thick. Remove from heat. Stir in butter and vanilla until well blended. Allow to cool.

To assemble:
1 cup whipping cream, whipped (or more)
1–2 cups fresh berries (raspberries are best)

1. Use either two cake layers or split the two you have horizontally, making four layers. Place a layer of berries and whipped cream between each of the layers. Build them up until all the cake layers have been used. Cover the whole cake with Richmond frosting. Dot the top with whatever berries you have left. Refrigerate until somewhat cooled.

of party attendees. Anniversaries are normally thought of as marking years of marriage and celebrated in decades and half decades: twenty, twenty-five (called Silver), fifty (called Golden), or even more. Usually, anniversaries are private between partners and perhaps children but longer ones such as Silver and Gold can be more elaborate with a wider circle of family members and friends attending. Like a wedding, a cake is almost always the centerpiece of a table.

There are other life markers, some religious and some secular, that occasion parties, especially for young people. School graduations are one of them, christenings another, confirmation among Catholics, bar and bat mitzvahs in Jewish traditions, and Quinceañera in Latino customs. A bar mitzvah ceremony takes place when a boy reaches the age of thirteen and takes on all the responsibilities of being a man; a bat mitzvah happens when a girl becomes twelve. Both events involve religious rituals and speeches but they are also reasons to have a party. Depending on how observant the family is, foods vary from strictly kosher to non-kosher, but most of the dishes are Ashkenazi, meaning Eastern European in origin. Served buffet style, the foods could include bagels with lox, knishes (stuffed baked rolls), smoked whitefish, potato latkes, blintzes, falafel, challah (a braided sweetened bread), and many sweets including cheesecakes, honey-nut cakes, cookies, ice cream, and birthday-style cakes. Quinceañera is celebrated when a girl reaches fifteen and is deemed to pass from girlhood to womanhood. Everyone dresses up in their best clothes and the young woman gets to pick out a special dress, usually a version of a wedding dress. There is always a party with plenty of food. These can be traditional like tamales, picadillo (seasoned ground beef eaten in a taco shell), barbacoa, enchiladas, and tamales, or more American appetizers, pizza and the like. A cake is always served, either home baked or a fancy decorated one from a bakery with a small doll on top. A really elaborate cake will have two or more layers with a staircase winding from the bottom to the top and up to fourteen dolls representing the years up to fifteen.

Since the 1960s when it began, Super Bowl parties have become one of the premier special occasions in America: some think that it is quasi-religious because of the fervor with which fans root for their favorite teams. This television event is perhaps the most commercial of any in the American calendar, companies paying enormous sums to make entertaining commercials that are rated by fans and critics. Beer and soft drink companies are among the largest advertisers and sales of beer to their home audience are their rewards. Food companies also pitch their products, snack foods being a main category. Chips and dips including guacamole feed avid fans while they sit in front of their television sets. Set out on tables for pre-half time and post-game times might be chili, chicken wings in several kinds of flavors such as Buffalo-style, chili, mac and cheese, spinach dips, meatballs, mozzarella sticks, cubed cheeses, crackers and breads, and plenty of desserts such as brownies. In terms of amounts of food consumed, Super Bowl parties might come close to Thanksgiving.

CHAPTER EIGHT

Street Food and Snacks

Americans have always eaten food while "on the go." Whether travelling, doing business, working at all kinds of jobs, or going to entertainment venues such as fairs, amusement parks, and ballgames, Americans developed a taste for eating in public and between meals. As Americans developed an industrialized food system, large-scale industries produced the kinds of portable foods they eat today. By definition, street food is sold from a public stand, food cart, food truck, or fixed location in a market or building where travel activities or business take place. Such foods are prepared quickly from premade ingredients and served quickly. Foods can also be prepackaged such as wrapped candy, snack bars and cookies, chips of various kinds, peanuts, and canned and bottled drinks. Vending machines are popular places where these kinds of snacks are sold. Some of the foods served in street food or snack vending venues are more substantial and nutritious than others. The line between street food and snack food is not firm since many snacks are eaten at home but they can be characterized as basic foodstuffs that provide nutrients, junk food with little or no nutritional value, and snacks that are in-between, meaning based on nutritious foods such as potatoes but processed with sugar, lots of salt, and fats. Dishes such as tacos or hot dogs are among the first kind, while cotton candy, candies, and similar sugar-based items have little dietary values. Potato chips, pretzels, and even deep-fried doughs have some basis in good nutrition, but are usually eaten because of taste rather than for basic food values.

History

Native American peoples who fed themselves by hunting and slash-and-burn agriculture and who traded widely took snack foods with them to eat while working. Pemmican, dried meat pounded together with fruits, is the best known of them but dried fruits and corn-based cakes were also eaten while on the move from place to place. Early European and African immigrants, such as French voyageurs who traded with Native peoples for furs, ate the same snacks. So did the pioneers who moved from the eastern coastal settlements into the interior; Daniel Boone ate the same dried meats and fruits and corn cakes as the Indian peoples he met. Modern vending machines and quick food places, such as gas stations, sell jerky that earlier peoples would have recognized, only now in vacuum-preserved packaging.

As American cities and towns developed, street food appeared and flourished. Street vendors and stalls in city markets served quick eats for shoppers and merchants alike. Colonial cities were served by street vendors who sold foods that came from local sources to imported products. In coastal cities, oysters from nearby bays and seas were hawked from open carts. Philadelphians could enjoy Caribbean-inflected hot pot while New Orleans was famous for gumbo. Savory pies were common as were baked buns and breads. The well-known story of young Benjamin Franklin newly arrived in Philadelphia buying two loaves of bread and carrying them in the street under his arms is an example of portable baked goods on city streets. Anyone coming to markets in these cities would also have found imported citrus fruits, local apples, pears, and peaches in season, as well as cheeses brought in from nearby farms. Nothing about the idea of American street and snack food is new, only how they're made and sold.

American street foods expanded as the population grew, mainly through immigration. From around 1850, German-speakers arrived in large numbers bringing their publicly-eaten foods with them, especially sausages and pretzels (along with light beers). Later in the nineteenth century, Southern Europeans, namely Italians and some Greeks, also immigrated along with Eastern Europeans such as Poles, Russians, Czechs, Bulgarians, Serbs, Croats, and Jews. All came with their own dishes and food habits, some of which migrated into street food. For instance, Germans created beer gardens— literally gardens or open spots in nearby woods—where families could gather on their days off to picnic. Sauerkraut, potato salad, sausages, pretzels, breads, and beer were popular and then migrated into mainstream American foodways. In the American Southwest and California with large Mexican American populations, tacos, enchiladas, tamales, and similar dishes had long been eaten by all people regardless of ethnic origin. These foods, such as hot dogs, tacos, peanuts, and popcorn migrated onto city streets and into the new popular entertainment venues: city parks, amusement parks such as boardwalks, and sporting events. They also appeared at country fairs and travelling shows across the nation.

In rural towns all over the newly expanding America, provisions were sold by either itinerant vendors or small grocery stores. Snacks in the form of preprepared foods were prominent. Grocery stores were the gathering place for people to shop, hear news of the day, and swap stories. Crackers, sold from barrels, were main snacks. Descended from sailors' biscuits, these were made to keep for long periods of time without spoiling. The phrase "cracker barrel" came into popular usage in many ways, but the barrels disappeared when crackers—and cookies—were industrialized around 1900. Made in large factories, they were put into waterproof packages and sold as regular grocery items. In the twentieth century, there was a packaging revolution that saw almost every kind of snack food sealed for long shelf life and today, the snack food industry is a major part of the American food production system.

Since the nineteenth century, coffee trucks have been popular in cities in the morning and, for most vendors, lunch is the busiest time of the day. However, Americans like to snack so street food is eaten all through the day, depending on what the food is. Some food trucks and carts serve dinner-sized entrees for people leaving work for home. Though people eat large amounts of usually high-calorie street foods, they are not the main source of calories for most Americans.

Street food, as separate from snacks, is mostly found on city streets, public amusements such as boardwalks, street fairs, country and state fairs, and at athletic events of all kinds, including auto and horse races.

Street food is especially important in ethnic communities, especially those with origins in Latin America and Southeast Asia. Street food was traditionally sold from pushcarts and these are still used on city streets such a New York City where there are about 3,000. Carts are also found on boardwalks and in parks often selling ice cream and ices, various kinds of popcorn, fruits, and, in places with Hispanic customers, tamales and elotes, or roasted ears of corn dosed with chili powder, among other items. Food booths or wagons are common at fairs and in the late twentieth century, food trucks have become highly popular in cities and towns that permit them; Seattle, Washington, and Austin, Texas are leading food truck cities but others are catching up. Many food trucks are run by chefs who see them not only ways to practice their crafts and make livings, but give themselves visibility to the diners and the media. One way to do this is by creating new dishes, often fusing one or more kind with another. Hot dogs topped with Korean condiments and tacos made with Asian fillings created in Los Angeles were among the first and remain popular. Attraction to interesting food truck cuisine had led to 30 percent of Americans having patronized them.

Types of Street Food

Foods served in wrappers are the most popular street foods; battered or breaded, deep-fried ones are common at fairs. Wrappers made of wheat in the form of white bread or buns are the usual versions, though flatbreads—pita usually—and wheat or corn-based flour tortillas are widely used. Sandwiches such as hot dogs, hamburgers, submarines, meatball, cheese, ham, and many others have been on American streets and in fast food restaurants since the nineteenth century. Tacos and foods served in other kinds of flatbread began in different part of the country but they serve the same function as street food and dishes in quick service restaurants and drive-thru places. Packaged tacos or the related wrap, burritos, are also available in vending machines. Small meat or vegetable turnovers, such as empanadas, tamales, and regional specialties such as knishes in New York, Cornish pasties in the Upper Midwest, and runzas or bierocks in Nebraska, are well-known.

Fresh Corn Fritters

Yield: Makes about 12

Ingredients
2 cups scraped corn (about 3 large ears or less)
2 eggs
½ tsp salt
1 tsp sugar
1–2 Tbsp flour
¼ cup cooking oil

1. To scrape corn ears, cut them lengthwise through each kernel so that milk is released. Then scrape, not cut, each ear along its length into a bowl.
2. Add eggs, salt, and sugar and mix until well blended; add flour to thicken, 1 tablespoon at a time (2 tablespoons may not be needed to make a batter).
3. Have ready a frying pan with cooking oil heated to smoking. Drop 1 tablespoonful of batter into pan. When fritters seem brown on the bottom, flip with a spatula and cook the other side. Should take about 3 minutes.

Serve as is for breakfast, lunch, or a side dish, or with honey or maple syrup.

Asian foods have become widespread, many food trucks now serving Chinese dumplings, Filipino lumpia, and Korean won, among others.

Baked goods have always been popular as witnessed by the eighteenth-century nursery rhyme "Simple Simon met a pie man going to the fair." Savory and sweet pies, buns, muffins, and scones often appear on carts and trucks, often ones that serve coffee and tea. Fancy cupcakes are a recent food fad and are now sold from trucks in a number of cities. Waffles, pancakes, and churros are always found at fairs and in trucks. Pizzas are the most popular baked food of all and mainstays of the food truck and fair food businesses.

A nineteenth-century British critic of American food said that they (Americans) were addicted to their frying pan. There is no escaping such preparations, especially the deep-fried versions, in almost all street and fair food venues. Traditional fried foods include French fried potatoes, battered fried cheese curds, corn dogs, fried tortilla chips (for nachos), chicken wings, and chicken. So are fried doughs, including doughnuts, funnel cakes, ice cream, bananas, and even beer and lemonade. None of these are healthy parts of anyone's diets, but are snacks eaten for pleasure.

Sweets have always been important items for street food vendors. Since the nineteenth century, ice creams, and ice-based sweets such as Italian ice, have been served outdoors in warm months. Popcorn—plain

---

Simple Caramel Popcorn

Yield: Serves 6

Ingredients
1 gallon can of popcorn, 12 ounces
1 cup light corn syrup
½ cup sugar
½ Tbsp cream of tartar

1. Place light corn syrup in a deep pan, add sugar, bring to boil, reduce heat, and cook until thin threads form when a spoon is inserted into the mixture.
2. Remove from heat and stir in cream of tartar well.
3. Pour on popcorn in can or big bowl, mix, and consume while warm.

Adapted from archived manuscript recipe in Deer Creek Public Library, IL.

and caramel-laced—sit side by side with fudge, salt water taffy, toffee, cotton candy, and numerous manufactured candies on fair midways, boardwalks, and even in some shopping malls. Sweetened beverages such as sodas (or pops), lemonade, and fruit drinks are served by almost all food stands and trucks. Although usually accompanying food, they are often served alone as refreshments for customers who are on the move.

Major Street Foods

Sandwiches

The most widely consumed types of food are those served between slices of wheat flour bread or split buns. The simplest kinds of sandwiches are slices of bread on either side of fillings, usually meats or cheese of various types and, after 1900 when it became popular, peanut butter often matched with a jam or jelly. Ham and cheese, BLT (bacon-lettuce-and tomato), egg salad, tuna fish or chicken salad, and melted cheese are well-loved examples. From the late nineteenth century onward, these were served from lunch wagons that served factory and office workers in America's cities. Motorized lunch wagons still sell various kinds of sandwiches, along with salads, and beverages to people working in urban and suburban industries and businesses areas across the country.

Some now popular sandwiches came from industrial work backgrounds. The best known might be the submarine sandwich, or hoagie, from Philadelphia. It was probably invented by Italian street vendors or by Italian delicatessen owners near industrial shipyards around 1900. The classic hoagie is long, crusty Italian-style roll, split down the center, and filled with ingredients common in Italian communities: cheeses, sliced cold meats, shredded lettuce, and thinly sliced tomatoes, sprinkled with olive oil and herbs such as oregano. The submarine sandwich has become the central item in several fast food chains, but it was and remains a feature of lunch trucks, food trucks, and food carts throughout the United States.

Hot Dogs

No sandwich is more iconic as street food than the hot dog. Hot dogs have been served as street food in American cities and at amusement areas, such as seaside boardwalks, since at least the 1860s and have been associated with sports events, especially baseball, for more than a century and a quarter. There is hardly a public event at which hot dog vendors do not appear. The hot dog is a member of the sausage family. It descends from

German sausages brought to America, namely frankfurters (supposedly from Frankfurt, Germany) and wieners (from Vienna, Austria), but was transformed into an all-American product. Before processing machinery was invented, sausages were made by butchers in their shops by grinding meat by hand and stuffing them into casing made from animal guts. Chopping and grinding machines were developed during the late nineteenth century, eventually leading to modern automated or semi-automating large-scale processing. Today's hot dogs come in two basic types, cased and skinless. Natural casing hot dogs are made in the traditional way, by stuffing very finely ground meat and other ingredients into a tube made from animal intestines or casings made from plant fibers. Natural casings give cooked hot dogs a "snap" texture when bitten into, something that most aficionados prefer. The sausages are then sent to large cabinets where they are cooked and often smoked for flavor. Skinless sausages are also finely chopped meat stuffed into artificial casings, but then the casing is stripped off. Skinless hot dogs outsell natural casing ones and the usual kinds found in supermarkets, because they are much cheaper to make and sell at lower prices. Cheap hot dogs are everywhere from gas stations to sports venues—skinless hot dogs in plain buns with perhaps mustard and sometimes ketchup—but they are not the same when sold from hot dog stands and hot dog restaurants.

Hot dogs are models of America's ethnic food history. After being introduced by German immigrants beginning in the 1850s, the business of making and selling them was taken up by people of other ethnicities: East European Jews, Greeks, Italians, and later Latin Americans and South Asians such as Pakistanis and Bangladeshis. They added new toppings, some based on dishes that came from their own traditional cuisine. For instance, Greek and Macedonian vendors put sauces spiced with cinnamon and nutmeg, among others that were similar to dishes such as moussaka. Some of these were laced with ground meat and called chili, though they are not classic Southwestern chili styles.

The basic hot dog found in many stands and carts or served from roller grilling appliances around the country is a heated sausage made with pork, beef, poultry, or some combinations of them, set into a slit bun and topped with mustard, perhaps onions and sometimes tomato ketchup. New Orleans' famous Lucky Dogs carts are like this, though they do serve some other toppings. Sometimes, toppings for these kinds of hot dogs include a thick cheese food sauce or shredded cheese, and cheese stuffed into hot dogs is another variation. However, the glory of American hot dogs is the great variety of regional and local styles.

In many places such as New York City, Chicago, and Los Angeles, all-beef dogs are preferred, but elsewhere sausages made of pork and beef are common. New York City has more street food carts than any other American city, many of them serving hot dogs. For much of the twentieth century, carts served "dirty water dogs," so-called because they are heated and held in water just under the boiling point. This style has faded in recent years as more and more carts serve other kinds of foods, namely grilled meats. The New York style is a small, natural casing 1½ ounce sausage served in a heated bun and topped with yellow mustard, chopped raw onions, or a light tomato-onions mixture. Sauerkraut is often a condiment. Some hot dogs are griddled until browned on a hot metal sheet and served with the same condiments.

Corn Dogs

Yield: Serves 6

Ingredients
Oil for deep frying, at 375°F
1⅓ cups cornmeal
⅔ cup flour
1 Tbsp sugar
1 tsp dry mustard
1 tsp baking powder
Salt to taste
½ cup milk
1 egg, lightly beaten
1 Tbsp melted shortening
6 frankfurters
6 skewers or sticks

1. Combine the cornmeal, flour, sugar, mustard, baking powder, and salt, mixing well.
2. Add the milk, egg, and shortening, mixing until very smooth. Pour the mixture into a tall glass.
3. Put the frankfurters on sticks. Dip them into the cornmeal batter to coat them evenly.
4. Deep fry in oil heated to 375°F until golden brown for about 2 minutes. Drain on paper towels.

Bruce Kraig and Colleen Sen. *Street Food: Everything You Need to Know about Open-Air Stands, Carts, and Food Trucks Across the Globe.* Evanston, IL: Agate Publishing, 2017.

Along America's East Coast and in the South, there are other styles. The most popular is a hot dog covered in a meat sauce, commonly called "chili." The chili is usually ground beef mixed with seasonings and a tomato-based sauce. Some sauces are thin, others thick. Shredded cheese and the usual topping and chopped onions are common additions. From Rhode Island (famous for its smaller hot dogs) down through West Virginia, North Carolina, Georgia, to Florida, chili dogs are the standard. In some parts of the South, chili is accompanied by coleslaw to make the famous "Slaw Dog." Shredded cabbage, and sometimes carrots, mixed with either a vinegar or mayonnaise dressing are the main slaw components. Chili dogs were invented mainly by Greek immigrant vendors and when topped with German/Dutch American slaw, the combination is an example of how Americans fused food traditions into something new.

In the Midwest, there are two basic hot dog forms: Chicago-style hot dog and Coneys. Chicago dogs are all-beef sausages, water bathed or steamed, set into heated buns, and topped with mustard, bright green relish, chopped fresh onions, tomato slices, pickle spears, and small spicy hot "sport peppers," and never, ever, with ketchup. Coneys come from the southeastern Michigan area, especially Detroit, Jackson, and Flint. They are flat griddled beef and pork sausages, served in buns and topped with mustard and a thick or thin meat sauce that in Flint are made with beef hearts. Both styles are served as take-out dishes everywhere from stands, diners, ballparks, and other amusement areas.

Since the 1980s, Arizona and other parts of the Southwest hot dogs have received blankets of culturally fused ingredients. The Sonoran Hot Dog, also known as the Mexican Hot Dog, or Tijuana Dog, and even "danger dog" in Los Angeles originated in Tucson, Arizona. When made "all the way" it is a griddled or grilled pork-based hot dog, wrapped in bacon—or covered in cooked bacon bits—then coated with cooked pinto beans, chopped onions, chopped tomatoes, mayonnaise, crumbled or shredded cheese, Mexican red or green salsa, mustard, sometimes ketchup, and can also have sliced radishes or cucumbers and a roasted mild Mexican pepper alongside it. There are about 200 Sonoran Hot Dog carts in Tucson, Arizona, alone, more in Phoenix, and in recent years other southwestern cities and into Los Angeles. In hot dog places that serve different regional variations, some version of this Mexican American specialty will be found on the menu.

Bratwurst

Bratwurst is a German word meaning "cooked," by various methods. Unlike frankfurters or wieners (hot dogs), bratwurst is usually prepared from its freshly made, raw state. Bratwursts are almost always cooked on open charcoal or gas grills during festivals of all kinds, in tailgating parties and in ballparks. The sausages are either cooked directly or first simmered in water or the preferred method using beer, and then cooked on the grill. Bratwursts are best served in special bratwurst buns that are larger, crustier, and chewier than a hot dog bun. Brown Düsseldorf mustard is popular as a condiment, along and onions and sauerkraut. Wisconsin is a bratwurst capital, every public event having bratwurst stands and usually lots of beer. But wherever there were German settlements, there are "brats and beer." For instance, since 1967, Bucyrus, Ohio, has held an annual Bratwurst Festival. Here, at least a dozen vendors sell grilled brats, some on buns, others on rye bread, and all with mustard, onions, and optional sauerkraut and horseradish.

Polish Sausage

Polish sausage is a name given to several kinds of Eastern European-based products. Polish is a thicker sausage, traditionally made with pork, pork and beef, all-beef coarsely chopped, and heavily seasoned with garlic. Some are fresh, especially when made by local butchers, others such as those sold in supermarkets are precooked and smoked, like hot dogs. They are almost always grilled or griddled before serving. The standard sandwich has mustard and chopped onions, though in some versions the onions are cooked on a griddle until caramelized. Chicago's famous Maxwell Street Polish is made with caramelized onions and is now found in other parts of the country. Like hot dogs, and largely based on people's concerns about health issues with red meats, turkey and chicken-based Polish sausages have become popular. Most of them are sold in the packaged meat sections of supermarkets, but some have made their way into upscale stands and restaurants.

Fusion and Gourmet "Dogs"

Beginning in the late 1990s, hot dogs and sausages made from other kinds of meats have been given upscale and fusion treatments in urban areas across the United States. Chef-owned food trucks and a few restaurants pioneered the trend. Asian ingredients such as Korean kimchi (spicy marinated vegetables) and galbi (marinated strips of grilled meats) began with Los Angeles and Seattle food trucks. Thai salads with mango, peanuts, fish sauce, and sriracha sauce, seaweed salad, teriyaki-grilled meats, spicy noodles, wine sauces, foie gras, and lots of other ingredients usually found in fine-dining restaurants have been put on sausages served in buns.

Sausages in these places might be made from less usual ingredients and with flavoring to match: duck, venison, elk, antelope, lamb made with North African seasonings, and Portuguese Linguica flavored with saffron are among many new varieties. Fine French and Spanish cheeses are also used to supplement toppings. Like American food itself, new flavors from around the world are being integrated into familiar street food dishes.

Wrapped Foods

Tacos, Enchiladas, Burritos, Flatbreads

Wrapped foods are like sandwiches except that the outer shells that encase fillings are generally thin. Like sandwiches, they do not always fully enclose fillings, but can be partly open. The name of the most popular of American wrapped foods originated in the American Mexican borderlands—the taco. The concept of eating food wrapped in a shell made of corn flour is old in Mexico but the taco, meaning "plug" or "wad" to be eaten on the run, became common in the Southwest and California around 1900. Tacos expanded out of their original Mexican neighborhoods into mainstream American cuisine beginning in the late 1950s. Fast food chains, especially Taco Bell, spread from California from the 1960s onward to become major forces in the industry. Still, tacos are made and sold by numerous independent purveyors from stands, carts, and trucks across the United States. With ingredients sold in supermarkets, they are also widely eaten at home for lunch and dinners.

Tacos are made with thin, flat cakes called tortillas. In most of Mexico, these are made from *masa de maiz*, dried corn soaked in lime water, then ground into dough, flattened into thin rounds, and toasted on a hot flat metal griddle. The shells can be soft, as in most of Mexico, or fried into hardened exteriors. Wheat flour tortillas are a common version in northern Mexico and the United States. Tacos are made by the vendor taking a tortilla in hand, filling it, and then handing it to the customer. In fast food restaurants, taco shells are set into metal holders with as little handling as possible. Fillings are made from shredded or ground meats, pork, beef, or chicken, that are mixed with chili pepper-flavored sauce and often topped with shredded cheese, chopped tomatoes, chopped onions, and a cream dressing. Countless variations exist, from fish tacos made from breaded or battered fried fish, to Korean-style tacos using with grilled beef and spicy pickled vegetables, and vegetarian options using boiled or fried beans, salads, and salsas.

Newer Mexican and Central American immigrants have brought some specialties to open air street food venues that earlier generations of Americans ate but rarely do now: brains, eyes, tongue, and tripe. One variation is now widely eaten, the fajita. It is a marinated skirt steak that is grilled and served

---

Tacos

Yield: Makes 12 tacos

Filling
1 Tbsp olive oil
1 onion, finely chopped
1 clove garlic, smashed and finely chopped
1 pound lean ground beef
1 tsp ground cumin
1 tsp ground guajillo chili powder (optional)
1–2 medium tomatoes, peeled and chopped
½ tsp salt

1. Heat olive oil in a frying pan. Add onion and garlic and sauté until transparent. Add beef and sauté stirring to break it up into small bits. As the beef browns, add cumin, tomatoes, and salt. Stir until cooked through. Remove from heat and drain fat from pan. Set filling aside.

To assemble:
1–2 tsp cooking oil
12 fresh corn tortillas
Shredded lettuce

Additional fillings:
Guacamole
Hot sauce

1. Heat small amount of oil in a heavy pan. Place as many tortillas as will fit and heat until they become puffy and soft. Do not allow them to become hard. Remove from pan and drain on paper towels, cover, and keep warm.
2. To assemble, hold a taco in hand, fill with meat filling, shredded lettuce, and other fillings of choice.

with spicy sauce, cooked sliced green peppers and onions, and sometimes shredded cheese on a taco. Street carts and stands with flat griddles usually serve some type of fajita.

Enchiladas are also tortilla wrapped creations, only larger and often a main course in restaurants where they are covered in Mexican-style sauces, cheese, and sour cream. Burritos, or "little donkeys," is a food invented in 1930s California. The burrito is a large wheat-flour tortilla fully wrapped around filling. These are usually shredded or ground meats meat cooked in sauce and mixed with beans and rice. The burrito is widespread across the country, often a breakfast dish (filled with scrambled eggs), and sold by fast food chains, food trucks, at take-out places, gas stations, and even in some vending machines. Foods simply called "wraps" have joined the burritos that they resemble. While burritos are Mexican inspired, wraps are often Asian in character like Vietnamese spring rolls. Wraps are found in the same take-out food places as sandwiches, from airport kiosks to vending machines and everything in between.

Flatbreads such as pitas are more or less like tacos since they are one piece of casing not fully enclosing fillings. Pitas are soft wheat-based breads that are prebaked in bakeries and heated before use. Middle Eastern shawarma, Greek gyros, and Turkish doner kebab, are familiar meat fillings for flatbreads of various kinds. They are all conglomerations of layered meats, normally lamb, skewered on long spit and roasted over an open flame. The meat is cut from the spit in thin slices and served on rolled up flatbread with a dressing or sauce. Presliced spit-roasted meats are also served from street stands, sometimes cooked on a flat griddle, and some food trucks cook the meat on the spot. Kebabs that are common everywhere from Europe to Afghanistan also serve as flatbread wrapped street food in America. Kebabs are meats such as lamb, beef, or chicken, skewered with onions, green peppers, and tomatoes, seasoned, and cooked over an open flame. In recent years, falafel (fried balls of ground garbanzo beans) from Middle Eastern countries including Israel have become popular ingredients for flatbreads, especially because they are delicious vegetarian alternatives to meats.

One kind of flatbread brought by immigrants is now among the most popular American foods, served in all venues of every kind including street food vehicles: pizza. Brought to the United States by southern Italian immigrants before 1900, pizza was made mostly in urban Italian American communities. In the late 1950s and 1960s, pizza began to spread across the United States where it morphed into many styles with many toppings. Pizza is a flat wheat flour dough round that is covered in a tomato sauce with

Burritos

Yield: Makes 6 burritos

Ingredients
2 Tbsp cooking oil
½ medium onion, coarsely chopped
1 clove garlic, mashed and finely chopped
1 pound lean ground beef
2 tsp chili powder
½ tsp ground cumin
Salt and pepper to taste
1 can (16 ounces) refried beans
8–12-ounce jar Mexican red chili sauce
6 large flour tortillas
Optional toppings: shredded Mexican cheese, sour cream, guacamole, chopped tomatoes, shredded lettuce

1. Preheat oven to 350°F. Pour cooking oil into a large skillet over medium heat and add onion and garlic; sauté until transparent.
2. Add ground beef and cook until meat is browned, stirring often to break up meat.
3. Drain fat from pan.
4. Stir chili powder, cumin, salt, and pepper into the meat mixture, bring to simmer, and cook for 10 minutes.
5. Add refried beans and half of the chili sauce. Heat thoroughly.
6. Lay out the tortillas on a board or plate.
7. Place about ½ cup of the ground beef mixture onto each tortilla, roll up, and place seam-side down on a baking dish. Do the same for the rest of the tortillas.
8. Place in preheated oven and bake for 10 minutes. Remove and serve as is or with optional accompaniments.

Bruce Kraig and Colleen Sen. *Street Food: Everything You Need to Know about Open-Air Stands, Carts, and Food Trucks Across the Globe.* Evanston, IL: Agate Publishing, 2017. (adapted from http://southernfood.about.com/od/groundbeefrecipes/r/bl31221e.htm)

cheese, and usually served with chopped toppings such as mushrooms, peppers, and often sausage. It is sold from carts, stands, and food trucks, some of the latter with fancy toppings. There is hardly an American who has not eaten pizza either from food purveyors or frozen and baked at home.

Stuffed Foods

Stuffed foods are those totally wrapped in a pastry and then either fried, steamed, or baked. The best-known stuffed foods are dumplings. They are found in almost every one of the world's food traditions, from Asian steamed or fried dumplings to Italian raviolis. Naturally immigrants brought many varieties of dumplings to America where they became restaurant, home, and street foods. Under the name dim sum, or "snacks," Chinese dumplings come in many varieties. Jiao are rice wrappers, filled with chopped meat or vegetables that are steamed or fried. Northern Chinese Bao are either thick wheat or rice flour doughs, stuffed and made into large balls that are steamed. Fried Guo Tie, or pot stickers and Shaomai are small steamed dumplings that can be found in food trucks and fairs. Thai, Vietnamese, Korean, and Japanese dumplings are similar to Chinese versions and are sold by many food trucks devoted to these national cuisines. The most popular of all Asian dumpling-like dishes are deep fried Cheun Gyun or spring/egg rolls along with increasingly popular Filipino lumpia. Italian raviolis are also fried as a street food, especially in St. Louis, Missouri where the style originated.

European and Latin American dumplings are also popular on the street food scene. Empanada is a generic name for foods made from a flour dough, rolled out, cut into circles, filled with chopped meat, or cheese, or vegetable fillings that are sealed, and then baked or fried. Hundreds of types of empanadas are made in Latin America and are widespread in the United States in food trucks and at fairs. One famous stuffed Mexican-based dish is the tamale. Made with fillings ranging from savory meat to sweet ones made with fruit, they are long rolls of corn dough filled, then wrapped in a corn or banana husk, tied into a bundle, and steamed. There are two kinds of tamales in North America. One is standard Mexican-style made with corn dough, the other is the Mississippi Delta tamale. Made with coarse corn meal, filled mainly with cooked pork and a spicy sauce, Mississippi tamales are found on street stands, carts, and fairs as far north as Chicago. Traditional Mexican tamales from different regions of that country are common across the United States.

One kind of stuffed food is so commonplace that Americans hardly think of it as "stuffed." Pies come in two basic forms: savory and sweet. Meat pies are made in several ways, one of which is the well-known Cornish Pasty from Michigan, Wisconsin, and parts of Minnesota. Originating in Cornwall, England, as lunch for hard-working tin miners, pasties are sold at every fair and festival in those states and beyond. Pasties are thick wheat-flour pastries, made into oblong, square, or round forms, filled with ground meat, chopped potatoes, often carrots and root vegetables, and then baked. The similar runza from Nebraska is also a meat and vegetable dumpling, but originated in Russia. Sweet pies of every sort, but usually made with fruit, are integral parts of any fair or festival and sold in food trucks. One sub-specialty is the fried pie. Supposedly Southern in origin, crispy deep-fried fruit-filled pies are found at fairs almost everywhere.

Deep-Fried Food

Americans love fried foods. It is the preparation of choice above all others and is always featured in fast food places, fairs, and festivals: it is hard to think of hamburgers without French fries accompanying them. There are two kinds of deep-fried foods: savory and sweet. French fried potatoes are America's favorite deep-fried food, while fried chicken might be America's best-known fried meat dish. Chicken can be done in many ways, from Southern American (Kentucky and New Orleans are the best-known styles because of food chains) to Asian. Deep-fried Buffalo chicken wings is a more recent addition to the fried chicken scene, these served with sour cream and a spicy hot sauce. Fried cheese curds and nachos (fried tortilla wedges swerved with a soft cheese food topping), and many others foods are dunked in hot oil to be served hot and crispy. Often, these foods are skewered on a stick before frying. Since the 1920s, corn dogs are the best-known fried food on a stick. Hot dogs are impaled on sticks, dipped in corn meal batter, and then deep fried to a golden brown. At state, county,

Deep-Fried America

Some food critics have said that deep frying is an American fetish. The Minnesota State Fair brags about its 75 deep-fried preparations, as do other fairs. Among them are the "muddy pig," bacon dipped in chocolate, battered macaroni and cheese, battered spam filled with fake cheese, Elvis on a Stick made of a battered banana with peanut butter and bacon, and Spaghetti and Meatballs on a Stick, spaghetti mixed into a meatball, battered, fried, skewered, and rolled in marinara sauce. Even less healthy are chocolate cake, S'mores, banana splits, fresh fruits, Oreo cookies, Twinkies, and candy bars, especially Snickers, Milky Way, Three Musketeers, Reese's Peanut Butter Cups, and Tootsie Rolls and jelly beans—all battered and deep fried. In America, almost nothing escapes deep hot oil and batters.

and local fairs there will always be corn dogs accompanied by other savory stick foods. Bacon, plain hot dogs, batter-dipped fish, patty sausage dipped in batter, pizza, macaroni and cheese, pickle slices, and battered spam are a few of an infinite variety of the often battered fried stick foods that fair goers relish.

Sweet Foods

Sweet foods are among the oldest street, fair, and boardwalk foods in America. Some made their first appearances at world's fairs, such as caramel corn in 1876, an early version of Cracker Jacks, in 1893, and ice cream cones and cotton candy in 1904. Candied and caramel apples appeared on New Jersey shore resorts after 1908 and are now features of Halloween and Thanksgiving food traditions. Cold sweets are even more popular. In the late nineteenth century, "hokey pokey" men sold ice cream from mobile carts. In the 1920s, motorized trucks sold newly invented chocolate-covered ice cream bars, the most famous being Good Humor Company trucks. Popsicles, including Mexican paletas and shaved ices—coarsely ground and syrup-flavored ices—are among the many frozen treats familiar to fairs and amusement areas.

There is not a fair or amusement park where the smell of pastries frying in hot oil do not fill the air. Fried batters, especially funnel cakes (poured into hot oil in strings and served with powdered sugar) are universal and, in recent years, Latin American buñuelos (fried dough balls), churros (fried dough sticks sprinkled with sugar and cinnamon), and elephant ears (flat, round pastries) have also become popular. The Dunkin Donuts chain's Dunkin Donut fries are very much like churros. The oldest of fried doughs, doughnuts and crullers are also sold in amusements areas, but are more common from food trucks where they come in plain and fancy versions. Other unusual battered creations include fried Coke (Coca-Cola), made by mixing cola syrup with batter, deep frying it, and pouring more syrup on top of the final product.

Packaged candies are street food since they are foods eaten on the go, but they are usually thought of as snacks. One candy is almost completely associated with the kinds of public eating done at seaside resorts, salt water taffy. Taffy originated in England around 1800 and spread to American coastal resorts such as Atlantic City, New Jersey, by the 1880s. There, it came to be called "salt water" because it was sold by the seaside. Taffy is a semi-soft candy made from sugar, cornstarch, corn syrup, and flavorings made by machines that pull and cut ribbons of candy before customers' eyes. Taffy machines are not confined to their original locations but are found at fairs and shops in tourist areas of the country. In these places, taffy is often joined by made-on-location fudges.

Snacks

Snacks are foods eaten between meals, at events such as movie theaters, concerts, and sports venues and are consumed at any time people are feeling somewhat hungry but not hungry enough for a full meal.

Nutritious Snacks

Before the appearance of industrialized, sugar rich, salt-laden snack foods, ingredients nutrition experts consider unhealthy, most snacks were natural. Nuts were the most common because they kept well, are portable, and taste good. Walnuts and hickory nuts were early American favorites as were chestnuts when roasted. Pecans and almonds were regional specialties; the native American pecans growing only from southern Illinois to Texas and almonds (a Mediterranean tree) being planted in California in the 1850s. Macadamia nuts, pistachios, and cashews (technically a fruit) were all later additions to the American nut inventory. The most popular nut, by far is not a nut, but a legume, the peanut. Native to South America, the peanut was used in the American South mainly as food for slaves and poor white people. Union soldiers in the Civil War and afterward brought peanuts back home with them to the North and roasted peanuts became instantly popular. In the South, peanuts are often boiled and salted, giving them a somewhat different flavor. Today, all of these nuts remain as snack foods with almonds favored because of their health values and peanuts because of flavor and relatively low prices.

Fruits

Fresh and dried fruits and berries have always have been popular snack foods. Of all fruits, apples are the most popular. They tend to keep for longer periods than other fruits and so are good for eating on the go. Introduced from Europe to the Americas, they spread rapidly across the nation to be used for cider-making and eating fresh. Eating varieties were developed beginning in the 1850s and over the next century and a half, mass apple production was devoted to breeds such a Delicious, Jonathan, and Macintosh, among others. In recent decades, old apple types have been reintroduced and new flavorful ones invented. Stayman Winesap and Pippins are old ones, while Honeycrisp and Fuji are popular new ones.

Pears and peaches, citrus fruits, especially easily peeled tangerines and mandarin oranges, are widely eaten as snacks. Mangoes, popular in Latin

America and India, are also eaten by people more recently arrived from those parts of the world. Americans love grapes, especially seedless varieties. Since they were developed in California beginning in the 1870s, white seedless Thompson grapes have been eaten fresh along with red versions developed later. However, grapes are even more popular when they are dried into raisins. Raisins are portable, sweet, and nutritious. Sold in snack packages, mixed with other dried fruits and nuts into trail mixes, and blended into nutrition bars, they are the most widely consumed fruits in America.

Energy or protein bars, granola, and other kinds of nut and fruit bars are a newer supposedly healthy snack in the American market. Originally invented in the 1960s for astronauts, these snack bars were made to have nutritionally balanced amounts of protein and carbohydrates with vitamins. Modern snack bars became mainstream in the late 1980s when Power Bars made high-protein products for athletes. Many more brands followed and there are dozens on grocery store shelves today. Some are high in high fructose corn syrup because the vegetable protein mixtures in the bars are not tasty, others like Lärabar and Kind are all organic "natural" products with lots of nuts and dried fruits in them.

Junk Food

Commercially made candies are the most widely consumed snack food in America. Candies are sugar-based sweets mostly made from cane sugar but some use corn (high fructose), molasses, sorghum syrups, and honey. Candies are of many types, from hard candies to soft and sticky and many are chocolate coated. From the nineteenth well into the twentieth century, hard "penny" candies such as lemon drops were the most popular. Lollipops followed in the 1920s. Peanut brittle, also hard, and soft fudges became widely sold in the early twentieth century. Perhaps the most popular are those made with chocolate. Local confectioners made chocolate candies, most often truffles, which are small candies coated in chocolate with fillings such as creams, caramels, nuts, or fruits. Wrapped bar candies came in the late nineteenth century with hundreds of companies competing in the national market. The best-known companies include Mars, Hershey, and Nestlé, each of whom made their own and in recent decades bought up other well-known companies. Bars can be solid chocolate, Hershey and Nestlé among the most common, or filled bars, such as Mars' Snickers and Milky Way. Nuts and nut products are often used in bars or cups, Reese's made with peanut butter is the best known. Nuts are certainly healthy but the rest of the ingredients are not. However, candy companies often advertise their products as daytime energy boosters. Sugar certainly plays such a role, if fleetingly.

Popcorn

Do you know what the world's most expensive food is, in terms of cost of raw ingredient against profits? It is something Americans eat to the tune of 17 billion quarts or about 45 quarts per person each year. The food is popcorn. One ounce of popcorn costing about 35 cents makes 1 quart of popcorn sold from $2.50 to $5.00 in movie theaters. Profits average 85 percent; a full service restaurant is lucky to net 10 percent. Popcorn sellers can thank Charles Cretors who in 1891 introduced the first portable steam-powered popcorn machine and, in the 1910s, the first electric-powered popcorn maker.

Cookies are among America's favorite snacks and have been for at least 300 years. Meaning "little cakes" in Dutch, cookies were sweet products made at home and in small bakeries until the late nineteenth century, when large-scale industrial baking arose. There are many kinds of cookies, both hard and soft, but almost all of them have large amounts of sugar in them. Chocolate chip, raisin, oatmeal, gingery, iced, and those filled with sugary spreads are displayed in profusion on grocery store shelves and on convenience store racks. Mondeléz makes the most popular cookie of all, cream-filled Oreos and Chip Ahoy, while Keebler (a division of Kellogg's) makes a variety including Chips Deluxe, Vanilla Wafers, and Animal Crackers. Other small cakes are equally popular as snacks. Twinkies, an oblong sponge cake filled with a vanilla cream, is the best known. Cupcakes, some filled with creams, with sugar icing on top are also widely consumed snack cakes. Hostess (which also makes Ding Dongs), Tastycake, Little Debbie, and Drake's are all popular brands.

Some snacks are in-between healthy and junk food status. Popcorn, made commercially viable in the 1880s and vital to the movie theater business, is a wholesome food. When loaded with artificial "butter" and lots of salt in theaters and ballparks, or when coated with caramel as in Cracker Jacks and other versions, it is anything but a healthy snack. Potato chips are similar since they begin as raw potatoes that are then fried in oil and sprinkled with large amounts of salt. The more recent category of nacho or tortilla chips are treated the same way, though some brands bake rather than fry them. Crackers are among the largest class of snacks, some eaten plain out of the box like Goldfish crackers, others serving as bases of other ingredients such as dips or cheeses. Like the better pretzels today, early crackers were made with wheat flour and leavening alone. This lives on in Saltines and oyster crackers, both made with baking soda. Ritz Crackers that have been popular since the mid-twentieth century are made with high fructose corn syrup and trans fats and so are Wheat Thins. Graham crackers, named for the nineteenth-century health food advocate Sylvester Graham, are also made with plenty of sugars and simple carbohydrates. Other crackers are far more nutritious. Triscuits invented early in the twentieth century are made from whole wheat and the Swedish Wasa Crisp Bread is high in fiber with no sugars added. In response to consumer demands for more nutritious crackers, companies have created new products. Kellogg's Special K Multi-Grain Crackers, Crunchmaster Original Multi-Seed Crackers, Back to Nature Harvest Whole Wheat, and Mary's Gone Crackers are among the many new healthier crackers now available.

CHAPTER NINE

Dining Out

The public dining industry is one of America's largest, amounting to about $400 billion and employing some 14 million people. According to the U.S. Department of Labor, the average household in the United States spent $3,365 eating out in 2018. That sum amounts to about 40–45 percent of the annual food budget, depending on the individual household's income and preferences: younger people spend more on restaurant and take-out food than older Americans. Eating out can be an extension of eating at home or it can be an adventure. Almost every American has eaten at some kind of restaurant during the year and the reasons for doing so are as varied as the restaurant types. People eat out while at work or doing other activities during the day in venues ranging from restaurants, cafeterias, fast food places, food stands, foods trucks, and street vendors. For the increasing number of Americans who cannot or do not want to cook or clean up afterward, eating out or getting take-out food is a common way to dine. Restaurants can be places for social gatherings such as informal clubs, meeting friends or family members, or people getting together after work for drinks and snacks or dinner. Dining places can be entertainments that are enjoyable because of their décor and food or for the aesthetics of fine dining. Restaurants can be educational because diners can have new taste experiences that may come from other culinary traditions or they can learn about interesting dishes that they will try to recreate at home. New food combinations, tastes for and ideas about ethnic cuisines, and ideas about wholesome and ethically sourced foods have been changing since the late twentieth century. Like the evolution of life on Earth, restaurants have filled all the niches created by these ideas and are evolving continuously. Mainly, though, Americans like to eat the foods that are familiar to them but with more interesting flavors or maybe of better quality because it is made by professionals.

Eateries are categorized by the restaurant industry in several ways: fast food, fast casual, casual (also called family style), contemporary casual, ethnic, fine dining, and pop-up. These categories are fluid, for example street food (see Chapter 8) is another class of public dining that overlaps with fast food and casual restaurants often change their styles and menus. Within each of the dining types are subcategories: pizzerias, hot dog stands, pubs and gastro pubs, cafés, brasseries, diners, ice cream shops, food trucks, truck stops, cafeterias, buffets, and coffee houses. Each one caters to perceived customer needs and many also fit into local neighborhood cultures. For instance, diners, coffee shops, or casual restaurants might be the places that people in a neighborhood regularly go for a family meal or when they do not want to cook at home. These are usually friendly places where the owner, staff, and customers know each other and dining is comfortable. The foods will be dishes to which they are accustomed, traditional American-like hamburgers, steaks or chicken, or perhaps ethnic ones that they have long known, the most popular of which are Italian, Mexican, and Chinese. These kinds of places help to define a neighborhood and shape what dining experiences are for most Americans.

Americans have been eating out since the eighteenth century, only not in restaurants as we know them today. Inns and taverns were places where travelers lodged and dined and where informal meetings took place: George Washington and all the American Revolutionary leaders regularly met at Fraunces Tavern in New York City and the Warren Tavern in Boston. The food was usually boiled and roasted meats, bread, and simple sauces accompanied by ale, hard cider, and liquor. France, where the modern restaurant was born, provided the model for fine dining first in hotels and in the 1820s and 1830s, freestanding restaurants such as the famous fine dining establishments Delmonico's New York. As cities grew rapidly, the need for

Iconic Local Foods

Some American foods have become "iconic local" foods because of different ingredient combinations or they have unique names. Many are big foods like the Horseshoe from Springfield, Illinois, two ground beef disks on white toast, covered in French fries and then coated in a cheesy Welsh rarebit sauce. Hot Brown another local calorie-laden Welsh rarebit-covered sandwich made with bacon and turkey was invented in the Brown Hotel in that city in 1926. The king of big local foods is the Rochester, New York, Garbage Plate, a layered dish with baked beans or macaroni salad together with French fries topped with hamburger, cheeseburger, hot dogs, Italian sausage, fried fish, fried ham, eggs, grilled cheese, onions, and a Coney sauce.

midday meals led to the development of lunch places. These ranged from full-scale meals for the upper-class businessmen, to middle-class cafeterias and buffets, lunch rooms that catered to young women who entered the workforce as clerical workers and sales staffs, working men's restaurants like Boston's Durgin-Park, bars that served free or cheap lunches to male customers, down to food wagons and pushcart vendors. In the latter nineteenth and early twentieth centuries, some of these places changed into clean, quick-service luncheonettes and cafeterias where simple dishes, namely sandwiches, frankfurters, soups, spaghetti, breads, and desserts, especially pies, were served. Some, like Schrafft's in New York and Howard Johnson's, nationally morphed into sit down restaurants with relatively inexpensive meals served fairly quickly for midday shoppers and families who could not afford fancy restaurants. A number of restaurants of this kind were local family-oriented places, often with booths along walls and tables in the middle, that still serve fairly simple menus and desserts at reasonable prices. Later in the twentieth century, a number of national and regional family-style restaurant chains were established and now dominate the restaurant market, even though locally owned ones are still abundant. Ethnic restaurants appeared as early as the 1850s when immigrants from German-speaking areas of Europe immigrated in large numbers: German and Viennese restaurants, cafés, and bakeries were once highly popular. Italians, especially from southern Italy opened small restaurants that became staples of the American dining scene at the same time as Chinese immigrants from Guangdong Province opened inexpensive and popular eating places in America's cities and later towns across the nation. Theme restaurants with décor to match their cuisines began in the 1920s with fish houses and later many others kinds including the once-popular Pacific Island style called "Polynesian." All of these varieties of dining places remain much the same, perhaps with different menus, in different locations, and with different decor, but the ideas on which they are based have not changed much.

Fast Food

Fast food means foods that are prepared in a usually small restaurant, wrapped up, and served across a counter or through a service window and eaten quickly on the spot or taken away to be eaten in one's car or elsewhere. A variation on this style is actually one of the earliest forms of fast take-out food, the drive-in; McDonald's began as one of these. Fast food restaurants date to the 1920s chain called White Castle, which began in Wichita, Kansas. Clean, efficient, and cheap, the restaurants specialized in small square hamburgers (colloquially called "sliders") that were cooked quickly on the spot. White Castle and many imitators were soon established in cities across the country. These were different from the numerous hot dog stands and local greasy spoons whose cleanliness often left something to be desired. When Americans took to the roads in their newly acquired cars in the 1920s, the first drive-thru and drive-ins began in Springfield, Illinois, and Dallas, Texas. The menus were simple, hamburgers, barbecue sandwiches, fries, and soft drinks. These kinds of restaurants boomed after World War II as the national road system was built, suburbs were established further and further away from city centers, and the number of cars on the roads increased vastly. McDonald's, Burger King, Burger Chef, Wendy's, A&W Root Beer, and Sonic (leading drive-in chains with a carhop service) became enormous successes based on limited menus and swift service. Later, fast service chains such as Kentucky Fried Chicken, Church's, Popeye's, and Chick-fil-A served fried chicken as the core menu item. Fast food chains from the 1970s onward moved into cities where they replaced the old cafeterias, lunch counters, and local eateries. The early drive-ins and drive-thrus catered to travelers who needed meals at all times of the day whether going to work, shopping, or out for leisure driving. In the 1950s, drive-ins became places were young people driving their often-old cars gathered to socialize. When they became adults, they took their children to the same places, which became destinations for parents and children; it is not an accident that fast food restaurants like McDonald's market themselves through advertising and promotions to children. In cities, fast food chains serve as lunch and snack food places.

Casual Restaurants

In between fast food and fine dining lies a wide range of public dining places that fall into several categories. Casual or family-style restaurants are the descendants of older middle-class restaurants and, like French bistros or modern versions of Italian trattorias, they are places that serve moderately priced dishes in a comfortable atmosphere with friendly waitstaff. The décor can be thematic, Mexican for example, or classic American with wooden trim on walls and room separators, plants, and pleasant pictures on the walls. Theoretically, the food is of better quality than fast food, prepared by professional staff and served by single wait persons, unlike fine dining places that have specialized staff for serving wine, among others. Knives, forks, and spoons are on the table with napkins and water glasses stood on one side and the food is served plated, meaning already arranged on a plate. Some specialized family restaurants serve food in bowls from which diners help themselves but these are mainly historical places as in

Pennsylvania Dutch country. The food is familiar to diners with signature dishes often linked to the restaurant style. Greek-owned family restaurants that are common in American cities and towns might serve hamburger platters with fries, steaks, pasta, and "Grecian chicken" (usually roasted chicken with sesame seeds) along with Greek salads and perhaps a soup, for example, avgolemono soup (chicken with lemon). The model for chain casual restaurants is Howard Johnson's, which began as an ice cream shop in Massachusetts. Marked by an orange roof and turquoise cupola, Howard Johnson's developed into a near thousand-unit chain by the 1970s, along highways, in towns, and near the newly developing suburbs. In places where few other family dining places existed, it became a go-to restaurant for families and travelers alike. The menu always included a grilled hamburger plate, minute steak, a sirloin steak sandwich, and a signature dish— fried clams either plain or in a platter with French fries. For desserts, there were a wide variety of sundaes based on the chain's famous "28 flavors" of ice cream. For a variety of reasons, Howard Johnson's restaurants changed into a hotel chain, but the idea lives on and older Americans remember the restaurants fondly because of the food and for memories of family meals.

Among the best known and largest casual chain restaurants are, Applebee's Neighborhood Grill + Bar, Buffalo Wild Wings (also a sports bar), The Cheesecake Factory, Chili's, Cracker Barrel, Denny's, Golden Corral (all-you-can eat buffet restaurants), Hooters (two chains), International House of Pancakes (IHOP), Longhorn Steak House, Outback Steakhouse, P. F. Chang's China Bistro, Pizza Hut, Red Robin, Red Lobster, Steak 'n Shake, Texas Roadhouse, TGI Friday, Waffle House, and Wingstop. Each restaurant chain fills geographic, social, and economic niches in the dining landscape. At the same time, each tries to differentiate itself from the competition with standard menu items, adding new ones, and by having different themes. For instance, most Denny's are located near highway intersections and service areas. Its menu is oriented toward hearty breakfasts including large omelets and pancakes along with classic American dinners such as meatloaf with mashed potatoes and gravy, pot roast, chicken tenders, spaghetti and meatballs, and grilled chicken. These are not meant to be family dining destinations unless it is a family that is travelling together. Denny's has also developed classic roadside diner restaurants that reproduce the old dining cars that once dotted highways across the country. Cracker Barrel followed a similar geographic recipe, putting restaurants along highways, but with a different theme and menu: Southern cooking. The décor is like a comfortable, homey Southern country store with a porch, rocking chairs, and stone fireplace with lots of old-fashioned bric-a-brac. Cracker Barrel serves large breakfasts all day that include large platters of eggs, turkey bacon, sausage, fried apples, hash brown potatoes and buttermilk biscuits, or a fried breakfast with chicken fried chicken or country fried steak. Lunches and dinners are in similar style with fried catfish, fried chicken livers, ham, fried chicken tenders, pork chops, and hamburger steak, with typical Southern sides of corn, fried apples, coleslaw, turnip greens, French fries, green beans, fried okra, and macaroni and cheese.

Other chains try to be even more family friendly. Applebee's Neighborhood Grill + Bar, owned by IHOP, is a franchise system meant to replicate old neighborhood restaurants, as their advertising says. They are both urban

---

Monday Meatloaf

Yield: Serves 8

Ingredients
3 eggs
1 medium onion chopped finely
1 Tbsp ground allspice
1 Tbsp dried dill weed
1 tsp prepared horseradish
1⅓ cups half and half creamer
⅓ loaf white bread pulled apart
3 pounds lean ground beef
1⅓ cups ketchup
⅓ cup brown sugar

1. Preheat oven to 350°F. Place eggs in a large bowl and beat until smooth. Add onion, allspice, dill, and horseradish, and mix well.
2. Add half and half creamer and stir; add bread and mix all together, making sure all the liquids and spices are absorbed into the bread. Add the ground beef and mix with your hands; however, don't over mix as that will make it tough.
3. Place mixture into a large loaf pan and pat evenly. You can poke holes into the mixture for the glaze to seep into the loaf if desired.
4. To make glaze, pour the ketchup and brown sugar into a bowl and mix well. Pour over the meatloaf mixture.
5. Place pan into a preheated oven and bake for 1–1½ hours, depending on the oven. When internal temperature reaches 160°F, remove from oven.

Courtesy of Flesor's Candy Kitchen, Tuscola, IL 61953. Ann F. Beck, co-owner and President of Flesor Family Confectionary.

and suburban regions, many in and near shopping areas. These locations are not residential neighborhoods but the restaurants have become places for families to hang out, giving out coloring books and crayons to children while parents can have alcoholic beverages. The menu is homey American, steaks and ribs, grilled chicken and chicken tenders, chicken parmesan, battered fish and shrimp, and a variety of creamy pasta dishes, hamburgers, and wraps. There is a children's menu that features corn dogs, chicken tenders, mac and cheese, and tacos. These dishes are updated versions and in greater varieties than the older restaurants that Applebee's intends to replace. Outback Steakhouse and The Cheesecake Factory are closer to the neighborhood concept, though one is Australian-themed and the other known for its array of rich cheesecakes and pastries. Both chains have freestanding restaurants mainly in suburban and in and near large malls. They are more or less destination restaurants because of their locations—people drive to them—and the menus are family friendly. Outback serves varieties of beef steaks, chicken and seafood, and a combination that was once very popular in American restaurants, surf and turf: a beefsteak with either a lobster tail or shrimp on the same plate. Its signature dish is a "blooming" onion, a large onion breaded and deep fried, cut in a way that it opens into a flower shape. The Cheesecake Factory has a very large menu with 250 items including the usual meats, salads, soups, and side dishes served in copious and often calorie-laden quantities. Unlike most casual restaurants, The Cheesecake Factory features a number of international entrees ranging from Italian to Mexican American, Japanese, Thai, and Hawaiian poke so that diners can have different food experiences if sharing or when returning. With its location in shopping areas, the chain does a large lunch business for shoppers and families.

In a competitive market, casual restaurants use different menu items and decorative styles to attract customers of different ages, tastes, and incomes. Olive Garden, begun by General Mills, is Italian American, building its brand on large amounts of pasta dishes—it once offered unlimited pasta to diners—unlimited breadsticks, and television advertising. Olive Garden has always appealed to older people and remains a favorite dining spot for senior citizens. Red Lobster specializes in seafood with prices that range from moderate fish and chips to expensive surf and turf. Once a dining adventure, a place for Americans to try different kinds of seafood, its customer base became older and patronage declined. In recent years, Red Lobster devised new dishes using fresh ingredients, emphasized sustainable seafood, and has become a fun and educational "night out" place for younger families, as well as older customers, who are interested in seafood. Chili's began as a friend's gathering together hamburger restaurant in Dallas, Texas, and has morphed into a mostly Tex-Mex chain. Its many locations include airports, city locations, and shopping districts. So popular were its burgers, ribs, quesadillas, and more Texas-Mexican inspired dishes as well as frequent special pricing and giveaways that it remains a "hang out" kind of place for families. TGI Fridays is similar, pitching itself as an after work gathering place as the name, meaning "thank God it's Friday" implies. Buffalo Wild Wings' concept is a sports bar that specializes in a Buffalo, New York, specialty: fried chicken wings dipped in a hot sauce and butter. The restaurants serve a variety of meat-based sandwiches, wraps, and salads in a setting that looks something like a sports stadium with seating along the sides and a number of television screens showing sports. It is promoted as a family friendly place for sports-minded patrons. International House of Pancakes (IHOP) is another themed restaurant chain, this one originally based on breakfasts and now serving a variety of sandwiches, meats, soups, and desserts. IHOP sells a variety of pancakes, waffles, egg dishes, and meat and egg combinations and is especially popular for weekend family breakfasts. IHOP's multigenerational orientation is seen in its children's menus that feature pancakes with smiley-faced toppings and a do-it-yourself pancake trimming plate, and also a senior citizens menu. There are a number of smaller pancake chains in the United States, but in the South, where waffles are often paired with varied ingredients including chicken, Waffle House has a wide distribution that rivals IHOP.

Fast Casual Restaurants

Because of changes in American lifestyles and ideas about food, the fastest growing segment of the restaurant market is called "fast casual." Mostly chains, at least 500 of them large and small, these restaurants offer foods that are of better quality than most fast food places. Hamburgers made from meat ground on the spot, or hand-cut French fries, breads that are baked on location, and, in a number of restaurants, fresh foods with better health benefits than traditional fast foods are among the kinds of dishes found at these places. In many fast-casual eateries, food is ordered at a counter and it is prepared in open kitchens. Seating is usually limited because diners are expected to eat more quickly than in a casual restaurants and utensils and dishes are likely to be disposable or recyclable. And take-out foods are also common features akin to standard fast food places. Some fast-casual restaurants are destination places for people who want better quality food quickly or for those who want the restaurant's specialty: Five Guys Burgers and Fries, Fuddruckers, Fatburgers and Smashburgers, or the Mongolian barbecue stir-fry at Genghis Grill are examples.

There are varieties of styles within this category, hybrids of fast food and fast casual. Steak 'n Shake, for instance, is a hamburger place dating to the 1930s that originally made its ground beef from steaks in its restaurant along with hand-mixed milkshakes. Now a national chain, locations usually have eat-in service, front-window, and drive-thru services. Other fast-casual restaurants chains are moving into this model. Panera, a leading chain, is among many now opening drive-thru windows in its locations, and using a mobile phone app for quick payments. Delivery is another hybrid, an old one that has been adopted by restaurant chains. Local take-out and delivery was a long-time practice, especially among urban Asian restaurants; the semi-pyramidal cardboard boxes are icons of American dining. From the mid-twentieth century, pizza chains like Domino's built their businesses on delivery of hot, freshly made pizza. Pizza Hut, which has always had a dine-in component, has been changing to a take-out and delivery service but remains a hybrid. Pizza has become a familiar comfort food eaten at any time of the day or night, but restaurants ranging from fine dining to upscale fast food are moving to the delivery model. Called "ghost" or "cloud" restaurants, these exist only in large catering facilities making dishes that might be found in fast-casual restaurants only for delivery. Delivery services such as Uber Eats, Grubhub, and Skip the Dishes run large-scale delivery services for existing restaurants and for ghost restaurants with which they have partnered. In large cities—New York, Chicago, and Los Angeles are leaders—there are new exclusively online restaurant companies such as Green Summit that make pastas, barbecue dishes, healthy soups, salads and wraps, poke bowls, fancy hamburgers, Asian-inspired dishes, and more that they will deliver themselves. This concept blurs the lines between dining out at fast-casual restaurants and home dining.

Sandwich shops are a fairly recent take on the hybrid restaurant style. These kinds of places make take-out, dine-in (though like fast-food places in spartan conditions), and many can do food delivery. The largest chain is Subway with roughly 40,000 units worldwide. Subway's specialty is the Italian American submarine sandwich done in several ways from cold to hot, using varieties of fillings that range from cold meats and cheeses to meatballs, roast beef, tuna fish, Buffalo wings, vegetarian, and more. Jersey Mike's is a rapidly growing submarine chain that advertises itself as having better, fresher ingredients than its competitors: fresh onions, lettuce, tomatoes, olive oil blend, red wine vinegar and spices, plus premium meats and bread. Jimmy John's also serves submarines but also large club sandwiches, inexpensive smaller ones, and recently a French-style baguette with Italian salami and cheese in it. Jimmy John's does a large delivery business offering twenty-minute service. Arby's, the nation's second largest sandwich chain, specializes in meat but not hamburgers. Founded in 1964 as an alternative to hamburger and fries fast food chains, Arby's has roast beef and beef brisket sandwiches along with an array of chicken sandwiches, tenders, and an even wider selection of side dishes including several kinds of fried potatoes. The chain's advertising does not claim that its food is healthy or modern, only that they have a lot of meat. A number of fast casual restaurants, Panera one of them, are doing similar kinds of delivery and drive-thru concepts in their restaurants, though often using third-party delivery services. All of these delivery services are geared toward a lunchtime clientele, though with differing customer preferences. Panera offers soups, salads, and wraps while Arby's is quite the opposite.

Chipotle Mexican Grill is considered by authorities on dining out to be the pioneer of the fast casual and of the fresh ingredients, healthy food concept. Begun in 1993 in Colorado as a San Francisco taqueria, the menu is limited to tacos, "Mission"-style burritos invented in San Francisco's Mission district in the 1960s (large flour tortillas filled with various meat, vegetables, and rice), burrito bowls, salads, quesadillas for children, guacamole, and chips. Tapping into younger diner's interests in wholesome food, Chipotle is transparent about its fifty-one ingredients and says that its food sourcing is mostly sustainable, socially conscious, and humane in animal treatment; it was a pioneer in using only free-range eggs. Though the chain has endured a number of controversies including bacterial outbreaks in some of its units, the ideas of inexpensive and environmentally conscious fresh food has propelled its continued growth. Other chains both national and local seeing changing public tastes have followed the model. Panera Bread Company begun in St. Louis, Missouri, in 1987 as a bakery-café with a wide variety of fresh breads and has become a major chain that serves a range of dishes from soups, sandwiches, salads, bowls (mac and cheese in several versions, including one for children) with their own baked-on-site breads and desserts. The company's food is self-described as "clean," meaning no artificial preservatives, flavors, or sweeteners and as free of allergens as is feasible. Like Chipotle, Panera is moving to a sustainable-as-possible food source model along with humane treatment of animals such as free-range eggs. The same kinds of ideas about food are behind a number of smaller restaurant chains that are located mainly in cities. Boston and New York, for example, has new ones that are "farm to counter," a take on the fine dining farm-to-table concept. This means seasonal foods that come directly from local farmers, much of it organically raised and prepared by innovative chefs. Many are vegetarian or vegan and are often influenced by Asian cookery. The Digg In chain in both New York and Boston works with nearby farmers who use organic and sustainable methods to produce dishes like their signature bowl: charred chicken (thigh), charred broccoli with lemon, roasted sweet potatoes, brown rice with parsley, and garlic aioli dressing. Together, these kinds of fast-casual restaurants are the leading edge of major changes in the food industry based on new ideas, especially in younger generation Americans, about health, nutrition, and the environment. Digg In and New York City-based fresh&co have even bought their own farms where they sustainably grow the vegetables that they use. These ideas have leaked over into mainstream cuisine as witnessed by the explosive growth of plant-based meat alternatives now appearing widely in hamburger chains. If restaurants intend to be comfortable places in which to eat then the newer emphasis on "clean" food appeals to diners who think more carefully about what they eat and how it is sourced.

Other fast casual chains distinguish themselves by having singular items or a greater variety of dishes that they know diners like. Boston Market, for instance, features the American favorite roasted chicken, turkey, barbequed ribs, and meatloaf accompanied by plenty of mashed potatoes, macaroni and cheese, green beans, creamed spinach and, in a nod to modern trends, bowls. Chick-fil-A has almost nothing but chicken dishes in numerous forms at modest prices as does the Mexican inflected El Pollo Loco. Panda Express started in mall food courts but has expanded to stand-alone fast-casual restaurants that serve the classic Chinese American creations: orange chicken, kung pao chicken, broccoli beef, chow mein, fried rice, steamed rice, and stir-fried vegetables. With more than 2,000 units Panda Express is a kind of modern version of the chow mein places so familiar in neighborhoods across the nation. Noodles and Company is Asian-inspired and similar to locally owned noodle shops in cities such as Chicago. Culver's, a mainly Midwestern chain, features "Butterburgers" (fresh hamburgers served in a buttered bun), chicken with no antibiotics and humanely raised, Wisconsin cheese curds, and its signature frozen custards. There will be other kinds of fast casual and hybrids popping up but two trends are clear: interest in world cuisines and desire for food that is raised and prepared in ways that are healthier for individuals and the environment. How these needs can be addressed when chain restaurants get their food either preprepared from central kitchens or the foods to be prepared on site comes from the chain's warehouses is a question often asked. Supply chains have become much more sophisticated in their purchasing of the ingredients that they want and swift transportation has allowed restaurants to have just as fresh food as might be found in grocery stores.

Two related kinds of fast-casual restaurants are among the quickest growing segment of the market; gastropubs and brewpubs. Gastropubs, from the Latin word for stomach and a shortened version of the British public

Chinese Chicken Salad with Crispy Angel Hair Pasta

Dishes like this are often on fast-casual restaurant menus.

Yield: Serves 4

Ingredients
1 3-pound chicken, roasted
2 Tbsp sesame oil
1 Tbsp rice wine vinegar
1 Tbsp soy sauce
¼ tsp kosher salt
¼ tsp white pepper
4 ounces dry capellini, cooked, drained thoroughly, and dried on paper towels or 4 ounces thin rice threads soaked until soft and dried
¼ cup cooking oil
Romaine lettuce leaves
1 red pepper cut into thin strips
1 green pepper cut into thin strips

1. Remove meat from roasted chicken and shred it with fingers into a nice edible size. Discard the bones.
2. Mix together sesame oil, rice wine vinegar, soy sauce, salt, and pepper in a bowl and add shredded chicken to it. Coat chicken with mixture and allow to stand at least 15 minutes.
3. Meanwhile, have cooked and drained pasta ready.
4. Heat cooking oil in a large frying pan to smoking point. Add pasta a little at a time and fry until it puffs up and becomes crispy. Remove from pan and drain on paper towels. Do this until all pasta is used. You may have to add more cooking oil to the pan. Allow to cool.
5. Place a bed of lettuce leaves on a plate. Mound one-quarter of the noodles on a plate. Heap chicken mixture on the noodles. Arrange red and green pepper strips around the noodle mound. Make 4 of these and serve.

house, began in Great Britain in the 1990s. Unlike older public houses that were drinking establishments with a few snacks or light dishes such as meat pies and pickled eggs, the new restaurants serve high-quality food prepared by trained chefs. Rotating seasonal menus with grilled meats, fish and vegetables, fancy sandwiches, often in Mediterranean style, are on the menu. They also feature varieties of craft beers, wines, and perhaps liquors from their own or local distilleries. All of these are sold at higher prices than most fast-casual restaurants. Gastropubs have spread across the United States as locally owned establishments and in chains such as BlackFinn Ameripub and Yard House. Because of surging interest in craft beers, especially among younger Americans, brewpubs have proliferated across the United States. These microbreweries make craft beers and ales on site in numerous styles according to the owner's tastes and what their patrons like. The most popular styles are India pale ale, light beer with heavy use of bitter hops, American pale ale, wheat beers, stouts, and porters. Each style can be made with different ingredients and flavorings and alcoholic strength so that each brewpub can have its own unique styles. The food served in brewpubs is not as elaborate as in gastropubs, more like sports bars with chicken wings, pizzas, and lots of fried side dishes.

Ethnic Restaurants

Ethnic restaurants featuring world cuisines have been popular since the nineteenth century and from the late twentieth into the twenty-first century have inspired a number of chefs and restaurant chains. Once considered by older generations of Americans to be foreign and unappetizing, German and Italian cuisine became integrated into everyday restaurant fare. Few chain restaurants do not serve hamburgers (from the German *hackfleisch,* ground or finely chopped meat, supposedly originating in Hamburg), and sausages that are German in origin (bratwurst and hot dogs) are also commonly sold. Polish, Czech, and other Central and Eastern European restaurants, including Jewish-American delicatessens, serve dishes that are similar to older American ones or were assimilated into mainstream American restaurant offerings: :almost all breakfast places serve some form of bagels. As for older Mexican American foods also thought to be exotic and alien in most of the country, they were mainstreamed even further by fast food chains such as Taco Bell.

There are not many chain restaurants that do not have Italian-style menu items; Italian restaurants are by far the most popular throughout the United States. Many of the dishes called Italian are Italian American because they were transformed from original recipes by immigrants who had access to new ingredients. For instance, impoverished immigrants from southern Italy and Sicily might have eaten meat once or twice a week, but in America they discovered abundant and inexpensive meat. Spaghetti with big meatballs, chicken parmigiana, fettucine alfredo (a thick roux-based cream sauce) with chicken, a heavy creamy artichoke spinach dip, Italian beef and Philadelphia cheesesteaks, and hoagies or submarines loaded with meats are among many foods that no Italian would recognize. Pizza margarita, a

Basic White Pizza

This pizza is mainly an East Coast specialty.

Yield: Makes two 10-inch pizzas

Dough
0.75 ounce dry yeast
1 tsp sugar
1 cup warm water (105°F)
3½ cups flour
1 tsp salt
2 Tbsp olive oil

1. Sprinkle yeast and sugar in bowl containing warm water. Stir gently to dissolve. Let stand in warm place for about 5 minutes or until proofed.
2. Place 3 cups of flour in a large bowl and mix with salt. Form a round hole in the middle of the flour and pour in the yeast mixture and olive oil. Mix together until a smooth dough is made.
3. Set dough on a floured surface and knead until dough is elastic for about 10 minutes. Add more flour as necessary. Place dough in a lightly oiled bowl, cover with a clean cloth or plastic wrap, and set in warm place. Allow to rise until doubled in bulk. Should take about 40 to 60 minutes.
4. When ready to use, punch down the dough and roll several times, folding between each rolling. Shape dough to proper round shapes to fit pizza 10-inch baking pan or pizza baking stone. Let stand at least 15 minutes before filling.

Filling
2 pounds fresh ricotta cheese
¼ cup grated Romano cheese
2 eggs, beaten
Freshly ground pepper to taste
¼ cup chopped fresh basil or oregano
1 pound mozzarella cheese, shredded

1. Mix all ingredients except mozzarella together in a large bowl.

Pizza
1. Preheat oven to 450°F. Roll out a 10-inch circle of dough. Lightly oil the pizza pan and set dough in it. Bake in preheated oven for 5 minutes or until crust is lightly browned.
2. Remove pan from oven and place half the filling on it. Replace in oven and bake for about 15 minutes or until almost dry.
3. Remove from oven and sprinkle half the shredded mozzarella cheese on it. Replace in oven and bake another 3 to 5 minutes or until cheese is melted. Cool slightly and serve.
4. Repeat process for second pizza or do two at a time.

dish native to Naples, is a thin soft flatbread with some chopped tomatoes, basil, mozzarella cheese (either cow or buffalo milk), and good olive oil. It is eaten rolled up. This is nothing like the pizzas mostly found in the United States and completely different from Chicago deep-dish pizza. Italian American food has become one of America's comfort foods, safe and familiar to restaurant goers.

Chinese food has two sides in America: one is Chinese American as seen in Panda Express and chop suey houses, and the other is food closer to their original forms and eaten by both Chinese who retain their culinary roots and non-Chinese diners who are interested in more "authentic" fare. Chinese restaurateurs in the late nineteenth century learned that Americans were carnivores, that they liked sweet dishes and, even more, liked thick gravy on their food. The result of adapting Chinese dishes was not only chop suey but General Tsao's chicken (crisply fried nuggets in a sweet glaze), sweet-sour pork, beef and broccoli, and fortune cookies. Chinese American restaurants also became family friendly with familiar foods famously among Jewish-American families who patronized them on Sunday nights.

Ethnic restaurants underwent an ongoing revolution beginning in the late twentieth century. Interest in new cuisines entered home cooking just as it did in restaurants, each influencing the other. New Chinese chefs brought regional foods beginning with hot and spicy Sichuan fare, filling northern foods, sweet and sour eastern cuisine, and subtly flavored fresh-food Cantonese dishes. Peking duck and Mongolian hot pots, barbequed duck, dim sum from Hong Kong and Taiwan, northern dumplings, and whole fish with the heads on and even chicken feet joined vegetables as varied as bitter melon to cabbage. With the influx of Thai, Vietnamese, Laotian, and Korean immigrants, restaurants featuring their foods have joined new Chinese as popular places for Americans to dine. Pad Thai noodles and green, red, yellow, and massaman curries are Thai favorites, as are Vietnamese phô' (pronounced Fah), bánh (many kinds of steamed rice cakes), and delicate spring rolls with nước chẩm (a somewhat sweet dipping sauce made with lime juice, sugar, fish sauce, and chili peppers). Laotian *larb*, ground meat mixed with fish sauce, lime juice, fermented fish juice, roasted ground rice, and fresh herbs served with lettuce leaf wraps has also become popular. Hearty Korean dishes, soups, barbecued beef ribs, and *bi bim bap* (a rice, meat, and vegetable bowl with an egg on top) have moved out of Korean restaurants and into fast casual and fast food places. Of all the varied Asian restaurants now found in cities and towns almost everywhere, one has become preeminent, Japanese. Americans' introduction to Japanese food began in the 1960s with teppanyaki steakhouses. Invented for Americans living in Japan after World War II, these feature meat and vegetables cooked by chefs on an open griddle in front of customers. In the 1970s, sushi and sashimi became popular because of television shows and movies featuring Japanese history and culture and because health authorities proclaimed the benefits of fish in American diets. New restaurants featuring sushi and ramen (noodles in soup) sprang up along with new Americanized creations such as California rolls (with avocado and crabmeat) and inside-out sushi (the seaweed wrap is on the inside not the outside). Today, there are at least 4,000 sushi restaurants in the United States and sushi is made in supermarkets for take out across the country. Raw fish, once disgusting to Americans, is now common in all of these venues. Instant ramen, the packaged version of classic Japanese quick service restaurants, is sold everywhere and is a mainstay of college students' diets.

Other ethnic restaurants have presences in areas where immigrants have settled and especially in cosmopolitan areas. The borough of Queens, New York, for instance is one of the most ethnically diverse regions of the United States with 138 languages spoken among people from Central and South America, Mexico and the Caribbean, South Asia, East Asia, the Philippines, Africa, the Middle East, and Europe. Restaurants representing almost all of these groups are sprinkled across the borough that attract not only local people who want familiar foods, but loads of culinary tourists from New York and around the country who are interested in new foods or who want certain dishes that they cannot find elsewhere. Other big cities boast the same kinds of food diversity. Even in smaller cities and town, when enough immigrants settle, they open restaurants that attract older residents. From the Hmong, mostly from Laos, in Minneapolis–St. Paul to mom-and-pop Mexican places making foods from the regions from which they came in small towns in the Midwest, America's dining experiences have broadened considerably and changed American ideas about food.

Fine Dining

In the hierarchy of restaurants, fine dining, also called white tablecloth, establishments stand at the top. These places have the greatest prestige among chefs and restaurateurs and confer this to the customers who dine there. The menus contain dishes made from the finest and often costly ingredients, the dishes made in house usually taking a lot of time and labor by chefs trained in schools or having learned by working with excellent chefs. The food service is done by specialists from wait staff to sommeliers or wine specialists whose job it is to make sure a leisurely meal is enjoyed by the patrons. A number of such restaurants are actually entertainments both in artful presentations of dishes as well as in the serving of them. These are expensive restaurants whose regular customers appreciate fine foods and wines and can afford it and by many people who would not ordinarily dine there except for special occasions such as birthdays, anniversaries, and wedding parties; reservations are required, sometimes months in advance. Among top restaurants there is a star culture, famous or rising chefs being attractions for diners who want the newest trends in food made by the celebrated culinary artists. On the other hand, ideas about fine dining depend on where restaurants are located. Usually, fine dining in rural America might be a restaurant that serves well-cooked steaks or roasted chicken, perhaps with French-style sauces, fresh vegetables, and well-priced wines. In more culinarily sophisticated areas, such a restaurant might be viewed as good but of middle rank, not in the same class or price range as one serving the latest molecular gastronomy.

Historically, fine dining has been associated with French restaurants. All culinary schools teach basic techniques of French cookery that were established in the nineteenth century: white, brown, tomato, and egg-based sauces, reductions, and demi-glaces (stock or sauces cooked down until very thick or gelatinized). Ways to roast, sauté, and poach meats and fish, along with vegetables using butter and cream as standard ingredients are all codified into practices that chefs must learn. The same rules apply to classic baked foods such as croissants. In the twentieth century, French cuisine was influenced by Japanese techniques and now emphasizes lighter sauces and fresh ingredients. Going to a French restaurant today, one can expect classic patés, mussels in wine sauce, beef bourguignon, coq au vin (chicken in wine sauce), confit de canard (slow cooked duck), gratin dauphinoise (sliced potatoes cooked with milk and butter and sometimes cheese), bouillabaisse (fish stew from Marseilles), ratatouille (vegetable stew), and the bistro classic steak frites (steak with fries), among many others.

Cioppino

This classic seafood stew from San Francisco began as a simple fisherman's stew that used local ingredients and seafood.

Yield: Serves 6–8

Ingredients
½ cup extra virgin olive oil
1½ cups green pepper, chopped
2 cups onion, chopped
1 cup celery, chopped
5 large cloves garlic, coarsely chopped
16 ounces clam juice
28 ounces canned diced tomatoes with juice
2 cups dry white wine
3 Tbsp tomato paste
2 bay leaves
¼ tsp red pepper flakes
½ tsp ground black pepper
½ tsp dried oregano leaf
1½ tsp salt
2 pounds halibut, or Alaskan cod, cut into 2-inch pieces
1 pound raw shrimp (about 21–25 pieces), peeled and deveined
1 pound crab, cut into 2-inch pieces
8 ounces scallops, cleaned
1 pound mussels in their shells
1 Tbsp lemon juice
3 Tbsp Italian parsley, finely chopped

1. Place olive oil in a large pot and heat to medium hot. Add green pepper, onion, celery, and garlic and sauté for 10 minutes or until the vegetables are very soft, but not browned.
2. Add clam juice, canned tomatoes and juice, white wine, tomato paste, bay leaves, red pepper flakes, black pepper, oregano leaf, and salt. Bring to a boil, reduce heat, and simmer for 15–20 minutes.
3. Add the fish and simmer for 5 minutes.
4. Add shrimp, crab, and scallops and simmer for 5 minutes.
5. Add mussels and simmer just until the mussels open.
6. Add lemon juice and parsley.

Serve with baguettes or sour dough.

From the 1970s, Italian has also become fine dining. In the 1970s, chefs from Rome and northern Italy came to the United States and opened upscale restaurants like those in their home country. Fine dining menus today might have appetizers of buffalo mozzarella with fresh tomatoes and balsamic vinegar, carpaccio (thinly sliced raw beef), *formaggi e salumi* (imported Italian cheeses and preserved meats), grilled octopus, mussels in tomato-wine broth, or scampi wrapped in prosciutto (thinly sliced aged ham). Pastas of various kinds will often be homemade, chicken grilled with white or Marsala (heavy red) sauces, meats roasted and grilled with sauces made from high-quality olive oils, capers, peppers, imported mushrooms, and herbs, perhaps roasted rabbit with polenta, and many more. In such restaurants, ingredients will be fresh and preparations deceptively simple: as chefs say, it is easy to ruin high-end Italian food by overcooking and over saucing.

Fresh Grilled Halibut with Cilantro and Tequila Lime Butter

Yield: Serves 4

Ingredients
4 7-ounce halibut steaks
Olive oil
4 Tbsp butter
Juice of ½ lime
¼ cup tequila
1 bunch cilantro leaves, chopped
Salt and freshly ground pepper to taste
Cilantro sprigs
Lime slices

1. Heat grill to 400°F. Coat swordfish steaks with olive oil. Place on grill and cook for no more than 2½ minutes each side. Meat should be translucent, not white.
2. In a small pan, melt the butter over high heat. Add lime juice and tequila. Allow to cook only for a moment or two to reduce slightly. Add chopped cilantro and salt and pepper to taste.
3. Pour sauce over tops of steaks.

Serve garnished with sprigs of cilantro and lime slices.

Since Italian restaurants are so popular, Americans have come to appreciate high-end Italian dishes and wines.

American fine dining has been influenced by the same ideas that have changed French and Italian restaurants: fresh food with different flavors and textures than older dishes. The phrase commonly used by these restaurants is "farm to table." Though all food that ends up in restaurants comes from farms, the phrase means locally sourced seasonal foods ideally from within a hundred mile radius. In northern climates where the growing season is limited, many restaurants use the numerous greenhouses that are sprouting in and around America's cities for supplies. Chefs are also interested in heritage breeds of plants and animals both for flavors and as ways to regenerate local environments from which they came. For example, there are breeding programs in the Midwest to bring back endangered prairie chickens both for the table and in the wild. American fine dining has been influenced by international/ethnic cuisines, especially Asian and Latin American. Asian ingredients such as lemongrass, soy sauce, ginger, pickled fish, coconut milk, black cardamom, bird chilies, baby vegetables, and artful presentations on the plate are all used in cutting-edge American restaurants. Mexican chilies and preparations, from fresh foods steamed in banana or corn husks, fanciful tacos, ceviche (pickled fish), to bold flavors of chilies, often appear on menus. New American chefs have created "fusion" cuisine in which disparate cooking traditions are brought together. A diner is as likely to find Korean short ribs on a taco as they are to see an egg roll stuffed with pastrami, hamburgers loaded with Korean kimchi, or pizza with artichokes and Japanese miso sauced vegetables. Fusion is not new, since all world cuisines are fusions of old ingredients with new ones. For instance, tomatoes were not widespread in Italy until the eighteenth century, but the new versions of fusion have brought very different ingredients and flavors together in ways that reflect the history of immigration to the United States as represented by public dining.

CHAPTER TEN

Food Issues and Dietary Concerns

Like all living things on Earth, human beings need food and drink since they are the substances that keep our biological engines running. Until only recent times, people spent most of their time catching or raising their food. From earliest days, farming has been a perilous occupation because yields of crops and animal products depend on the environments in which food sources were located. Unlike most other animals, beavers and ants exceptions, people have manipulated their environments since the last Ice Age, but getting reliable sources of food has always been perilous. There are countless examples of cultures, states, and empires disappearing because of climate change or misuse of land that reduced the amounts of food needed to sustain large populations. Even in the mostly climatically stable nineteenth and twentieth centuries, ecological disasters occurred, such as the Dust Bowl of the 1930s. Water is becoming a major problem in American agriculture. Too little of it in dry areas leads to drainage of what resources remain, especially aquifers and rivers, and too much of it in major flooding in the nation's interior destroys farmland and prevents crop planting. On the continent's lowland coasts, rising sea levels and ocean warmth threaten lowland farming and seafood sources. These events are in the news every day and disquiet many Americans.

There have always been concerns that what people consume might not be pure or unhealthy. Before the Pure Food and Drug Act and the Meat Act of 1906, and state pure milk laws were passed, Americans worried about food-borne illnesses from unsanitary food processors. They still are. Before 1990–2000s laws requiring that food be labelled with all ingredients, additives, and nutritional information, buyers were not fully informed about their purchases; often they still are not. Marketers extoll products as healthful, nutritious, low calorie, high in fiber, high in protein, able to help children grow big, strong, and smart, but can they be trusted? Highly sugared cereals that have marginal nutritional values are marketed to children, while many heavily processed food products declare themselves to be "organic" and thus better for human health and the environment. Food values have to do with health issues such as obesity, diabetes, and heart disease, all growing challenges in modern life. Americans might be puzzled about whether genetically modified organisms are deleterious to human health or how much pesticide or herbicide residue remains in what is put on the plate. Increasingly, younger Americans are concerned about animal welfare and the impact of husbandry and industrial agriculture on the planetary ecosystem. And especially around holiday times when charitable donations to food banks peaks, how many Americans who can afford decent and abundant food think about the millions of Americans who are food insecure?

These and a number of other issues that face American food consumers can be categorized in three levels of interest. One is wide spectrum and long-range problems that do not seem to immediately affect ordinary people but that can reach a second level of local or community concern. For instance, environmental issues are worrisome to an increasing number of Americans, but are usually not something people think about when shopping for or cooking food. The environment does gain immediacy in people's minds when water quality changes for whole communities due to climate-driven changes in water sources such as algal growths or drought. Community problems can relate to larger political and social structures—urban and rural poverty, food deserts, and food insecurity that are very real. A third level of unease is immediate for individuals and families—nutrition, safety from food-borne illnesses and possible food allergies, and personal health. What people buy to eat in stores and restaurants has to do with perceptions of what is dangerous and what is safe to eat. For these reasons, familiarity with foods and recipes in home cooking is important for home cooks and people who regularly buy prepared meals; they are also the reasons why grocery shoppers in stores stand in aisles looking at the ingredients listed on many of the foods that they buy. Familiarity and assumed safety are also important to people who dine out in restaurants and one reason why numerous chain restaurant menus resemble each other.

Wide Spectrum Issues

Environment—Climate Change

According to surveys taken in 2019, about 60 percent of Americans think that climate change is happening and that it will affect their communities, their families, and themselves personally. Climate change has come about due to rising global temperatures since the Industrial Revolution began in the nineteenth century with the most rapid rise occurring in the early twenty-first century. The cause is emission of heat trapping greenhouse gases, particularly carbon dioxide (CO_2). Scientists have long known that 350 parts per million of atmospheric CO_2 would cause perhaps irreversible warming that cannot be reversed easily. In 1958, the amount was already 315 ppm and in 2019 it was up to 415 ppm, the highest levels in three million years. The effects of global warming are shown on media every day: melting polar ice caps, melting mountain snow caps, consequently rising sea levels with flooding of coastal cities, low-lying nations in danger of sinking beneath oceans, droughts striking various parts of the world, wild fires, and animals that are adapted to colder climates either migrating or dying off. In fact, some one million species of plants and animals will die off by 2050 unless global warming can be reversed.

Climate change describes other elements of warming that more directly affect the nation's and the world's food. Weather patterns have been changing dramatically, especially during the late twentieth and early twenty-first century. Extreme weather events such as storms, river flooding, and erratic rainfall have become familiar to Americans in many parts of the country. Farmers count on reliable weather to know when to plant and harvest, but sudden freezes, massive destructive storms, and deluges of rain in areas such as the Midwest, America's soybean and corn belt, have caused declines in production. Since most of the corn and soybeans grown are used to feed livestock, meat production will be impacted; so will the popular plant-based meat alternatives based on soy. Severe heatwaves have become more common leading to drying out of forests in places like northern California, resulting in massive forest fires. Fires have destroyed rangelands for cattle, dairy farms, the citrus and avocado industries, and even made wine in the area taste ashen. Worse still, one-sixth of the world's grain, mostly wheat, production comes from America's High Plains. The water used comes from the vast Ogallala Aquifer that supplies 30 percent of all irrigated land in the United States. Fed by rainwater and snowmelt, the Aquifer is being depleted by high demand for irrigation on the semi-arid High Plains that are affected by heat and lack recharging water largely because of global warming. Experts say that within thirty years, most of the Aquifer will be depleted leaving the once rich wheat lands barren and America's food supply endangered.

Droughts and lack of water can have catastrophic impacts on people's food supplies because of loss of agricultural land. Droughts in Syria led to a long civil war and large migrations from Central America through Mexico to the United States. Not all water is potable, the salty oceans are unusable for terrestrial farming, but even here global warming has had major effects on human food. Oceans have warmed faster than the atmosphere, changing the distribution of fish living in them. Images of dead coral on Australia's Great Barrier make common appearances on television and magazines. Killed by ocean warming, they cannot move like fish that migrate to cooler waters. Fish stocks in warm seas such as the Indian Ocean and off the coast of West Africa that help support large populations have declined and will soon be at only 40 percent of prewarming levels. Fish supplies are already stressed by overfishing but when they virtually run out in the Indian subcontinent, more migration and political disorder will ensue.

Younger Americans are more keenly aware of environmental issues such as global warming and know quite a lot about the causes and possible cures. Millions of young people worldwide have seen Swedish teenaged environmentalist Greta Thunberg talking about the dangers and have followed her lead in staging informational demonstrations in schools. As she says, carbon emissions are the main cause with methane, a stronger greenhouse gas, second. Most greenhouse gas emissions are produced by manufacturing, generation of electricity, and transportation. Agriculture directly accounts for about 9 percent of emissions but when connected to the other causes through growing, transportation, and manufacturing of food it is about 30 percent of emissions. One cause is concentrated animal feeding operations (CAFOs), also known as factory farms. Animals, especially pigs and poultry, are raised in large numbers in sheds where they are not permitted to move much and do not see the light of day. Living over grates, their waste is collected in and sent to huge pits where it affects air through the release of methane gasses. Anyone driving by such farms will recognize them by the stench alone. Similarly, dairy cows and beef cattle produce a great deal of similar wastes including large amounts of gas through belching. Such wastes, especially from hog farms, have been a major contributor to water pollution in several states. Electricity and fossil fuels used to process and package foods and to transport them add to the environmental problem since most food in grocery stores comes from 1,500 to 2,000 miles way. Lastly, Americans waste at least 40 percent of the food that they buy, food that ends up in garbage dumps where it rots producing greenhouse gasses that amount to about 2 percent of all emissions. If food production causes global warming, warming affects the quality of the food that Americans eat. Studies show that excessive atmospheric carbon can increase the growth of plants like rice but significantly decreases its vitamin content. The same might apply to other edible fruits, vegetables, and grains; it does for grasses on the Great Plains where a good portion of the nation's cattle graze. One more effect of climate change on America's food supply is insects because 84 percent of all commercial food production depends on insect pollination. Some of these, like honey bees, have suffered major losses in recent years partly due to climatic effects such as sudden freezes that kill colonies, and parasites that may spread through global warming. Bees are the most important insects that have suffered colony collapse, endangering crops such as California almonds where about 80 percent of the world's supply originates. At least thirty-nine other major crops depend on insects for pollination and insect loss has become a problem that entomologists across the globe have described as an insect apocalypse. No doubt widespread use of pesticides on crops is another main cause of decline in useful insects.

Pollution

Because whole communities and food supplies have been affected, pollution of water and food sources has received a good deal of media attention over the years since. Lead found in the water supplies of Flint, Michigan, in 2015 has been a major new story since excessive lead damages nerves, the heart, and kidneys and impairs mental abilities in children. It is not a new story in American communities that have battled diseases borne in water supplies since the nineteenth century. Increased rainfall and flooding due to climate change has seen backup of waste management systems into drinking supplies as well as homes and businesses. Runoff from CAFOs into streams and rivers are usually due to breaks in waste confinement pits and areas, and when the increasing numbers of storms strike them, has caused lethal bacteria to enter community water supplies. More common is the runoff of agricultural chemicals into the nation's waters with serious effects on food systems. Chemical fertilizers, namely nitrogen, phosphorus, and potassium, enrich agricultural land but used in excess they can leach nutrients from the soil and pollute groundwater leading to less nutritious foods. Heavily applied to fields, fertilizers wash into rivers such as the Mississippi and lakes such as Lake Erie. So much fertilizer from farms, golf courses, and even home lawns flows down the Mississippi that the Gulf of Mexico into which it flows has a huge zone where no aquatic life exists. This dead zone is caused by blooms of algae fed by fertilizers that die and suck up all the water's oxygen. Lake Erie has had similar problems. In the Gulf, wild shrimp, shellfish, and finned fish that once flourished in these waters cannot exist in such conditions. Other pollutants have likely added to problems in the Gulf as they have in the Great Lakes. An explosion and fire on the Deep Water Horizon oil drilling rig in the Gulf led large amounts of oil being released into the Gulf, killing thousands of birds, turtles, and fish. The full effects are not yet known though it seems to cause heart problems and delays in reproduction in fish. In 2019, this spill is still going on at a rate perhaps a thousand times higher than previously thought and long-term problems with seafood are likely to occur.

Air and soil pollution are also a major threat to food supplies and human health. One of these is ozone that forms a main element in smog. Although ozone can be used as an antibacterial agent when mixed with nitrogen oxide, gas pipe and industrial pollutants such as coal ash are still toxic. It can kill seeds, weaken food plants making them less resistant to pests and cold, and inhibit growth of existing plants. Wheat is especially susceptible to this kind of contamination. Industrial plants, mining wastes, sewer system effluents, seepage from garbage dumps, contaminated water from storms, as well as air pollution poisons existing and potentially arable land. Heavy metals such as mercury, lead, chromium, arsenic and others have serious health effects when humans are exposed to them or ingested. In cities, abandoned industrial sites called "brownfields" are repositories of such heavy metals than ooze into groundwater and on dry days blow toxic dust into neighborhoods. There is a rise in urban farming and an interest

---

Zucchini Bake

Yield: Serves 4

Ingredients
1 pound zucchini squash unpeeled (to retain vitamins)
Oil for frying
1 clove garlic, finely chopped
1 medium tomato, chopped
1 medium onion, finely chopped
1–2 jalapeño chilies, seeded and sliced (optional)
Salt and pepper to taste
½ cup shredded fresh cheese (Mexican melting cheese is best)

1. Preheat oven to 350°F. Wash zucchini well, trim stem end, place in a small amount of water, and cook in saucepan until somewhat soft (not mushy). Remove at once, drain zucchini, and slice it thinly.
2. Meanwhile, heat 2 tablespoons of oil in a large frying pan. Add garlic and sauté until just transparent. Add tomato, onion, and chilies and sauté for 2–3 minutes. Add zucchini and cook for a few minutes longer. Salt and pepper to taste.
3. Place in a baking dish, cover with cheese, set in oven, and bake until cheese has melted (about 9 minutes).

by civic leaders in transforming brownfields into productive gardens, but they require considerable and safe cleanup. The cheapest way to do cleanup is by using microbes that consume and nullify toxic elements and specific plants that absorb the substances and that can be recycled. These remedies are difficult to do on extensive farmland so heavy metals remain a problem in the American food system.

Intermediate Issues

Food insecurity is a problem that affects not only individuals and families but whole communities. About 12 percent of Americans numbering 40 million, of whom 12 million are children, face food insecurity during the year. The number of food insecure Americans correlates almost exactly with incomes near or below the official poverty line. There are different levels within the term ranging from having normal amounts of food eaten by a family disrupted at times during a month to people having to skip meals or being worried about not being able to afford food by the end of a week or month, to outright hunger on any given day or week. It is always difficult for people beset with food insecurity to eat healthy meals, malnutrition and undernutrition being noted by many health authorities. Many Americans live closer to the official poverty line than they would like, 40 percent of them reported unable to pay a $400 bill for an emergency and, for those people, cheap, highly processed food is commonly consumed to the detriment of their health. Of the food insecure areas, three-quarters of rural counties account for the highest rates of food insecurity, with an estimated 2.4 million rural families in danger of hunger; 10.2 million Americans above the age of 60 are also insecure with some having to choose between buying medicines and food. Minority groups such as African Americans and Latinos also suffer from higher poverty rates than non-Hispanic whites. Undernutrition and malnutrition do their worst on children with underachievement in school among several deleterious effects. There are long-standing Federal and some state programs that try to remedy lack of access to food. The Supplemental Nutrition Assistance Program, or SNAP, is the latest version of programs that date back to the Great Depression of the 1930s. Recipients can buy healthy foods such as fruits, vegetables, meats and poultry, breads, and cereals. Though the program helps millions, and both farmers and food retailers like it, SNAP is often under attack by some political groups as wasteful of the nation's resources.

Where there is poverty and food insecurity, there are food deserts. These are residential areas, often urban, where there are no food stores or stores stocking nutrient-rich foods within easy access to residents. Usually, these are places where people do not own cars. Either no grocery stores are located in area of perhaps a mile or two or there is no public transportation to get to those outside the area. Any city with high poverty rates will have food deserts but so do poor rural regions as well. Surprisingly, some suburbs have seen nearby grocery stores close leaving them as kinds of food deserts. As a result, access to fresh, wholesome foods is limited for residents who likely have little income to spend on such foods. Also, the lack of stores, and therefore activity of shoppers, makes these communities seem deserted, blighted, affecting the quality of life in them. A number of municipalities have made efforts to have grocery stores located in food deserts and, where that happens, life for residents changes for the better. The more

---

Stuffed Eggplant

Yield: Serves 4 as an appetizer

Ingredients
1 medium eggplant, peeled, sliced vertically (¼ inch thick)
2–3 Tbsp salt
1 Tbsp butter
1 clove garlic, crushed
1 medium onion, finely minced
¼ cup fresh mushrooms, sliced
1 cup cooked shrimp, chopped
1 Tbsp fresh basil, chopped
Salt and pepper to taste
¼ cup sherry
½ cup shredded Gruyere or aged cheddar cheese

1. Preheat oven to 350°F. Slice eggplant and set in a bowl and cover each slice with salt; let stand for 15 minutes to remove moisture.
2. In a frying pan, melt butter over medium heat, add garlic and onion and sauté butter until transparent. Add mushrooms and sauté gently until soft. Add cooked shrimp, basil, and salt and pepper to taste. Add sherry. Sauté over medium heat until sherry evaporates. Set aside.
3. Gently wipe each eggplant slice to remove salt. Place one tablespoon of the garlic-onion-shrimp mixture in the center of each slice and roll up like a jelly roll. Place rolls in a baking dish, cover with cheese and set in oven (or under a broiler). Bake or broil until cheese completely melts, about 15 minutes.

upscale Whole Foods is one of the companies that has made the commitment in cities such as Chicago.

In a land where food insecurity on one hand and getting nutritious food on the other are important issues, it is a paradox that Americans throw away about a third of their food, including some 50 percent of their fresh fruits and vegetables. That amounts to 150,000 tons of edible food each day taking 30 million acres of land, 4 trillion gallons of water, and 2 billion pounds of fertilizer to produce. Americans are one of the most food wasteful people on Earth. Among the kinds of food thrown in the garbage and sent to dumps are foods that have rotted or gone past the expiration dates on their packaging, or fruits and vegetables that do not meet some ideal visual standards, such as bananas that might have a brown spot or two, or slightly misshapen products. Edible vegetable parts like potato skins or broccoli stems, and animal parts such as organ meats, also fill dumps. Restaurants have been one of the worst sources of waste because not all the food on diners' plates is eaten, especially vegetables, and even fast food customers leave plenty of scraps behind. Food that restaurants make and do not sell also goes into the garbage. The effects of food waste on the environment are severe. Organic decay in dumps is the largest producer of the greenhouse gas methane and runoff pollutes water sources. Both governmental and private organizations have stepped up to combat waste. Restaurants, manufacturers, food retailers, and foodservice companies around the country have joined organizations such as Feeding America and Rescuing Leftover Cuisine to collect potentially wasted food and sending it to food pantries where it can be distributed to people in need. Americans need to learn how to better utilize all the food that they buy for the health of the planet, if not human health.

Family and Personal Issues

Food Safety

Everyone wants to know if their food is safe to eat. The questions are, is the food nutritious, will the food make one ill, is the food what one likes to eat, meaning is it familiar or dangerous? The last question is really about food taboos both formal and informal. Nutrition and toxicity in food are matters of science. People have always known that most rotted foods or putrid liquids are unsafe to eat (fermented food are actually rotted but generally among the most popular of all foods and beverages). Only with the rise of germ theory in the nineteenth century did scientists learn what organisms caused food and water-borne diseases. Because of many abuses by food processors, the federal government stepped in with a series of laws beginning in 1906 dealing with rotten and adulterated foods, continuing with the creation of the Food and Drug Administration (FDA) in 1930 and, among a number of other regulations, to the Food Safety Modernization Act (FSMA) in 2010–2011. Individual states also have laws that try to insure the safety of America's foods. Aided by the newest technology, these agencies are charged with preventing food contamination by harmful chemicals such as pesticides, herbicides, heavy metals, harmful coloring and flavoring agents, and preservatives. Nonetheless, at least a third of American consumers are not confident that their food is entirely safe to eat and with reason: there is hardly a week that passes without media reports of food recalls because of contamination by foreign substances or pathogens.

The most common pathogens found in American foods are *Campylobacter, Salmonella, Staphylococcus aureus, Clostridium perfringens, Listeria monocytogenes,* and certain strains of *E. coli.* Most of these are transmitted in uncooked or undercooked foods, especially meats such as beef and chicken, milk and some cheeses, eggs, and even wheat. However, *Salmonella* has recently made its way into cucumbers and peanut products and the organism seems to have developed resistance to antibiotics. *E coli* is a large class of bacteria that includes types that live symbiotically in human guts where they help digest foods. Other varieties of the bacteria cause illnesses ranging from diarrhea to death. They come from fecal matter that might be left from animal slaughter or contaminated irrigation waters. If beef is cooked to 160°F then the bacteria are killed but an outbreak of undercooked hamburgers at a fast food chain in 1993 made hundreds of people ill, killing several of them. In 2019, *E. coli* contaminated Romaine lettuce grown in California and sickened dozens of people, requiring its recall from markets all over the United States. The cause was irrigation ditches contaminated by animal fecal matter and the fact that even washing this kind of lettuce does not remove the bacteria. Even with inspections, not all raw or cooked food will be completely safe. The USDA and other health authorities have issued numerous guidelines for preparing and cooking foods that are prone to carrying potentially deadly pathogens. Most people cooking at home try to be sanitary such as using separate cutting boards for meat and vegetables, thorough cooking, washing dishes and utensils, and even using solutions of bleach and hydrogen peroxide for cleanup.

The battle against microbes is never ending and will never be definitively won. One reason is farmers' use large amounts of antibiotics to keep animal herds and flocks that live mainly on factory farms free from diseases. Small-scale farms do not use massive amounts of pharmaceuticals. About

80 percent of all human-grade antibiotics are used this way with two related natural side effects. The first is that microorganisms constantly evolve to become resistant to antibiotics and these evolved life forms, some of them disease-causing, can spread into human populations. The second effect is that antibiotics fed to animals flow into the human food and water where they are consumed in enough quantities to reduce people's ability to fight diseases, even when given more antibiotics. Resistant bacteria can be carried by farm workers, can blow off farms in the form of dust, are spread by flying insects, and often contaminate water. Animals do not digest most of the antibiotics that they are routinely fed, so when factory farms, especially hog farms, spread sewage on fields near their operations, these medications leach into groundwater, then into streams, and into drinking water systems. Flooding of manure containment ponds during storms is an even worse problem. The effects of multidrug-resistant organisms (MDROs) are serious ranging from difficult to treat infections *Staphylococcus*, to *E. coli*, and *Klebsiella pneumoniae*, among others. Researchers estimate that in 2010 alone about 160,000 people died from infections by MDROs. No one wants to be immune to formerly effective therapies for infections.

Organic and Genetically Modified Foods

Anyone looking at food labels in grocery stores will notice that an increasing number of products have "Organic" and perhaps "Non-GMO" labels on them. Concerns for what conventional farming using pesticides and synthetic or inorganic fertilizers leaves in food products has led to a large increase in organically raised foods. The United States Department of Agriculture's (USDA) definition of organic is food produced by farmers who use renewable resources and to enhance the environmental qualities of soils and water. Plant and animal products such as dairy and eggs must be raised using only natural occurring fertilizers such as manures and compost that is worked into farm soils. Milk cows should be feed only natural grasses that they eat in pastures, hay and grains, and organic eggs must come from chickens fed exclusively on organically produced food. Nor should animals be fed antibiotics or growth hormones that may pass on to human consumers. One of the underlying assumptions in organic food production is that animals are treated humanely, unlike many confined feeding operations. In order to have the organic label, producers must pass federal government inspection and certification. Only foods that are fully organic can have the "100% Organic" designation. Most organic sales are in fruits and vegetables but dairy, packaged foods such as breakfast cereals, and breads are also rising in sales. Before the end of twentieth century, organic food was confined to a small number of health food and farmers market shoppers. By 2019, the organic market had grown to 5 percent of the total food market and is rapidly rising. So popular are organic foods that a number of food processors now market their products as "natural." In reality, this has little meaning beyond the USDA's requirement that such foods not have artificial flavorings and coloring. "Natural" food might have pesticides, herbicides, or hormones and they are not USDA certified. Most organic food is more costly than conventional ones but supermarket chains such as the nation's largest Kroger and Albertsons have extensive private label brands that have brought prices down to nearly the same as non-organic foods.

Since the 1990s, there has been a hot debate and much concern about plants and animals that are genetically manipulated to meet farmers' and food processors' production needs. The biotechnology used creates genetically modified organisms and genetically engineered organisms (both usually called GMOs). The USDA defines GMO tools as means to alter

---

Spinach Soup

Yield: Serves 8

Ingredients
2 Tbsp cooking oil
1 onion, chopped
3 cloves garlic, chopped
2 large tomatoes, peeled, seeded, and chopped
8 cups chicken or vegetable broth
1 pound spinach leaves, minus stems
½ tsp salt
¼ tsp pepper
Lime wedges

1. Place cooking oil in a deep soup pan and heat over medium heat. When hot, add onion and garlic and sauté in a small amount of oil until transparent. Add tomatoes and cook until pulpy.
2. Place broth in pan and heat. When hot, add spinach. Bring liquid to boil, reduce heat to simmer, and cook until spinach is soft for about 10 minutes. Add salt and pepper.
3. When done, spoon out into serving bowls and serve with freshly cut limes.

organisms in order to modify products, to improve plants or animals, or to develop microorganisms for specific agricultural uses. These techniques can include traditional breeding techniques, meaning cross pollination and breed selection to produce new versions of plants and animals. Almost all varieties of fruits, vegetables, and animals that Americans eat were developed by time-consuming traditional methods. Genetic engineering means manipulating or introducing genes from other organisms into plants and animals to create new versions of them. Recombinant DNA techniques and clustered regularly interspaced short palindromic repeats (CRISPR) are the most common methods of engineering organisms. The reasons for engineering plants are to improve nutritional values of food. One of these is Golden Rice, which has been modified to produce beta-carotene, a source of vitamin A, a substance lacking in countries that depend on rice as a staple food. Genetically engineered foods were also invented to save time and money for farmers and perhaps cut back on pesticide usage. For instance, some GMO crops resist infestations of corn borers, cotton bollworm, pink bollworm, and the Colorado potato beetle. Others kinds are immune to the powerful herbicide glyphosate that is widely used as an agricultural weed killer.

These may sound like good ideas for industrial-scale food production but when GMO food products were first proposed for human consumption in the 1990s, major scientific and public debates broke out. These include the effects on human health of the genetic modification, the use of pesticides and their effects on humans, other plants, and animals, and ethical issues about ownership of the modified plants and the profits derived from them. Called by critics "Frankenfoods" in a reference to the Frankenstein's monster of popular culture, these foods are said to increase susceptibility to allergies, cancers, and pulmonary diseases, among others. Virtually all of the corn and soybeans grown in the United States is GMO and most of that goes to animal feeds. In this way, GMOs move up the food chain into humans. Herbicide-resistant plants means that more chemicals are used in fields and since weeds evolve almost as quickly as microorganisms, new kinds of these plants abet monocropping and give rise to herbicide-resistant weeds. "Superweeds" have evolved necessitating even heavier applications of chemicals to combat them. Such weeds have escaped into the wider environment where they become invasive species. Companies that create GMOs have been accused of putting profit before the general good in their various business and lobbying practices.

In 2016, The National Academies of Sciences Engineering and Medicine published a report of GMO foods using the best science available. It concluded that no convincing evidence showing that GMO foods have major impacts on human health. It also found that genetically modified plants do not significantly increase crop yields. Further of all the world's farmland, only 12 percent of it is planted with GMO crops. Despite this convincing report, the controversy continues as more and more food is being gene-edited such as salmon and tilapia with more to come. As in some European countries where GMO foods are banned, most of the consuming public is wary of GMOs. As a result, more and more American food companies have removed GMO ingredients in their products and display Non-GMO symbols on their packages.

Additives, Ingredients, and Allergies

Food additives are one way to preserve foods from pathogens and they are also used to enhance flavor, color, texture, and nutrition in food preparations. Without them, hardly any processed food would be manufactured. People viewing a food label might be puzzled by the chemical names and the numbers of them in the food product. While most additives have not been proven harmful, questions remain in consumers' minds about whether that is true for all people. Additives are not the same as ingredients; salt—the oldest preservative and flavor enhancer—is an ingredient while glutamic acid is a flavor-enhancing additive. Food chemists have developed a number of flavoring agents, most of them derived now from natural plants. Banana flavor, for instance, when not from the whole fruits themselves is imparted by a derivative, isoamyl acetate. Sucrose (table sugar), glucose, and fructose and are plant-based sweeteners that work somewhat differently in the body. One of them, high fructose corn syrup (HFC), a cheaper sugar substitute, is thought to produce fat storage and high cholesterol in the body. For that reason, a number of manufacturers and soft drink makers (one of the largest users of HFCs) have begun to market more "natural" beverages using sugar alone. Other ingredients in processed foods are anti-caking agents that prevent dry substances from clumping, emulsifiers such as monoglycerides, diglycerides, propylene glycol esters of fats that allow different ingredients to mix together, gums from bushes and seaweed as thickeners, acids to change alkalinity or acidity, artificial colors, and vitamins that enhance the nutritional quality of the product. Because of public fears about these substances, governments around the world regulate their usage, but public opinion often drives the market. For example, sodium nitrate has been used for centuries as a meat preservative because it breaks down bacteria in foods and adds flavor to foods. It is a critical additive to preserved and smoked meats such as lunchmeats and hot dogs. Eaten in excess, it can damage hemoglobin levels in the blood and might be carcinogenic. Exact measures of how much is dangerous have not been fully established, but manufacturers of "natural" sausages and lunchmeats now use plant-based nitrate-rich celery and beet juices because of the nitrate scare.

There is no doubt that some foods and some ingredients in other manufactured foods can cause allergic reactions in some people. Food allergies happen when a human immune system fails to recognize something eaten as safe and attacks it as it would an alien virus or bacterium. Most of such reactions are localized, such as rashes for instance, but some are so severe, such as anaphylactic shock that can be deadly. Authorities in the field of allergies and immunology estimate that about 4 percent of adults and 8 to 10 percent of America's children have some form of food allergy. Many more people, about 19 percent, think that they have food allergies. Though the main offending foods are mainly tree nuts, wheat, soybeans, shellfish, milk and eggs, and especially peanuts; others include members of the nightshade family—eggplants, tomatoes, and peppers. It is thought that the incidence of allergies has been rising in the twenty-first century for reasons that are not precisely clear. Some think that the heavy use of peanut and soybean oils in other products have overloaded peoples' immunities to them. Others blame large amounts of toxins released in the air, water, and soils. Whatever the causes, food products are routinely labelled as having nuts, contact with nuts on processing, or not on labels. Schools routinely have epinephrine pens available for use in the event of someone having anaphylactic shock.

There are other human reactions to food that may seem to be allergies but they are not. Lactose intolerance is a condition when people lack an

Lab Meats

Will Americans soon be eating meat without the animals from which it comes? Concerns about the effects of raising livestock on the environment, on the ethics of animal treatment, and of meat consumption on human health have led to a new plant-protein-based industry. Plant-based meat substitutes that taste like traditional hamburgers are the fastest growing sector of the food business. The newest technology is meat grown in laboratories. Using cells from cows, chickens, and pigs, a number of companies including major meat producers are competing to produce edible meats made in vats or bioreactors. Many food specialists think that these products will be widely available by 2030 at low cost and saving 30 percent of greenhouse gas emissions and 70 percent of groundwater use.

enzyme that breaks down sugars in milk. Actually, about 65 percent of the world's people cannot digest lactose. While not fatal, lactose intolerance causes severe gastric distress. Celiac disease affects about 1 percent or less of American people. Gluten, a mixture of two proteins in wheat barley and rye that are responsible for elasticity in doughs, trigger autoimmune reactions in people with celiac disease. This can damage intestines and can cause children not to absorb nutrients from the foods that they eat. Since the start of the twenty-first century, about 20 percent of Americans have become convinced that they have been harmed by eating gluten, though this has not been proven scientifically. The power of market demand now has led to gluten-free products, especially baked goods, are commonly found on grocer's shelves. Products that would not naturally contain gluten, such as corn-based ones and even ice creams, are labelled "gluten free" to attract customers.

Nutrition

People want to know whether the food that they consume is healthful and because of food labelling laws many foods bought in stores display their caloric, protein, carbohydrate, fiber, sugar, and fat content-along with lists of additives. They also show a number of micronutrients such as vitamins, macro-minerals—calcium and potassium among them—and trace minerals like zinc and copper that are important in maintaining body and mind functions. These lists are intended to allow consumers to make healthy nutritional choices and there is no doubt that many consumers read package labels in stores and at home. They also buy large amounts of vitamins and other nutritional supplements, some $40 billion worth annually. By 1900, scientists knew that proteins, fats, carbohydrates, and certain minerals were main elements of good nutrition, but in 1911, Casimir Funk discovered another critical fundamental in human diets—vitamin B_3, also known as niacin. Later discoveries such as cholesterol, its effects on the human body, and the role of diet have led to changes in food processing and various trends in food marketing and peoples' dietary preferences. Knowing that they need a balanced diet of the substances mentioned above, people usually purchase foods that fulfil these requirements or avoid those that do not. Cholesterol, a waxy appearing substance that the body uses in digestion and to produce vitamin D, is an example of apparent dietary dangers. The medical profession and nutritionists want to limit certain kinds of cholesterol called low density lipids (LDLs) because they accumulate in arteries, clogging them and leading to heart disease—the leading cause of death among Americans. High density lipids (HDLs), on the other hand, are thought to be healthy. Among the foods that elevate LDLs are hydroge-nated oils (old-fashioned margarine and cooking solids such as Crisco that contain trans-fats), fatty red meats containing saturated fats, sugary bak-ery items, and full-fat dairy products. LDL-lowering foods include nuts, fish, beans, fruits, vegetables, and other foods high in soluble fibers such as oats. In the 1990s, oatmeal had a renaissance as a breakfast food when Quaker Oats and other manufacturers heavily advertised their products as heart healthy.

The media is filled with advice on how to achieve a diet that reduced cardiac risks, including eating five servings of fresh fruit and vegetables, whole grains like brown rice, healthy oils such as olive oil, and lean meats.

Fruit Soup

Yield: Serves 4–6 as party dish or dessert

Ingredients
1 cup of dried apples
1 cup of dried pears
1 cup of raisins
Water to cover
2 cups cranberries
Water to cover
1 cup sugar
2 Tbsp corn starch

1. Cut the apples and pears into small pieces, place in a large bowl with raisins, cover with lukewarm water, and soak one hour.
2. In a large pan or soup pot, place the cranberries and cover with water. Bring to boil and cook for 15 minutes. When soft, drain water and mash with a fork until they are small pieces.
3. Return to the pan and add the apples, pears, raisins, and sugar. Cover with water, bring to boil, reduce heat, and simmer for about 30 minutes until the mixture thickens into a syrup.

Note: Fresh apples and pears can be used in this recipe at the ratio of 2 pounds of fresh fruit per cup of dried.

From Sarah Tyson Rorer. *Mrs. Rorer's Philadelphia Cook Book: A Manual of Home Economies.* Philadelphia: George H. Buchanan and Company, 1886.

The term "Mediterranean Diet" is often used to describe the kinds of foods that should be eaten to remain not only heart healthy but healthy in general. Nonetheless, there is considerable discussion about what foods lead to rising LDL levels in humans. A great deal of research shows that saturated fats do not raise LDL levels, though trans-fats do. Eggs, which have been on and off the banned food list for years, are good nutritional sources, many processed oils thought to be healthy are not, and a large percentage of people who have suffered heart attacks had normal LDL levels. Amid this confusion, consumers often have difficulty deciding what foods are healthy. A number of diets have been put forward over the years that their creators claim to be the keys to healthy living. Low-fat, high-carbohydrate diets, for instance, were very popular because they were said to eliminate bad cholesterol. In fact, they do not. High-protein and high-fat diets, now called ketogenic diets, have been popular off and on for many years—the first ones dating to the nineteenth century. They can work on weight loss for a short time but can also lead to malnutrition kidney damage. In short, most experts say that the Mediterranean diet beloved of Italians, but perhaps minus the smoked and preserved meats and not so much pasta made from refined wheats, is the most likely to keep people heathier longer. But there is still uncertainty among a public that insists on eating potato chips and a whole range of fast and highly processed foods.

Obesity

One area of nutrition has had a great deal of attention over the last fifty years as perhaps the greatest threat to Americans' health: obesity. Obesity is calculated by measuring an individual's body mass index (BMI) which, in simple terms, consists of the person's weight as a ratio of their height. Invented in the nineteenth century, this index became widely used in the 1990s as a public health tool because health workers realized that obesity had grown so rapidly in the later twentieth century as to be declared an epidemic. The index in the United States places people with BMIs of 18.5 to 24.9 in the normal range, overweight is thought to be 25–29.9, and moderately obese to hyper obese include BMIs from 30 to 60. Although somewhat arbitrary in its categories—for instance, before 1998, the normal index number ran up to 27.5—the index is a quick guide to potential health issues for people with obesity issues. Today, some 40 percent of American adults and 19 percent of youths are considered to be obese. That is far and away the world's highest number, about double the world average. Obesity is a health threat because it is a factor in cardiovascular (heart) diseases, type 2 diabetes, high blood pressure and stroke, cancer, breathing disorders,

Southern-Style Greens

Yield: Serves 4–6

Ingredients
1 pound mixed greens, such as mustard greens, collard greens, turnip greens, kale, and spinach
2 Tbsp extra virgin olive oil
6 ounces smoked bacon, chopped
1 small onion, chopped
¼ tsp salt
2 cloves garlic, finely chopped
1 cup water
2 Tbsp vinegar (apple cider is better)
1 Tbsp brown sugar
¼ tsp ground black pepper
¼ tsp ground cayenne pepper
2 tsp lemon juice

1. Clean greens well by submerging them into a sink of water and rubbing vigorously. Rinse greens 2–3 times, until completely free from grit. Dry on a towel or in a salad spinner. Remove thick stems from greens and cut leaves into 1-inch pieces.
2. In a large, heavy pot, heat the oil over medium heat until very warm. Add bacon and cook until crisp-tender, about 5 minutes per side. Remove bacon from pan with tongs, and chop coarsely.
3. Add the onions and salt to the pot and cook for about 8–10 minutes, stirring constantly, until the onions are wilted and starting to brown. Add the garlic and cook 1 minute.
4. Add the greens to the pot and turn up the heat to high. Sauté for 3 minutes, stirring constantly.
5. Add water and bacon to the pot and stir. Turn the heat to low, place the cover on the pot, and cook for 3–4 hours.
6. Mix together vinegar, brown sugar, black pepper, and cayenne. Stir into cooked greens. Cook greens for 15 more minutes with the lid off to let the flavors meld and let some liquid evaporate. Stir in lemon juice. Season to taste with additional salt, sugar, cayenne, or vinegar and serve.

liver disease, and more. There is a social aspect to obesity with lower income people more subject to it than economically better off Americans; also, older people have higher obesity rates than younger ones. The annual public cost of obesity-related illnesses is around $147 billion and individuals beset with obesity problems spend about $1,500 more on healthcare than if they were not afflicted. More than money, obesity affects people's quality of life with depression and low self-esteem (and perhaps drug-taking to combat them) as serious problems. That popular culture presents thin, usually seriously underweight, people as role models does not help.

The causes of obesity are many. For some, genetics are at play since some people store fat more readily—more efficiently perhaps—than others. Mainly diet and lack of exercise seem to be the main culprits in the rising levels of obesity. The phrase "calories in, calories out" summarizes the problem. Human bodies use calories eaten to function but if more calories are taken in than are used then they are stored in the form of fat. Of course, what the calories consist of is important. Nutrient-dense foods are better utilized than those with "empty" calories—vegetables and whole grains with lots of fiber are better than doughnuts or candy. Americans eat a great many processed foods that are high in sugar and salt and consume drinks that are loaded with sugar and high fructose corn syrups, both empty calories. There are two main prescriptions to combat obesity: diet and exercise. Not only should a plant-based, lean proteins, high-fiber diet be followed but portions must be proportioned to the actual amount of calories to be used during the day and evening. It is well-known that Americans have become more sedentary than in days past when more physical labor was needed for food production and manufacturing. More people work at desks and more children play video and computer games than actually working on farms and in factories and playing physical games. Even walking, perhaps the most effective of all exercises, has declined dramatically as automobiles have replaced human legs to take people places. People who routinely walk in cities may be more fit than those who drive to grocery stores and shopping centers. People who do exercise regularly tend not to suffer from obesity and certainly feel physically better.

Glossary

à la Carte
Ordering single dishes from a restaurant menu rather than a preset combination of dishes.

à la King
Food covered in a cream sauce with mushrooms, green peppers, and pimentos. Often conflated with Alfredo sauces.

à la Mode
A French phrase usually used for pie topped with ice cream.

American Cheese
Various style of cheeses mostly in the Cheddar style made in nineteenth-century America, now associated with processed cheese made by companies such as Kraft.

Anchovy
Any of a number of small herring-like fishes. Usually salted and pickled.

Appetizer
A small portion of food or drink served as a first course, to stimulate the appetite.

Au Gratin
Food baked with bread crumb covering until browned.

Bake
To cook in an oven; mostly applies to flour-based dishes such as bread and sweets.

Baking Powder
Several types of quick leaving agent used in baked goods such as biscuits, cakes, and cookies.

Barbecue
To cook food slowly over a dried wood or charcoal fire, usually basted with sauces.

Baste
To wet food as it cooks with juices from the pan or other liquids.

Batter
A thin mixture containing flour, liquid, and often eggs, for making pancakes and as batters for coating.

Beat
To mix ingredients thoroughly by a rapid rotary motion with a whip or a spoon to make a smooth mixture.

Bisque
A thick, rich soup made thickened with pureed vegetables and cream.

Bistro
A small casual restaurant originating in France serving simple but hearty foods.

Blend
To mix ingredients until combined well.

Blender
An electrical machine with a cylindrical vessel fitted into a chopping blade. It is used to blend drinks, and chop and puree foods.

Boil
To cook food in water at boiling point 212°F.

Bouquet Garni
A loosely woven bag containing herbs such as parsley, onions, bay leaf, thyme, marjoram, and sage, set in a soup pot while simmering and removed when done.

Bourguignon
A meat dish braised in red Burgundy wine.

Braise
To cook meat by searing, then simmering in a covered pot with a small amount of liquid. Used on tough meats.

Breading
The product to be dipped must be damp or moist. First season it, then dip in flour to make the breading stick, then dip in beaten egg and milk, and lastly in fine breadcrumbs.

Brie
A soft. mild French cheese from the district of Brie, France.

Brine
Saltwater, or vinegar and water. Used to soak meats or marinate meats before cooking. Spices and herbs often added.

Broth
l. Liquid in which meat has been gently simmered. 2. A thin or simple soup.

Brown
To make brown by scorching slightly in an oven, a pan, a steam kettle, or in hot fat.

Brown Rice
Rice removed from hulls but not polished, retaining the bran layers and most of the germs.

Brown Sauce
Flour browned in fat, added to drippings and crusted juices from the roast, dissolved with brown stock or water.

Brown Stock
Stock made from beef or a mixture of meats that were first browned to give color.

Brunswick Stew
A stew of squirrel, rabbit, chicken, or veal with corn, onions, tomatoes, potatoes, beans, and salt pork. Usually made with beef in modern days.

Café
Originally a coffee house but now a type of casual restaurant with quicker service.

Canapé
A hors d'oeuvre made with a square or round of bread, toast, or cracker topped with various ingredients from cheese to caviar.

Caramelize
To heat sugar slowly until it colors and thickens.

Casserole
A pottery pot used for serving hot food; better known as an American baked food.

Caviar
The prepared and salted roe of the sturgeon and certain other large fish.

Charlotte
A mold or dish lined with strips of bread or cake, filled with fruit and custard, and topped with whipped cream and gelatin.

Cheddar
A semi-hard yellow cheese originally from England but the most popular of American cheeses.

Chicken Fried
A steak cubed or pounded, seasoned, floured, and deep fried.

Chili
The fruit of a plant in the Capsicum genus. The word usually means spicy hot peppers of the *frutescens* species. Bell peppers are the sweet relatives.

Chili Con Carne
Various cuts of browned beef simmered with tomatoes and chilies or chili powder, with beans or without. Can be made with poultry or pork.

Chives
A slender, green-leaved plant allied to the onion, with a mild flavor. Used for flavor and garnishing.

Chop
To cut into small pieces.

Chowder
A soup or thick soupy liquid with cooked seafood; clam chowder, cioppino, and bouillabaisse are versions.

Coat
To cover the entire surface of a food with another substance.

Cobbler
A deep-dish fruit pie covered with biscuit dough or pastry.

Cocktail
1. An appetizer of pickled vegetables, shellfish, or fruit. 2. An alcoholic beverage.

Coleslaw
Shredded cabbage with well-seasoned mayonnaise cream dressing, French, or similar dressing.

Combine
To mix two or more ingredients together.

Compote
Fruits stewed in syrup in such a way as to keep their shape.

Condiment
1. A seasoning such as mustard, pepper, spice, usually pungent added to a food. 2. A table sauce such as ketchup, gravy, or vinegar.

Cooking Oil
Edible oils such as canola, soy, sunflower, corn, or peanut oil, or mixtures with olive oil.

Cream
1. To beat fat and sugar until the combination becomes fluffy. 2. Various degrees of fat separated from whole milk.

Cream Sauce
A roux (see *roux*) to which hot milk is added to make a thick sauce.

Croutons
Small cubes of toasted and seasoned bread used in soups and salads; the basis for bread stuffings.

Crumbs
Soft crumbs made from day-old bread or hard crumbs from toasted bread, plain or seasoned.

Cube
To cut in ¼–2-½ inch square pieces.

Cuisine
1. A style of cooking. 2. The food usually prepared by a chef.

Cure
To preserve by drying, salting, or pickling in a brine solution.

Curries
Condiment or sauces widely used in South Asia containing a number of pungent spices.

Cut In
To divide shortening into firm pieces with a knife or knives until each particle of the shortening is covered with the flour to which it has been added.

Deep-Dish Pie
A pie with a top crust only, baked in a deep dish. Usually a fruit pie.

Deep Fat Fryer
A kettle in which foods are immersed in hot fat and fried.

Deviled
1. Cooked chicken, ham, or eggs chopped fine and highly seasoned, usually with hot condiments such as pepper or mustard. 2. Dressed with "hot" condiments.

Dice
To cut into long strips ¼ inch in diameter and then into ¼-inch smaller cubes.

Dip
A condiment in the form of thick or thin sauce for dipping bits of food by hand before eating.

Dissolve
To make a solution; to melt or liquefy.

Double Boiler
Two cooking pans, one for boiling water, the other fitted into it for cooking the food. Used to cook delicate dishes without burning.

Dough
A thick kneadable paste made of moistened flour or meal that is the basis of breads, pies, and other baked goods.

Dredge
Coating a food in flour or meal before cooking or baking.

Dress
1. To clean or stuff a meat such as fowl. 2. To cover with sauce as in salads.

Drippings
Juice and particles that drip from the meat after is it roasted. Used as gravy, plain or thickened.

Emulsify
To blend oil and water so as to prevent their separation.

Entrée
In American usage, this is a meal's main dish.

Fat
Any fatty or oily substance such as butter, margarine, lard, bacon fat, drippings, vegetable oils, salad oils, and so on.

Fermentation
A process using yeast to convert plant sugars to alcohol; used to make beer and wine. Sour dough breads are also fermented.

Filet Mignon
A small 5 or 6-ounce tenderloin steak.

Fillet
A narrow flat strip of meat or fish.

Flavoring
Adding a flavor to foods, especially baked goods and sweet dishes using extracts of vanilla, lemon, and others.

Flour
Finely milled wheat grains in many varieties.

Fold
To add egg or cream to a mixture and blend in, turning gently with a spoon or rubber spatula.

Food Processor
A machine with a wider bowl than a blender used for cutting, shredding, puree-ing, or kneading foods.

French Toast
Bread dipped in egg and milk batter and fried.

Frijoles
Spanish word for beans, used in innumerable Latin American dishes such as refried beans.

Fritters
Foods both savory or sweet dipped in batter and deep fried.

Fry

To cook on a stovetop in fat or oil at moderately hot temperatures until outside of food is crispy. Deep frying is immersing the food completely in hot oil.

Garbanzos

Chickpeas, dried or canned.

Giblets

Heart. liver, and gizzard of poultry.

Grate

To break into small particles by rubbing on a grater or anything rough and dented.

Grease

To coat a pan or griddle with a thin film of fat, usually with a brush.

Griddle

A large flat metal plate with heat applied from the bottom.

Grill

To cook on an outdoor grill uncovered or on an indoor grill or broiler.

Grind

To put through a food chopper or meat grinder using a coarse, medium, or fine blade.

Grits

Coarsely ground cornmeal cooked into a cereal.

Guacamole

A dip made of mashed avocado.

Gumbo

Specialty of New Orleans, a thick soupy dish made with chicken, sausages, onions, peppers, tomatoes, and thickened with okra.

Hard Sauce

Creamed butter and powdered sugar. Brandy, rum, or vanilla extract is often added.

Herbs

Savory leaves such as parsley, mint, tarragon, bay leaf, and others.

Hollandaise Sauce

Egg yolks emulsified with melted butter, lemon juice, or wine, with white or cayenne pepper.

Hors d'Oeuvre

Small snacks served at parties or at the beginning of meals.

Knead

To work dough by manipulating it, folding it over and over.

Kosher
Butchered and cooked according to Jewish certification authorities.

Lard
Pork fat. Leaf lard used in baking comes from the kidney area.

Leavening
Anything that produces fermentation or produces gas that creates air pockets in a food that is to be baked.

Marinade
An acid-based spice or herb mixture such as vinegar, wine, or soy sauce in which meat or fish is set to tenderize and flavor it.

Mash
To reduce to a soft, pulpy state by beating or pressing.

Mayonnaise
Salad dressing made of egg, oil, vinegar, lemon juice, and various seasonings emulsified by beating.

Melt
To dissolve items such as sugar or butter in a heated pan.

Menu
The listing of dishes in a restaurant.

Meringue
Egg whites and powdered sugar, beaten to peaks.

Microwave Oven
An electronic device that heats and cooks using microwaves to excite molecules in the food.

Mix
To blend two or more ingredients by stirring.

Mixer
1. An electric machine with two whisks or paddle attachments and removable bowl used to mix various ingredients. 2. A handheld stick mixer with one blade for mixing or pureeing food in its cooking pot.

Mousse
1. A dessert of whipped cream, sugar, and flavorings thickened with gelatin or eggs. 2. A puree of meat, fish or fowl, whipped cream, solidified with gelatin.

Parboil
To partially cook in boiling water.

Parmesan
A hard grating cheese from Parma, Italy.

Pastry Bag and Tube
A paper or canvas bag fitted with various types of tubes for decorating foods.

Pâté de Foie Gras
A thick paste made of seasoned fat goose livers often with truffles.

Petit Fours
Small square cakes with icing.

Piquant
Pleasantly sharp flavor in a food.

Pot Pie
Meat cut into small pieces, mixed with vegetables and a sauce, and baked in a pie crust.

Pot Roast
Meat that is seared and cooked with root vegetables in a small amount of liquid on a stovetop or oven for several hours.

Pressure Cooker
A device that seals in steam to cook foods quickly and seal in flavors. Widely popular as Instant Pots.

Pungent
Highly seasoned or umami-flavored

Puree
To press fruit or vegetables through a sieve, ricer, or in a food processor or hand blender.

Reduce
To decrease in volume or to concentrate the essence, by simmering a liquid for a long time.

Roux
A mixture of equal parts of flour and butter cooked together either quickly or browned slowly, used to thicken soups and sauces.

Sauté
Lightly fried in a pan on a stovetop with a small amount of fat or oil.

Sear
To brown the surface of meat in a pan with fat or cooking oil before further cooking it.

Shallot
A bulb of the onion family but stronger in flavor, widely used in fine cooking.

Shortening
Any cooking fat used in baking.

Shred
To cut into very fine strips or slices using a knife or cutting device called a mandolin.

Sift
To pour dry ingredients such as flour, baking powder, and soda through a sieve to aerate and blend.

Simmer
To cook in liquid at a low temperature, covered or uncovered; also called "poaching."

Smorgasbord
1. Swedish in origin, an array of appetizers. 2. Restaurants featuring a wide choice of self-service foods, also known as buffets.

Soy Sauce
Sauces fermented from soybeans in various strengths and salt levels.

Steaming
To cook over a steam source or surrounded by steam.

Stew
Meat and vegetables seasoned and simmered in a liquid on a stovetop or oven for several hours.

Stir
To blend ingredients using a circular motion with a utensil.

Stir Frying
An Asian cooking technique, quickly frying small pieces of meat and vegetables over very high heat, usually in a wide pan called a wok.

Stock
A base for soups and sauces, the liquid left from cooking meat, fish, or vegetables.

Succotash
Native American dish of corn and beans.

Syrup
Sugar and water boiled together until the sugar dissolves into a thick liquid.

Tabasco Sauce
Made in Louisiana from hot red peppers.

Tacos
A tortilla heated, topped with various fillings, folded, and eaten out of hand. Major street food.

Tamales
A Latin American wrapped food made of corn dough, filled with meat and sauce or sweets, and steamed in corn or banana husks.

Tapioca
Powdered cassava starch used in puddings and for thickening soups; similar to corn starch.

Toast
To brown by direct heat or in a hot oven.

Tortillas
Thin flat cake made from finely ground corn dough baked on a heated iron or stone.

Toss
To mix lightly, such as a salad.

Tostados
Tortillas fried flat then often heaped with chopped meats or covered in melted cheese or semi-liquid cheese food.

Truffle
A black mushroom-like fungus with a distinctive earthlike flavor.

Vanilla
The dried pods of a Central American orchid used for flavoring.

Vinaigrette Sauce
A standard salad dressing of vinegar whisked together with oil, shallots or garlic, herbs, and salt and pepper.

Whip
To beat rapidly with a whisk or electric beater to aerate and increase volume.

Selected Bibliography

Abbott, Abigail. *Three Squares: The Invention of the American Meal.* New York: Basic Books, 2013.

Albala, Ken. *Beans: A Global History.* London: Reaktion Books, 2007.

Albala, Ken. *Noodle Soup, Recipes, Techniques, Obsession.* Urbana: University of Illinois Press, 2018.

Albala, Ken (ed.). *The Sage Encyclopedia of Food Issues* [3 volumes]. Thousand Oaks, CA: Sage Publications, 2015.

Arellano, Gustavo. *Taco USA: How Mexican Food Conquered America.* New York: Scribner, 2012.

Barr, Andrew. *Drink: A Social History of America.* New York: Carroll and Graff, 1999.

Beard, James. *James Beard's American Cookery.* Boston: Little Brown and Company, 1972.

Beard, James. *James Beard's Theory and Practice of Good Cooking.* New York: Alfred A. Knopf, 1977.

Beard, James. *Beard on Bread.* New York: Alfred A. Knopf, 1995.

Belasco, Warren. *Meals to Come: The Future of American Food.* Berkeley and Los Angeles: University of California Press, 2006.

Beranbaum, Rose Levy. *The Baking Bible.* Boston: Houghton Mifflin Harcourt, 2014.

Beranbaum, Rose Levy. *The Cake Bible.* New York: William Morrow Cookbooks, 1988.

Berzok, Linda Murray. *American Indian Food.* Westport, CT: Greenwood Press, 2005.

Bobrow-Strain, Aaron. *White Bread: A Social History of the Store-Bought Loaf.* Boston: Beacon Press, 2012.

Brown, Deni. *The Herb Society of America Encyclopedia of Herbs and Their Uses.* London and New York: Dorling Kindersley, 2005.

Brown, W.W. (compiler). *The Illinois Cook Book; From Recipes Contributed by the Ladies of Paris, and published for the benefit of Grace (Episcopal) Church.* Claremont, NH: The Claremont Manufacturing Company, 1881.

Burhans, Dirk. *Crunch! A History of the Great American Potato Chip.* Madison, WI: Terrace, 2008.

Cahn, William. *Out of the Cracker Barrel: The Nabisco Story, from Animal Crackers to Zuzus.* New York, Simon and Schuster, 1969.

Carruthers, John, John Scholl, and Jesse Valenciana. *Eat Street: The ManBQue Guide to Making Street Food at Home.* Philadelphia: Running Press, 2016.

Coe, Andrew. *Chop Suey: A Cultural History of Chinese Food in the United States.* New York and Oxford: Oxford University Press, 2009.

Crume, Richard (ed.). *Environmental Health in the 21st Century: From Air Pollution to Zoonotic Diseases* [2 volumes]. Santa Barbara, CA: ABC-CLIO, 2018.

Culinary Institute of America (CIA). *Hors D'Oeuvre at Home with the Culinary Institute of America.* Hoboken, NJ: John Wiley & Sons, 2007.

Curtis, Isabel Gordon. *Mrs. Curtis's Cook Book: A Manual of Instruction in the Art of Everyday Cookery.* New York: The Success Company, 1909.

Czarra, Fred. *Spices: A Global History.* London: Reaktion Books, 2009.

DeGroff, Dale. *The Craft of the Cocktail.* New York: Clarkson Potter Publications, 2002.

Denker, Joel. *The World on a Plate: A Tour through the History of America's Ethnic Cuisine.* Boulder, CO: Westview Press, 2003.

Deville, Nancy. *Death by Supermarket: The Fattening, Dumbing Down, and Poisoning of America.* Fort Lee, NJ: Barricade Books, 2007.

Diner, Hasia. *Hungering for America: Italian, Irish, and Jewish Foodways in the Age of Migration.* Cambridge, MA: Harvard University Press, 2003.

Dirks, Robert. *Food in the Gilded Age: What Ordinary Americans Ate.* Lanham, MD: Rowman & Littlefield, 2016.

Edge, John T. *Apple Pie: An American Story.* New York: G.P. Putnam's Sons, 2004.

Edge, John T. *Fried Chicken: An American Story.* New York: G.P. Putnam's Sons, 2004.

Fussell, Betty. *The Story of Corn: The Myths and History, the Culture and Agriculture, the Art and Science of America's Quintessential Crop.* New York: Alfred A. Knopf, 1992.

Gabaccia, Donna. *We Are What We Eat: Ethnic Food and the Making of Americans.* Cambridge, MA: Harvard University Press, 2000.

Genoways, Ted. *The Chain: Farm, Factory, and the Fate of Our Food.* New York: HarperCollins Publishers, 2014.

Gutman, Richard J.S. *The American Diner, Then and Now.* Baltimore: Johns Hopkins University Press, 1993.

Hamilton, Alissa. *Squeezed: What You Don't Know about Orange Juice.* New Haven, CT: Yale University Press, 2010.

Horowitz, Roger. *Putting Meat on the American Table: Taste, Technology, Transformation.* Baltimore: Johns Hopkins University Press, 2005.

Huckelbridge, Dane. *The United States of Beer: A Freewheeling History of the All-American Drink.* New York: William Morrow, 2016.

Jackle, John A., and Keith A. Sculle. *Fast Food, Roadside Restaurants in the Automobile Age.* Baltimore: Johns Hopkins University Press, 1999.

Jordan, Jennifer. *Edible Memory: The Lure of Heirloom Tomatoes and Other Forgotten Foods.* Chicago: University of Chicago Press, 2015.

Kellner, Jenny, and Richard Rosenblatt. *The All-American Chili Cookbook: The Official Cookbook of the International Chili Society.* New York: Hearst, 1995.

Kenneally, Joyce A. (ed.). *The Good Housekeeping Illustrated Microwave Cookbook.* New York: Hearst Books, 1990.

Kirkpatrick, Melanie. *Thanksgiving: The Holiday at the Heart of the American Experience.* New York: Encounter, 2016.

Kolbert, Elizabeth. *The Sixth Extinction: An Unnatural History.* New York: Henry Holt, 2014.

Kraig, Bruce. *Hot Dog: A Global History.* London: Reaktion Books, 2009.

Kraig, Bruce, and Colleen Sen. *Street Food around the World: An Encyclopedia of Food and Culture.* Santa Barbara, CA: ABC-CLIO, 2013.

Kraig, Bruce, and Colleen Taylor Sen. *Street Food: Everything You Need to Know about Open-Air Stands, Carts, and Food Trucks across the Globe.* Evanston, IL: Agate Publishing, 2017.

Lee, Edward. *Buttermilk Graffiti: A Chef's Journey to Discover America's New Melting-Pot Cuisine.* New York: Artisan, 2018.

Long, Lucy M. *Regional American Food Culture.* Santa Barbara, CA: ABC-CLIO, 2009.

Mariani, John. *America Eats Out: An Illustrated History of Restaurants, Taverns, Coffee Shops, Speakeasies, and Other Establishments That Have Fed Us for 350 Years.* New York: William Morrow, 1991.

Mclean, Alice L. *Asian American Food Culture.* Santa Barbara, CA: ABC-CLIO, 2015.

Mendelson, Anne. *Milk: The Surprising Story of Milk through the Ages.* New York: Alfred A. Knopf, 2008.

Miller, Adrian. *Soul Food: The Surprising Story of an American Cuisine, One Plate at a Time.* Charlotte: University of North Carolina Press, 2013.

Mintzer, Rich. *Start Your Own Restaurant Business and More: Pizzeria, Coffeehouse, Deli, Bakery, Catering Business* (5th ed.). Irvine, CA: Entrepreneur Press, 2016.

Nestle, Marion. *What to Eat: An Aisle-by-Aisle Guide to Savvy Food Choices and Good Eating.* New York: North Point Press, 2006.

Newton, David E. *GMO Food: A Reference Handbook.* Santa Barbara, CA: ABC-CLIO, 2014.

Nissenbaum, Stephen. *The Battle for Christmas: A Social and Cultural History of Our Most Cherished Holiday.* New York: Vintage, 1997.

Payn, Michael. *Food Truths from Farm to Table: 25 Surprising Ways to Shop & Eat without Guilt.* Santa Barbara, CA: ABC-CLIO, 2017.

Pollan, Michael. *In Defense of Food: An Eater's Manifesto.* New York: Penguin Press, 2008.

Ray, Krishnendu. *The Ethnic Restaurateur.* London and New York: Bloomsbury, 2016.

Recipes and Recollections. Carmi, IL: White County Historical Society, 2005.

Redman, Nina E., and Michele Morrone. *Food Safety: A Reference Handbook* (3rd ed.). Santa Barbara, CA: ABC-CLIO, 2017.

Robinson, Jancis. *Vines, Grapes & Wines.* London: Mitchell Beazley, 1992.

Rombauer, Irma S., Marion Rombauer Becker, Ethan Becker, John Becker, and Megan Scott. *Joy of Cooking: 2019 Edition Fully Revised and Updated.* New York: Scribner, 2019.

Rorer, Sarah Tyson. *Mrs. Rorer's Philadelphia Cook Book: A Manual of Home Economies.* Philadelphia: George H. Buchanan and Company, 1886, reprinted. Bedford, MA: Applewood Books, 2008.

Schlosser, Eric. *Fast Food Nation: The Dark Side of the All-American Meal.* Boston: Houghton Mifflin Harcourt, 2001.

Schmidt, Stephen. *Master Recipes* (2nd ed.). Santa Fe, NM: Clear Light Publishing, 1998.

Shapiro, Laura. *Something from the Oven: Reinventing Dinner in 1950s America.* New York: Viking, 2004.

Smith, Andrew F. *Fast Food and Junk Food: An Encyclopedia of What We Love to Eat* [2 volumes]. Santa Barbara, CA: Greenwood, 2011.

Smith, Andrew F. *Food in America: The Past, Present, and Future of Food, Farming, and the Family Meal* [3 volumes]. Santa Barbara, CA: ABC-CLIO, 2017.

Smith, Andrew F. *Hamburger: A Global History.* London: Reaktion Books, 2008.

Smith, Andrew F. (ed.). *The Oxford Encyclopedia of Food and Drink in America* [3 volumes]. New York: Oxford University Press, 2013.

Spieler, Marlena. *Macaroni & Cheese.* San Francisco: Chronicle, 2006.

Stern, Jane, and Michael Stern. *Roadfood Sandwiches: Recipes and Lore from Our Favorite Shops Coast to Coast.* Boston: Houghton Mifflin, 2007.

Szathmáry, Louis (compiler). *Fifty Years of Prairie Cooking.* Introduction and suggested recipes by Louis Szathmáry. New York: Arno, 1973.

Szathmáry, Louis (compiler). *Southwestern Cookery: Indian and Spanish Influences.* Introduction and suggested recipes by Louis Szathmáry. New York: Arno, 1973.

Tiedjens, Victor A. *The Vegetable Encyclopedia and Gardner's Guide.* New York: Avanel Books, 1943.

Turner, Katherine Leonard. *How the Other Half Ate: A History of Working Class Meals at the Turn of the Century.* Berkeley and Los Angeles: University of California Press, 2014.

Villas, James. *Crazy for Casseroles: 275 All-American Hot-Dish Classics.* Boston: Harvard Common, 2003.

Wyman, Carolyn. *Jell-O: A Biography—The History and Mystery of "America's Most Famous Dessert."* San Diego, CA: Harcourt, 2001.

Yepsen, Roger B. *Apples* (revised and updated). New York: The Countryman Press, 2017.

Zanger, Mark. *The American Ethnic Cookbook for Students.* Phoenix, AZ: Oryx, 2001.

Index

ABOUT THE AUTHOR

Bruce Kraig, PhD, is professor emeritus in history and humanities at Roosevelt University in Chicago and former adjunct faculty at the Culinary School of Kendall College, Chicago. He has published ten books on culinary history and cookery, including as coauthor of *Street Food around the World* (ABC-CLIO), author of *Mexican American Plain Cooking*, *Hot Dog: A Global History*, *Man Bites Dog: Hot Dog Culture in America*, and *A Rich and Fertile Land: America's Food History*, and coeditor of *The Chicago Food Encyclopedia*. He has written numerous articles on food and food history, world cultures, and American and Midwestern food. He also served as an editor of *The Oxford Encyclopedia of Food and Drink in America* and is series editor of book series "Heartland Foodways," for the University of Illinois Press.